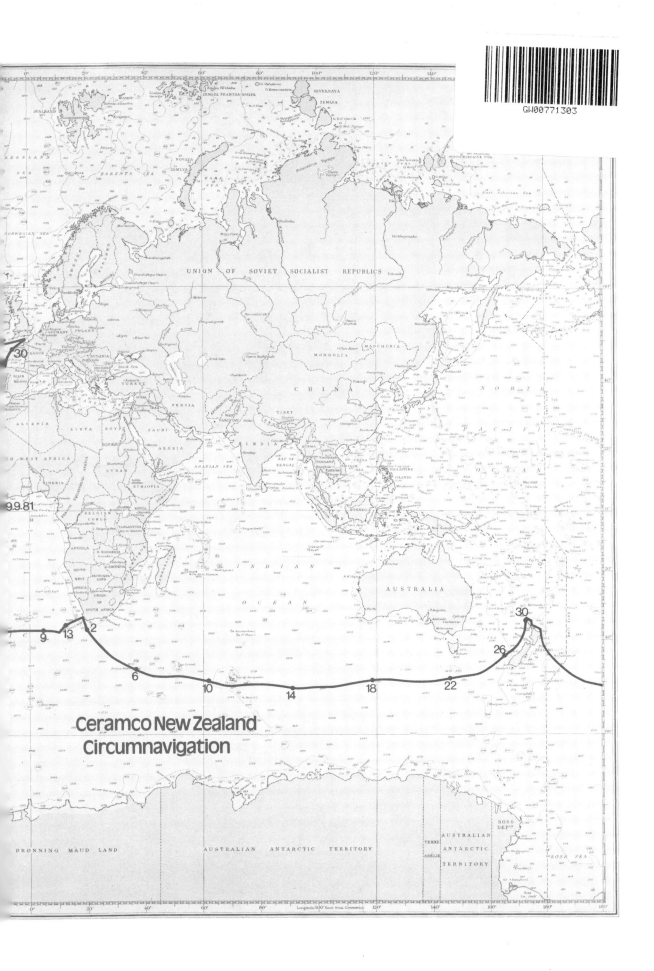

Ceramco New Zealand
Circumnavigation

BLAKE'S ODYSSEY

BLAKE'S ODYSSEY
THE ROUND THE WORLD RACE WITH CERAMCO NEW ZEALAND

PETER BLAKE · ALAN SEFTON

HODDER AND STOUGHTON
AUCKLAND LONDON SYDNEY

Jacket and book design by Tom Elliott.

Typesetting by Carter More Limited, Auckland.

Colour separations and plates by SupaScan Studios Ltd. Printed by
Woolmore Printing Ltd, bound by Trade Ruling and Binding Co. Ltd,
Auckland.

CONTENTS

FOREWORD

When *Ceramco New Zealand*, competing in the 1981-82 Whitbread Round the World race, lost her mast in the South Atlantic, three things happened aboard *Flyer*.

The first reaction was one of sadness — that such bad luck had befallen our number one competitor. At the same time we realised that with *Ceramco* out of the first leg our chances of taking line honours in the race were enhanced, if we could keep our show together. So we immediately steered off 10 degrees to lessen the strain on our mast and rigging as we punched into the south-east trades.

The crew of *Ceramco* soon had a jury rig set and we all began to appreciate the excellent leadership qualities and seamanship of Peter Blake. He and his crew continued to race to Cape Town so that they could go on to prove themselves over the next three legs of the race, which they did.

On *Flyer*, we did not always enjoy having *Ceramco* breathing down our neck nor, for that matter, ahead of us. But it inspired both crews to push the boats well beyond their limits. At the same time, it strengthened the appreciation and friendship among the two crews, which is what the race, mainly, is all about.

The exhilarating match racing between our two boats set new trends and paved the way for a maxi division in the 1985-86 Round the World race.

I sincerely hope that, in future, others will be fortunate enough to experience the excitement and good sportsmanship that we on *Flyer* and *Ceramco New Zealand* have shared.

Conny van Rietschoten
June 1982

7

ACKNOWLEDGMENTS

An undertaking as multi-faceted and complex as the *Ceramco New Zealand* project involves many people. We have endeavoured to record everyone involved in the appendices to this book. But special thanks must go to: Joyce and Brian Blake, Judy and John Glanville, Martin Foster, Warwick White, Peter Cornes, Tom Clark, Alan Topham, Peter Montgomery, Alan Sefton, The Ceramco Group of Companies, Air New Zealand, British Airways, Healing Industries (Epiglass), Feltex NZ Ltd, Columbus Martime Services Ltd, the Royal New Zealand Yacht Squadron, the Devonport Yacht Club, and the people of New Zealand.

Peter Blake
June 1982.

1. COUNTDOWN TO DISASTER

Oh Lord, have pity on me. Thy sea is so great and my boat is so small.
— A Breton Fisherman's Prayer

SEPTEMBER 21, 1981: The 1981-82 Whitbread Round the World race is 23 days old. On *Ceramco New Zealand*, 120 miles to the north of the Ascension Islands in the South Atlantic, everything is going to plan. The boat is performing right up to expectations, pacing the 76ft *Flyer* at the head of the fleet and averaging 9½ to 10 knots, just cracked off with the No. 4 jib and one reef in the mainsail.

Skipper Peter Blake records in the log: 'Going like a rocket.' The accompanying entries are terse but tell their own story.

'Monday, 0100 hrs: Course 210 degrees, full and bye. Wind SSE 28 knots, sea moderate. Position 3.47S, 13.48W. Taking over a few wet ones.'

The wind swings south-east and settles to 25 knots.

0400hrs: 'No. 3 jib. 2 reefs. Lovely sailing.'

0600hrs: 'Sea tatapatchish, rocketing along.'

0800hrs: 'Wind 25 knots SE, sea lumpy. Fast sailing.'

Then...

1235hrs: 'Mast came down — f..k it.'

There had been a crack like a field gun firing. The lower intermediate shroud had parted at the bend over the lower spreaders. Lacking the support it required, the radically slender (for a Round the World race boat) spar folded and broke at the middle spreader and then again at the bottom spreader. The whole top half went over the side.

In a matter of seconds Blake's dream of winning the 27,000-mile Whitbread race was shattered, a nation's hopes dimmed.

In the two years of build-up to this event, Blake had frequently said 'To win you first have to get around the world, so top priorities are a hull, a mast and a rudder which will stand up to the job.'

Yet here was *Ceramco*, 2455 miles from the first stopping point of Cape Town, with her wings savagely clipped.

The shocked crew was quick to react to the emergency. First priority was to get the rig back on board — to salvage as much as possible but, immediately, to prevent the 45ft top section of the spar, which was still attached to the rest of the crumbled rig by internal halyards and wiring, and by the head foil, jib and mainsail, from punching a hole in the hull.

It was demanding, heartbreaking work which took the rest of the day.

Blake assessed his options.

Monrovia, 800 miles to the north, was familiar territory. He'd been there when *Heath's Condor* had lost her mast on the first leg of the 1977-78 Whitbread. To go back to Monrovia would mean the end of the race for *Ceramco*.

Cape Town, nearly 2500 miles upwind from *Ceramco*'s position, was dauntingly far for a boat which had no chance of sailing an efficient course under jury rig.

This left only the downwind route, to Cape Town around the western side of the infamous South Atlantic high pressure system. It would be anything from 1000 to 1500 miles longer, but it held the promise of stronger, favourable reaching and running conditions and, if Huey, the Kiwi yachtie's wind God, was kind, might yet provide a way out of this seemingly hopeless mess.

There was one other choice — to withdraw from the leg, pick up fuel at the Ascension Islands and motor to Cape Town. But that was unthinkable with so much pride and the hopes of so many people involved.

The downwind route it had to be.

Blake gathered his tired crew in the cockpit to announce his decision. *Ceramco* was crawling south under trisail and No. 6 jib set on the bottom section of the mast which was still in place and jutting 16ft above deck.

'That's it then,' he concluded. 'Tomorrow we set about hoisting the 45ft top section into place and lashing it to the 16ft stump so that we can get more sail on. Meanwhile, if anyone is going to get demoralized, come and see me and we'll get demoralized together.'

2. FROM DREAM TO REALITY

I must down to the seas again,   And all I ask is a tall ship
to the lonely sea and the sky,   and a star to steer her by, ...
— *John Masefield*, Sea Fever

IT WAS ON *Burton Cutter*, an 80ft John Sharp design, with Les Williams that I did the inaugural Whitbread Round the World race, in 1973-74, and began to form my own ideas of what was required for this event, both in terms of boat and tactics.

We completed only two legs on that occasion — Portsmouth to Cape Town and Rio to Portsmouth. The aluminium hull construction wasn't strong enough and we were forced back to Cape Town with large cracks in the forward sections, so missing the two Southern Ocean legs. But Sharp had embodied some interesting characteristics in *Burton Cutter*, not the least of which was the ability to sail faster downwind, although not planing, than was theoretically possible.

For the second Whitbread, in 1977-78, Les and Robin Knox-Johnston had enough faith in Sharp to go to him for the 76ft design that was to be *Heath's Condor*. Their brief was for a sloop with maximised windward performance but with the downwind ability of *Burton Cutter*.

11

Meanwhile, I was already pursuing my own thinking, much of it based on the fact that at least 60 per cent of the Round the World race is sailed in strong tail winds. I returned to New Zealand to confer with a long-time friend Martin Foster and sort out the basic concept for what I hoped would be a New Zealand entry in the 1977-78 race. Late in 1975, we approached the Bruce Farr office for a 65-footer that would be a downwind machine. Farr, a young New Zealander, had cut his design teeth on unrestricted 12-footers and flying 18-footers, winning the world championships in both classes. He'd just won the Quarter Ton Cup in France with the radical, light-displacement *45 South* and was in the process of revolutionising offshore racing with that same light-displacement approach. I liked his boats and his fractional rigs. They made sense for an around-the-world race because of ease of handling and readiness to surf quickly and maintain high speeds under complete control.

Martin and I spent a lot of money and time trying to get this boat off the ground, touting it all around Auckland in search of a backer, or backers. We were unsuccessful mainly, I think, because the Whitbread race had yet to make an impression on New Zealanders. The first race had visited Sydney and not Auckland and Kiwi companies were unconvinced of the commercial merit in pouring a lot of money-into a young man's pipedream. One of the people who did give us an interested hearing, however, was Tom Clark of Crown Lynn Potteries, a man who later proved to be an invaluable friend and supporter.

Unable to do my own thing, I jumped at the chance of sailing in the 1977-78 Whitbread on *Heath's Condor* with Les and Robin. The boat was behind schedule and we were still rigging the experimental fibreglass mast on the morning of the start, August 27. Nineteen days later, as *Condor* punched into 15 to 20-knot tradewinds with a huge lead on the fleet, the mast broke in two places, at the upper and lower spreaders. With a jury rig on the bottom third of the mast, which was still in place in the boat, we limped 400 miles to Monrovia to replace the fibreglass spar with a conventional aluminium mast which had been flown in from England.

For the second time running, the boat I was on had been stopped in her tracks. This time, however, we completed the race, taking line honours in the Cape Town-Auckland and then the Rio de Janeiro-Portsmouth legs. My opinions of what was required to win this race were strengthened and New Zealand had been exposed to the glamour and excitement of receiving a Whitbread fleet.

Tom Clark

Warwick White (left) and Peter Cornes

12

Aucklanders in particular love the sea and had been weaned to an unusual interest in offshore racing on a diet of international success — *Fidelis* taking line honours in the 1966 Sydney-Hobart; *Rainbow II* winning the 1967 Hobart and then the 1969 One Ton Cup; *Pathfinder, Runaway* and *Wai-Aniwa* finishing one, two and three in the 1971 Hobart to clinch the Southern Cross Cup; *Wai-Aniwa* winning the 1972 One Ton Cup; *45 South* winning the 1975 Quarter Ton Cup; *The Magic Bus* winning the 1976 Quarter Ton Cup; *Gunboat Rangiriri* winning the 1977 Half Ton Cup; *Waverider* winning the Half Ton Cup in 1978 and 1979. The sport had achieved a national following and image, particularly as most of those successes were achieved in light-displacement yachts designed by young Kiwis, developed to a high competitive pitch in Auckland and raced to unprecedented success with a mixture of New Zealand do-it-yourself and natural flair.

It was against this background that Martin and I rekindled the ambition to race an all-New Zealand boat in the Whitbread. On *Condor*'s return to Britain, from the 1977-78 Round the World race, she was renamed *Condor of Bermuda* and joined the ranks of the maxi-racers which roam the world to compete in the major events such as the so-called classic ocean races, the Fastnet, the Bermuda and the Hobart. I took over as *Condor*'s skipper and, with Martin along for the ride, we set off for Florida and the 1979 Southern Ocean Racing Conference (SORC). We discussed our ideas and recent developments at length during that trip and decided it was time to try again. I was convinced we had the right boat in the Farr 65-footer we'd taken to the preliminary drawing stage in 1975. Seeing the heavy-displacement, upwind-orientated yachts struggling to cope with the Southern Ocean in the 1978-79 Whitbread had only confirmed my views. Despite the attention which had gone into *Heath's Condor*, my reaction to the most severe occasions were 'This is the wrong sort of boat — heavy displacement and masthead rig'.

Martin flew back to New Zealand to see what could be done. If our reading of the situation was correct, the commercial sector back there might now be ready to reconsider our dream of a New Zealand crew tackling the Whitbread and the world in an all-New Zealand, light-displacement, fractional rig machine.

This time, things began to gell almost immediately. Martin had talks with the then commodore of the Royal New Zealand Yacht Squadron, Warwick White, whose son Stephen had done the second half of the 1978-79 Whitbread with Rob James on *Great Britain II*. It had already been confirmed that the 1981-82 race

Martin Foster

Alan Topham

Pippa Blake

would again use Auckland as the South Pacific stopping point and Warwick too was fired with the prospect of a full-on New Zealand entry. It was to be a happy marriage of ambitions. Martin showed Warwick the work we had done involving design, costings, construction and logistics. Warwick outlined the effort he'd already put in to prepare the ground. Peter Cornes, with a proven track record in project administration (he was deeply involved in the organisation of and managed New Zealand's 1975 Admiral's Cup challenge), was recruited and these three became the New Zealand 1981 Round the World Race Challenge Committee, with the task of organising the funding and construction of a challenger.

They moved quickly. By April 1979, I was flown home from Florida for the announcement of a challenge which had by now received the endorsement of the Royal New Zealand Yacht Squadron and the Devonport Yacht Club. The boat was to be of New Zealand design, built in New Zealand and raced by an all-New Zealand crew.

The first problem to solve was finance. Few New Zealand companies have the sort of advertising budget that can absorb the costs of building and campaigning a round-the-world racer with a large crew. The solution was innovative and ingenious. The Ceramco group of companies, whose managing director was Tom Clark, agreed to underwrite most of the cost of building the yacht as well as contribute to the general expenses of the challenge. Tom Clark, a noted yachtsman in his own right (he compaigned the 73ft John Spencer design *Buccaneer* on the maxi circuit) commented at the time: 'The boat will be a showcase for New Zealand enterprise, demonstrating our skills in design, construction and sailing and in the manufacture of equipment. It will thus make a significant contribution to New Zealand exports.' Ceramco's commitment meant the project could begin immediately. But the major funding still had to be obtained — and this was the ingenious part of the total solution. The committee decided to launch a public syndication scheme through which the people of New Zealand could become shareholders in the boat by purchasing $500 debentures. The challenger would be truly a people's yacht and the project would command an automatic following. When the boat was sold at the finish of the race, the shareholders would be repaid. What, in effect, they were being asked for was an interest-free loan for something like three years with, hopefully, little risk to their capital. The 1981-82 challenge was under way.

We'd been doing our homework on design and construction. The Farr office was by no means an automatic choice, even though they had been involved in 1975. New Zealand had other designers of international fame — Laurie Davidson, Ron Holland, Paul Whiting and Jim Young — who had much to offer. But Farr got the nod. He was the acknowledged expert in light displacement and fractional rigs and, importantly, was Auckland-based and had the engineering know-how which would be vital to the success of the boat we wanted. His design brief was for a yacht which closely resembled his 1975 design for Martin and myself, but with less emphasis on the rating rule. We didn't want hull-line distortion for rating purposes. My *Condor* experience told me distortion meant control problems in Southern Ocean seas. We wanted a fair, fast hull — a boat which could maintain high speeds readily and stay with the weather systems for longer without exhausting the crew. I was convinced that such a boat would sail to her rating, providing it wasn't cripplingly high, and have a royal chance of line honours as well. This would later help the resale value of the yacht as full-on rating boats tend to date quickly and are frequently difficult to quit.

There was only one hitch — the Farr office had been approached by an Italian group which wanted a 62-footer for the race. This concerned us. We didn't want another country in there with a boat similar in pedigree, size and rating. It would tend to negate much of the edge we fully intended to gain from a close association with Farr and his team, and from the considerable input we had to offer. The outcome was that the committee negotiated exclusivity within a 10ft rating band — from 62ft to 72ft. The Farr office could not do anyone else a design in that range. To ensure that we would be in the clear, we increased the overall length requirement for our boat, from 65ft to 68ft. It was also the biggest we could go without the boat becoming a full-on maxi with all the attendant problems that would involve. We wanted a yacht which would have every chance of line honours on the two Southern Ocean legs, because of its performance and not because of its size. That boat had to be small enough, and the rig loads light enough, to be crewed to full potential by a maximum crew of 12 people. If the boat and rig were bigger, the gear to handle sails would be heavier and more expensive and we'd need more people. If there were more people, the food and water needs would increase and we'd nullify our whole light-displacement concept. It was also the biggest we could go within the budget that had been so carefully prepared. Most of what we would require in the way of deck gear for the boat was available off the shelf. Maxi equipment has to be mostly custom-made and is many times more expensive. We simply couldn't afford that.

The design requirements settled, the committee turned its attentions to a builder. Again, New Zealand was well endowed in this field and the choice was wide, but construction material narrowed the field. After a lot of deliberation we decided on aluminium. If we were going to be charging along with ice in the vicinity, I'd feel a lot more comfortable in an alloy hull. If we hit something hard, there was a good chance it would only dent instead of shatter, which would probably be the case with fibreglass or timber.

There were comfort considerations — alloy conducts more heat and cold and so would be more susceptible to the extremes we would encounter in the tropics and on the edge of the Antarctic. But this could be largely overcome with modern insulating materials. Provision was made to line the underside of the decks and inside of the hull with thick polyurethene foam. This would be covered with sound-deadening vinyl or synthetic carpet. This combination would keep the boat nice and quiet down below as well as comfortable. The only areas which would not be treated thus were the forepeak, which would be closed off and relatively unused anyway, and the steering flat in the stern.

The yard chosen was McMullen and Wing, on Auckland's Tamaki River. They had a world-wide reputation of building in alloy (*Escapade*, *Wai-Aniwa*, *Corinthian*, *Anticipation*, *Shockwave* were all built there) and, having done major underwater surgery on *Kialoa*, were fully conversant with big boat construction.

Everything was decided and construction was scheduled to start in January 1980 for an October launching. The construction would be 'monocoque' decks and cabin-top welded to the hull so that the possibility of leakage was reduced to a minimum. For the same reason, fittings would be welded to the deck instead of through-bolted.

The interior layout was carefully designed with the galley, living quarters and navigatorium located in a 35ft section of the boat where weight and movement would be least harmful to·performance. This meant that the crew would be sleeping in the same area where the food, water and fuel were stowed (and, when

CERAMCO NEW ZEALAND

(Plan by Edwin Meayers)

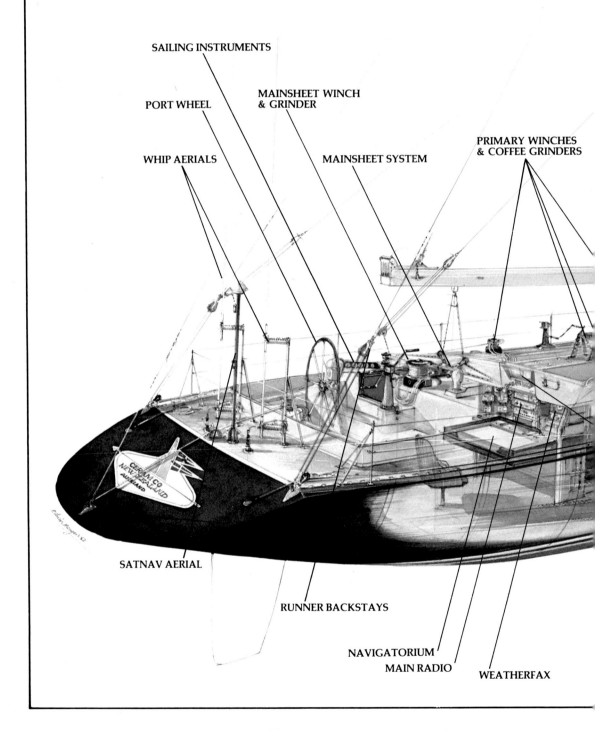

SAILING INSTRUMENTS

MAINSHEET WINCH
& GRINDER

PORT WHEEL

PRIMARY WINCHES
& COFFEE GRINDERS

MAINSHEET SYSTEM

WHIP AERIALS

SATNAV AERIAL

RUNNER BACKSTAYS

NAVIGATORIUM

MAIN RADIO

WEATHERFAX

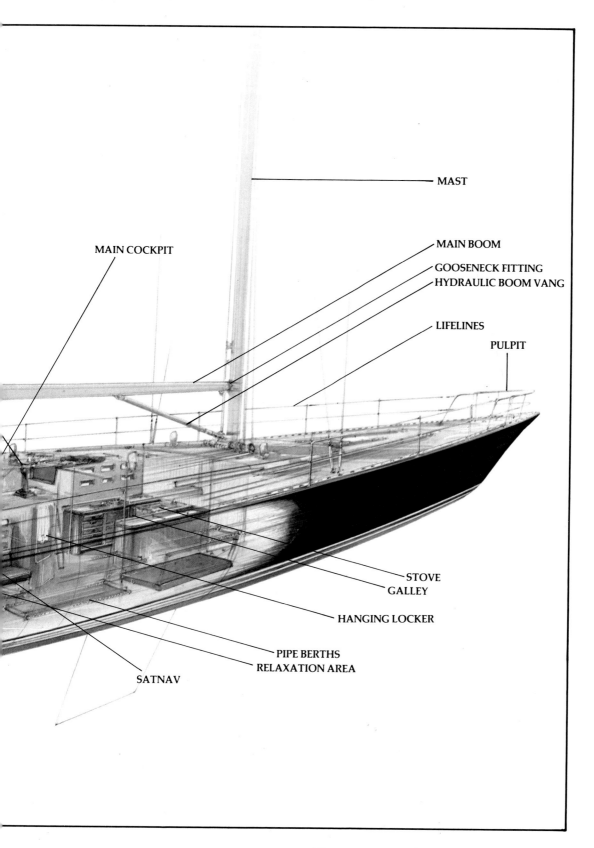

MAST

MAIN BOOM

GOOSENECK FITTING
HYDRAULIC BOOM VANG

LIFELINES

PULPIT

MAIN COCKPIT

STOVE
GALLEY

HANGING LOCKER

PIPE BERTHS
RELAXATION AREA

SATNAV

we were racing, the sails). The only thing in the forward section would be the engine, there for rating reasons which would allow the designer to put the keel further aft and so enhance our reaching and running potential. The bunks — 14 of them — would be planned so that crew weight could be concentrated to windward or to leeward, depending on whether the weather was fresh or light. In a situation where it was blowing hard from astern, the off-watch crew weight could similarly be concentrated near the stern.

The whole interior would be light, functional and comfortable because this yacht was going to be sailed like a harbour racer for a month at a stretch.

The same attention to detail went into deck layout and gear. The rig would be a triple spreader set-up, heavily tapered at the top, with jumper struts. It was custom-designed and engineered by the Farr office, and then especially extruded by Alspar in Australia, so that it had all the bend characteristics we wanted.

The coffee grinders and winches would be the best money could buy — our choice was Lewmar — because they would dictate how efficiently and reliably we could control sail shape and trim. The standing rigging would be Navtec rod which had a top reputation on the racing circuit even though I still saw much to recommend wire. There would be two steering wheels, mainly for visibility — the boat would be wide at the stern and the helmsman would need to be able to see the headsail luffs — but also because we could rig them independently to the steering quadrant. Then, if one set of steering wires broke, we'd still have the other wheel. There was another factor in this decision too. In very heavy downwind running the helmsman often needs an extra bit of grunt to keep the boat on the rails and out of a broach. We'd have a second helmsman riding 'shotgun' on the second wheel to provide this back-up when it was required.

The rudder was specially designed and engineered for where we would be going — to be wound hard over, if necessary, while the boat was doing 25 knots and not bend or break. If the loads got too high, the steering wires would break first. The bottom half of the rudder blade would bend or sheer off before any deflection in the rudder stock could take place. There had been a lot of rudder failures in recent times. We would be running with an unsupported spade rudder and we wanted to be sure of it. This was the basis of our whole approach. You don't win races if your hull isn't up to the job, if the mast falls down or if your rudder breaks. You have to get around the course.

Having settled all the major design and construction decisions with the committee, designers and builders, on another flying visit from the other side of the world, I returned to complete my commitments to Bob Bell and *Condor*. This included taking the boat to Sydney for the 1979 Southern Cross series and Sydney-Hobart and then on across the Tasman to Auckland, coincidentally to the McMullen and Wing yard, for a refit. At that stage I would step off to become full-time project manager for the Around the World boat, which was to be called *Ceramco New Zealand.*

Before leaving Britain for Sydney, though, I had a rather important appointment with a minister at a church in Emsworth in the south of England. An attractive young English lady, Pippa Glanville, had consented to be my wife and we'd decided that the opportune time to 'tie the knot' would be before *Condor* set sail for down under. The delivery trip to Australia would be our honeymoon. It was all highly romantic — getting married and dashing off to sea to exotic sounding ports. But we were both aware that the way the schedule was shaping, it might be the last opportunity to do things properly. With *Ceramco New Zealand,*

I was tackling a project which would dominate my life for the next three years and I didn't want to do it without Pippa.

While we were enjoying the trip on *Condor*, Messrs White, Foster and Cornes, now with the backing of the Ceramco group and, in particular, Tom Clark's corporate manager Alan Topham, were busily enlisting the support of New Zealand industry and the public. Offers of equipment, materials and supplies came rolling in and the concept of a people's syndicated boat promised to be a big success. By the time I brought *Condor* into Auckland harbour in January 1980, everything was 'go'. Chris McMullen was lofting the boat, construction materials were on hand and the yard team was assembled. It was an exciting moment, to see everything beginning to come to fruition. But it was tinged with sadness too. Coming across the Tasman in *Condor* we'd struck a severe storm which we rode out reasonably comfortably in a 76-footer. Behind us, the New Zealand team yachts returning from the Southern Cross Cup got a real hiding in 80-knot winds and huge seas. The One Tonner *Smackwater Jack*, with designer Paul Whiting and his wife Alison in the crew of four, was lost without trace. The Whiting family in Auckland is a boating institution and everyone shared their grief.

The next 10 months flew by in a whirl of activity. We had to be in the water on time if we were to race *Ceramco New Zealand* in the 1980 Sydney-Hobart. The delivery trip to Australia would provide an ideal shakedown cruise for boat and crew, we'd be able to check the yacht's potential against top opposition in one of the world's classic ocean races, and then we'd have the opportunity to dip down into the Southern Ocean on the way home to give everyone a taste of things to come. There were the inevitable problems associated with building a boat as big and sophisticated as *Ceramco*, with parts and equipment coming in from various points of the globe. But the yard absorbed them and kept to the schedule. There were headaches for the committee, costs were escalating faster than the money was becoming evident. We had generous banking arrangemnts but Messrs White, Foster and Cornes still had to personally guarantee large sums of money to enable the project to proceed. Then there was the distraction of *Condor* going aground on Tetiaroa Atoll, in Tahiti, while on her delivery trip to Hawaii for the Pan Am Clipper Cup series. Bob Bell flew in both myself and Chris McMullen to help assess whether his completely refurbished pride and joy could be salvaged from the coral despite the massive hole that had been gouged in her port side. She eventually was, after a major operation in tricky circumstances, brought back to Auckland by freighter. Poor old *Condor* was a tragic sight as she waited to take over the shed space soon to be vacated by the resplendent *Ceramco New Zealand*, about to emerge for her launching.

Ceramco took to the water, in a blaze of publicity. Dame Norma Holyoake, wife of the then Governor-General of New Zealand, Sir Keith Holyoake, did the honours with the traditional bottle of bubbly, in front of 600 invited guests, including all the shareholders and people who had helped get the project this far. It was one of the great parties and went on well into the night. But this was really only the beginning and I couldn't help but reflect on Tom Clark's speech, in which he noted: 'Where this boat and these guys are going, if you get into trouble it's no good calling for mum.'

Condor of Bermuda *spreads her wings going to Hobart.*

The 'inside a whale' look as Ceramco *is framed up.*

Plating begins on the stern sections.

Stern plates on.

The 'sharp end' finished.

Dame Norma Holyoake sends Ceramco *on her way, with a bit of help from Warwick White.*

All dressed up and ready to go.

21

3. BLAKE'S XI

To honour we call you, not press you like slaves,
For who are so free as the sons of the waves?
— David Garrick, Heart of Oak

A TRAMPERS' HUT, perched high on a 2000ft bluff overlooking a remote lake, late on a bitterly cold spring night, is hardly the place or time you'd expect to encounter a group of 19 would-be Round the World race yachtsmen. But that's where we were in September 1980, as I went through the difficult final process of selecting the 11 men who would be my crew on *Ceramco New Zealand*.

Lake Waikaremoana, 1920ft above sea level and tucked away in the rugged Urewera National Park to the east of the centre of the North Island, had been chosen because of its isolation. In the three days it would take to walk and scramble around its shoreline, I hoped to gain an insight into the people and personalities to help me make my choice.

Time was getting short. *Ceramco* was nearly ready for launching and I owed it to the ones who had made the final 'squad' of 18 to let them know as quickly as possible whether they'd made the crew itself.

The process had already been long and involved. I'd sifted through 140 applicants, from all walks of life and the length and breadth of the country, whittled those down to 40 who were interviewed and then down to the 18 who made the tramp. The first sorting had been relatively simple. I wanted a crew with experience and specialist skills and these criteria ruled out the majority of applicants. Getting down to 18 had been considerably more difficult.

Now I was left with a group of men who I would happily take to sea and do the race — but I could pick only 11 of them. Would Waikaremoana ('Sea of Rippling Waters') help me decide? I knew there was some scepticism about the exercise. Alan Sefton, together with Martin Foster and Pippa, was with us to satisfy his own curiosity, not convinced that a tramp was the way to pick a yachting crew. As we started into the steep first stage from the lake shore to the Panekiri Hut, where we'd spend the first night, I heard Simon Gundry call to him: 'Hey Alan, when they pick a New Zealand tramping team what do they do, put them all on a yacht in the Noumea race?'

Happily, Waikaremoana did help. The long and often strenuous trek around the lake and the cramped living quarters in the huts revealed little idiosyncrasies which, in days on end of hard running in the Southern Ocean, might cause personality clashes. I discussed my findings with nobody but was quietly pleased when Alan told me he'd found the expedition highly constructive. I learned later that he'd written down the 11 he thought I'd go for, sealed the list in an envelope and taken it out again only after the crew was announced. He was one out.

In the 11 berths to be filled, there were certain specialist categories. I wanted a doctor, a cook, a rigger, a sailmaker and someone with a mechanical bent. I'm an engineer by trade, but I wanted someone who could take responsibility in that area because I would have my own work to do, skippering and navigating the boat.

The doctor decision was straightforward. We had three applications. One didn't turn up for his interview. He was scrubbed. Another was admirably qualified as a sailing doctor, but he wanted to do only two legs. The third was Trevor Agnew, a cardiologist from Auckland's Greenlane Hospital. Trevor had written, asking for a berth, before the selection procedure was even announced. I had him to dinner and we got on extremely well. Whilst he didn't have the offshore racing experience at that stage, hadn't done any ocean miles at all, I felt that at his age (46) with his personality, he'd be a good levelling influence on what inevitably was going to be a fairly young and hard team.

The choice of cook was almost as clearcut. Paul von Zalinsky made the 40 for interview as a straight-out crew. He had an impressive list of references as to the number of ocean miles he'd done. At the interview, with Martin and myself, he revealed that he wanted to be the cook. He'd cooked a lot at sea and it had become something of a hobby. Problem solved — but, as with the doctor, Vonny still had to prove that he would fit in with the rest of the group.

The same was true of several others. I knew, deep down, that I wanted Don Wright as the rigger. I'd worked with him as a sparmaker, sailed with him on *Quando* and *Condor of Bermuda*, and knew him to be always cool and calm, even in a crisis. Although he would be the baby in the crew, in terms of years, he had already done thousands of miles on big boats, was utterly reliable and highly likeable. He had to do the tramp like everyone else, but as far as I was concerned he was in.

I'd known Don England since school, he used to live just down the road from me. I'd sailed with him on *Quando* in the Sydney-Hobart, knew he was a strong character, a real worker, and particularly good in emergencies. He also had an engineering background and I was convinced he would be worth having around.

I wanted Geoff Stagg, a proven performer as a skipper and known to be a good, hard-driving man, which I would need. But he wasn't easy to get. I asked him when he was going to apply for a berth while running a film evening at the Royal Port Nicholson Yacht Club in Wellington, fairly early in the piece. He looked incredulous and retorted: 'Who me, do a race like that. You've got to be joking.' But he must have given it a lot of thought and, once he made up his mind that it was going to be a full-on racing effort, he was in.

Keith Chapman had a bit of inside running. He came highly recommended having done a lot of sailing offshore on good boats as well as 18-footers with Don England. He would be prepared to work on deck all night and every night. He was pencilled in, subject to my finding out how he would fit in with the group I had, and there were absolutely no problems in that direction.

The other five berths were selected without any such influences or preferences. Owen Rutter had sailed with me on *Condor of Bermuda* in the 1979 Sydney-Hobart and then from Hobart to Auckland. He was strong, fit, pulled his weight

'The Doc': Trevor Agnew (46), Auckland cardiologist — hadn't done the ocean miles but 'impressed as a good levelling influence'.

'Chappy': Keith Chapman (28), Auckland school-teacher — came highly recommended with leadership qualities.

'Don': Don England (27), plumber/welder from Auckland — 'a strong character and particularly good in emergencies'.

'Simon': Simon Gundry (29), Auckland contractor — experienced and a powerhouse who 'totally wanted to do the race'.

'Molly': Richard MacAlister (23), marine biology student from Wellington — 'a good all-rounder, got on with people and was utterly dedicated'.

'Newt': John Newton (32), Auckland lawyer — strong and fit, and always joking, 'the selection procedure was worth it just to get him'.

and got on with everyone — plus he had some big boat experience. He got the nod.

Richard White started with a handicap. He was the committee chairman's son and I was sure I'd be accused of taking him because of that, if he was selected. But Richard really picked himself. He'd done a lot of sailing, including a Pan Am Clipper Cup series on *Kialoa*, had travelled extensively and mixed easily with people, was young, fit and strong. Confirming him turned out to be one of my easiest decisions.

Simon Gundry had a bit of a reputation as a 'larakin', but didn't put a foot wrong. He totally wanted to do the race, was always there when there was work to be done and was experienced on boats of a similar size to *Ceramco*. On top of that, he was immensely powerful and showed on the tramp that he would go until he dropped — which would be long after everyone else. He would be extremely valuable.

'OC': Owen Rutter (25), Auckland schoolteacher — 'sailed with me on Condor, strong and fit with big boat experience'.

'Staggy': Geoff Stagg (33), production manager from Wellington — 'a proven performer and a hard-driving man'.

'Lui': Richard White (25), Auckland builder — 'strong and had done a lot of sailing, including a series on Kialoa'.

'Jaws': Don Wright (22), Auckland sparmaker — 'thousands of miles on big boats, excellent helmsman, cool and calm in a crisis'.

'Vonny': Paul von Zalinski (37), Auckland bookseller — 'a good yachtsman who wanted to cook'.

The skipper: Peter Blake (32), professional seaman.

Richard MacAlister was completely unknown to me but had Geoff Stagg's recommendation. He had done a considerable amount of ocean miles to the Pacific islands and turned out to be utterly dedicated to making the crew, moving to Auckland to live on the boat and help out until the crew was announced. His good humour and compatability tipped the scale in his favour.

That left one position to fill — and John Newton got it. He was one of the doubtful candidates right up to the last week before the crew was named. He'd done a lot of racing around the harbour, including 18-footers, but was short on ocean racing miles. He finally made it on personality and humour, apart from the fact that he too was strong and very fit. The look on his face, when I told him he was in, was one of pure surprise and delight. He must have been convinced he'd miss out.

Having to inform the ones who didn't make it was one of the most difficult tasks of my life. We were working the boat up quietly by this stage. All 18 were involved, and they were all good enough to make the cut-off — but there was only room for 11. One particular evening, I postponed the work-up sail and asked the guys to come down below to see me, one by one.

I explained everything to those who didn't make it and offered them help to get a ride on another Round the World boat if they wanted it. Only Grant Dalton took me up on that, and he went on to become a highly respected member of *Flyer*'s crew. For the other six, I think, I must have represented the biggest bastard in the world just then.

My decisions weren't over either. I still had to name two watch captains who would be largely responsible for the performance of the boat, 24 hours of every day, as a lot of my time in the race would be taken up with navigation, tactics and radio.

Staggy was an automatic choice because of his nature, ability and track record. He was one of New Zealand's best-known skippers in his own right, with boats such as the Spencer designs *Whispers II* and *Whispers of Wellington* and then the Farr design *Granny Apple*. He'd won the 1973 Auckland-Suva race in *Whispers of Wellington*. He might have a bit of trouble fitting in under me, but I was sure that could be overcome.

To lead the other watch, I opted for Keith Chapman. I don't think Chappy had any aspirations to be anything else but a crew member. He would have been quite happy to sail where he was appointed. But I'd watched him closely and saw leadership potential. He had no qualms about asking people to do things, or about delegating jobs, even when he was just one of 18. He quickly proved to be a natural and I think he quietly surprised himself as well as a few others.

There were criticisms around town of course. Auckland has a large but tight-knit yachting fraternity and by now the *Ceramco New Zealand* challenge had become national news. The boat and the crew were public property, almost like an All Black team. People asked 'Who the hell does Blake think he is, why is he skippering the boat?' My answer to that was that I was the one who had got off his chuff to start the wheels in motion. In more normal circumstances, you can dismiss the critics. If you are doing the race for a wealthy owner you can sit back and ignore them. But because *Ceramco* was public property, we were subject to a lot of pressure. To raise money, we had to make the boat even more public — opening her every evening between 5.00 pm and 8.00 pm and conducting tour parties at $1 a head. This didn't help our sailing one iota.

But there was a plus side to it all. The constant interest in the yacht and the publicity she attracted helped morale enormously. The fact that ordinary, everyday people would queue and pay money to have a look through *Ceramco*, and ask for autographs, made the crew realise they were involved in something special. They were also aware of the criticism, that some people thought the crew I'd selected wasn't good enough. This only made them work harder and keep driving. They had a point to prove.

The feeling that was generated became quite surprising, as were the lengths to which some people went in an effort to make their point. One leading Auckland skipper — who must remain anonymous, for his sake — even tried to get the whole project stopped because Blake, he felt, was on an ego trip and the crew selected wasn't high powered enough. Tom Clark refused to see this 'gentleman' and I simply got on with the job at hand, confident I had a crew that would make everyone proud. In the main, the people who criticised the crew selection didn't have a clue of what was involved. If I'd stacked the boat with 'heavies' we wouldn't have got further than the end of the dock without an argument. That was the last thing I needed. Ahead were 18 months of living in each other's pocket and it was absolutely essential that we got on well together.

We were copping criticism in other directions too — our mast wasn't strong enough and we'd gone to the wrong sailmaker. Anyone who has not lived and sailed in Auckland, and experienced the intense interest in ocean racing, may find all this somewhat difficult to believe. But *Ceramco* by now was a sporting entity and wrapped up in her was a lot of national hope and pride. I was beginning to wonder whether we'd created a monster.

The mast would have to prove the doubters wrong. It was tall and slender, even by modern standards, but it was also expertly engineered and constructed — and immensely strong. The section was small, but it was also heavy-walled, designed to whip a lot like a fishing pole. Maybe it was too radical in some people's view but it had all the characteristics we wanted and I had faith in the designers.

The sailmaker choice was complex, involving a number of considerations. The leading big-boat loft in the world at the time unquestionably was Hoods, and originally there was no choice as far as I was concerned. The sails would be from Hood. However, we asked for quotations from the various lofts, as we were still working to a tightly controlled budget, and there were service facilities at the various ports of call to discuss.

The best quote and most interest came from Lidgard Sails, an up-and-coming Auckland loft to which I hadn't given much thought. When I got down to it, though, Jimmy Lidgard probably had more experience with fractional rig Farr boats than anyone else. He'd been brought up with fractional rigs on Mullet boats and 18-footers and, with his brother Don, had headed the syndicate which owned and campaigned the Farr centreboarder *Smir-Noff-Agen* in the 1977 One Ton Cup and Southern Cross Cup. He also had a fractional Farr design, *Roperunner*, building for the 1981 Admiral's Cup trials. Jimmy was prepared to build *Ceramco's* sails to whatever detail and specification I required, and this was important because my requirements were not the norm. I wanted specialist features in the sails to provide for the extra demands of Round the World racing. I wasn't interested in, for instance, a mainsail of lighter material to save weight aloft because, in my opinion, you lose far more time through blow-outs in a race like the Whitbread than you do if you have a sail which is probably a bit too heavy, but can take the punishment and holds its shape.

All of a sudden, I was highly interested. The clincher was that Jimmy was prepared to fly to England, Cape Town and Mar del Plata, at his loft's expense, to personally take care of our sail needs. The Lidgard loft got the job, adding more fuel to the flames.

But soon there was to be a storybook ending to our popularity and credibility problems — the 1980 Sydney-Hobart classic. If someone had sat down and written a *Boys Own* adventure book script, they couldn't have improved on the actual events of December 1980 and January 1981.

Ceramco New Zealand had shown her potential in a handful of local races before we set out for Sydney, but we'd lacked a yardstick of our own size. Across the Tasman waited the 66ft Joe Adams design *Helsal II,* a stripped-out running and reaching machine which would really put our Farr boat to the test. There was a lot more in store however. We left Auckland on an early summer afternoon to waft up the coast under spinnaker in a light south-westerly. We were only 30 miles into our journey when, without warning, we were knocked flat by a 50-knot squall. *Ceramco* did a 'Chinese gybe' with no runner backstays on and lay on her ear until we were able to throw the spinnaker and get her back on her feet. If the mast had been at all suspect, it would have gone then. But it stood firm as a telegraph pole. Somewhat chastened, we continued on our way, the only damage a blown out spinnaker and a cupboard panel cracked by a flying milk bottle.

The rest of the trip was uneventful, but there was a storm of controversy awaiting us at Sydney's Cruising Yacht Club of Australia. Melbourne skipper Graham Warner, of the Sydney-Hobart entry *Noeleen III,* objected to the koru emblem on either side of *Ceramco*'s bow. Before we'd even gone to the Hobart start line we faced a protest under Rule 26.1, which deals with advertising on hulls, gear or crew. The koru is Maori in origin and has been adopted as a national symbol by Air New Zealand and the New Zealand Shipping Line. Warner regarded our bow regalia as advertising and it didn't help that we constantly flew an Air New Zealand koru flag as a 'battle banner' while tied up to the dock.

I countered by giving notice that I would protest the entire Hobart fleet, all 102 boats, under the same rule if, as required in the sailing instructions, they flew the officially supplied yellow identification flag until they were outside Sydney Heads after the start. That official flag just happened to bear the logo of the race sponsor Hitachi. All hell broke lose. Warner's protest was successful and we were told to remove or cover up the korus. This was no hassle as I'd already had Pippa go up town to buy enough tape to do just that. But the CYCA was in a flap about its Hitachi flags. No flags, no extra sponsor mileage through the live telecast of the start. We were reluctant adversaries in this issue however and arrived at a trade-off. I would refrain from protest provided the club reversed an earlier decision to prohibit me from communicating by radio telephone with the New Zealand media. All I wanted to do was go racing and explore *Ceramco*'s potential. If I could drum up publicity back home at the same time, all the better.

The compromise was agreed and, at noon on Boxing Day, in a lightish east-south-easterly, the Hobart race got away to its usual spectacular start. We were close hauled for the short leg down Sydney Harbour to the Heads and the relatively narrow exit to the Tasman, already churned up by the huge spectator fleet. From a safe position down the line and away from the pin-end traffic jam, we cleared our air and started to tramp. With the light No. 1 genoa (a full, baggy sail) and crew weight forward, we punched our way through the churned-up harbour to be first out into the ocean, making surprisingly easy work of the

First through Sydney Heads and bound for the Hobart race double.   *Inset: Peter Montgomery*

washing-machine-like water in the Heads.

Once clear, we held out to sea. The former 12-metre *Gretel* skirted the cliffs on down to Botany Bay to take time out of us. *Helsal* had been slow out of the blocks, but followed the same track as *Gretel* and she too closed in. Off Jervis Bay, some 70 miles later, the three of us were in line abreast. The breeze freshened that evening and shifted to the east. *Ceramco* and *Helsal* dropped *Gretel* astern as we started to reach. Still in smooth water, *Helsal* nudged ahead of us but as the sea got up we held our own. Early the next day we went for 2.2oz heavy, flat kite with the pole right on the forestay. *Helsal* followed suit and there was nothing in it for speed. By 3.00 pm on the second day we were into Bass Strait with the breeze starting to kick in. In 20 to 25 knots across the deck and right on the beam we went for it. The last we saw of *Helsal* at nightfall, she was hull and half the rig down on the horizon ahead of us. By morning, after a sizzling ride across the Strait, we were on our own. We'd either done a number on *Helsal* or she had done one on us. The log told me we'd averaged 11.5 knots throughout the night but when I got some RDF readings off Flinders Island, I found we were well to the south of our calculated position on DR (direct reckoning). The current through Bass Strait had kicked us to windward, which we'd planned for, and the log had been under-reading 25 per cent in the heavy surfing conditions. We'd averaged 14 knots across Bass Strait, surfing at 20 knots. We roared on down the Tasmanian

29

coast, the boat performing like it was on rails, with *Helsal* reporting her position eight miles astern. We found that *Ceramco* would flat run just like a big dinghy, lifting her bow out and riding on top of the seas as straight as an arrow. We were elated. No control problems and no broaches — just the characteristics we wanted for the Southern Ocean.

We were so engrossed in our tussle with *Helsal* for line honours, it almost escaped our notice that we were on schedule to break the record for the 630-mile course, 2 days 14 hours 36 minutes 33 seconds set by the 79ft *Kialoa II* in 1975. A big flat spot off Tasman Island, just 40 miles from the finish, put paid to that. We worked like hell but still covered only nine miles in seven hours. Finally we picked up a light north-westerly and beat towards the Iron Pot at the entrance to the Derwent River. The wind then swung south-west enabling us to hoist the big kite, shooter and full main for the blast up the river to the finish. *Ceramco* missed the record by 4 hours 9 minutes 7 seconds, reaching Hobart in 2 days 18 hours 45 minutes 40 seconds. *Helsal* was 1 hour 48 minutes 51 seconds astern. We'd achieved our objective — line honours in our first major race and confirmed too that *Ceramco New Zealand* was a thoroughbred downwind machine. She wasn't exactly slow upwind either. That wasn't all. Behind us the breeze died and then filtered in again from the south. The big fleet still at sea was slowed to a crawl and headed. One by one, the challengers on rating missed their deadlines. *Ceramco* emerged handicap winner as well. The line and handicap double, first up. It was almost too good to be true. The double had been done only three times before in the 36-year history of the race — by Captain John Illingworth's *Rani* in 1945 (the inaugural Hobart race), by Ted Turner's *American Eagle* in 1972, and by Jim Kilroy's *Kialoa* in 1977. *Ceramco* was already in august company.

There was little time to celebrate. We had a date with the Southern Ocean and, on January 3, slipped quietly out of Hobart for a dip down to 47 South on our way back across the Tasman to Milford Sound on the majestic west coast of New Zealand's South Island. We were looking for a taste of what was ahead in the Whitbread race, and didn't have to go far to get it. We left the Derwent in miserable weather and took it with us all the way, 40 to 45-knot south-westerlies building up big seas. *Ceramco* ripped off the 1100 miles to Milford Sound in four days, with noon runs of 260 and 270 miles. Much of the time we were coasting with four reefs in the main and storm jib. I couldn't have been happier. I'd asked for a boat which would maintain consistently high speeds for lengthy periods without grinding the crew to a standstill, and I'd obviously got one.

We were barely able to see famous Mitre Peak on our starboard beam as we headed for the one berthing area near the hotel that caters for the tens of thousands of tourists who visit this part of New Zealand's Fiordland every year. There was no chance of anchoring as the sound plummets straight down to a depth of 950ft Mitre Peak, almost sugarloaf in appearance, is reckoned one of the tallest mountains in the world, jutting straight out of the depths to a height of 5560ft above sea level. The sheer grandeur of this place made *Ceramco* and what we'd been doing seem insignificant. But our coming caused quite a stir. On board with us for the return Tasman crossing we had Peter Montgomery, Radio New Zealand's yachting commentator, who had been doing live broadcasts on a national network of stations. The word was out that *Ceramco*'s first stop after her Hobart triumph was Milford. As the next day dawned clear and sunny, the traffic started to build up. Farmers arrived by air from Invercargill, 200 miles away on the tip of the South Island, one with a very pregnant wife, offering to buy debentures in the boat if one of the crew would give them a few lessons on handling trailer sailers. Holidaymakers drove in through the Homer Tunnel from Lake Te Anau. Inquisitive helicopter deer cullers just happened to drop in from their base at Queenstown and a television crew arrived by light aircraft from Dunedin. It was the beginning of what we came to regard as 'Ceramco fever'.

The Sydney-Hobart performance had made a big impression. New Zealanders love nothing better than to beat their Tasman neighbours the Australians in the sporting arena and the Hobart race, with all its media attention, is a particularly juicy prize.

Ceramco's schedule on leaving Milford Sound involved a whistle-stop tour of some of the country's major ports to fly the flag and beat the fundraising drum. First on the list was Nelson, in Tasman Bay on the northern coast of the South Island. The reception was overpowering, tugs playing their water cannons as they and dozens of small craft escorted Ceramco in to be received by the city's mayor, the town band and what seemed a large proportion of Nelson's population. A key part of this exercise was the fact that Ceramco had the capability to talk live on air to all the local radio stations in the ports to be visited. Peter Montgomery made full use of this facility and brought the people out in their thousands.

The Cook Strait crossing to Wellington was remarkably quiet in a near calm — most unusual for a stretch of water, separating the two main islands of New Zealand, which is generally regarded as a wind factory. We entered the capital city's imposing harbour to be greeted by a large Royal Port Nicholson Yacht Club contingent, there to ensure that local boys Geoff Stagg and Richard MacAlister got a big welcome home. Peter had done his stuff on the radio again and the boat was besieged by supporters and well-wishers. No firm figure was established, but we calculated that the challenge fund was $26,000 the richer for that nine-hour stopover.

Next came Lyttelton, the port of Christchurch, which is the main South Island population centre. It was the same story, the crew flat out conducting tours through the boat and selling special Ceramco souvenirs. Out off Milford Sound on the way to Nelson we'd received a radio-telephone call from the mayor of Timaru, almost 100 miles south-west of Christchurch, inviting Ceramco to his city. We had to decline because of an already established schedule, but we were beginning to fully appreciate the extent of the support for what we were doing, right through the country. From Lyttelton we headed north-east to Napier, the population centre of agriculturally rich Hawke's Bay, on the east coast of the North Island. The city itself owned two $500 shares in the boat. Then it was an overnight trip on up the coast to Gisborne for more incredible hospitality. Gisborne is in Poverty Bay, the southern extremity of which is Young Nick's Head, the first part of New Zealand sighted by Captain Cook's Endeavour and named after a cabin boy with a keen pair of eyes.

Gisborne was the last call before the return to our home port Auckland although we took the opportunity to overnight at the lovely Great Barrier Island, the north-eastern extremity of the Hauraki Gulf, before completing the final 45 miles to Ceramco's permanent berth at Marsden Wharf. We sailed into the Waitemata on a beautiful summer Saturday afternoon, the harbour and inner gulf crowded with racing and cruising boats. It was a big moment for the crew as we clipped close to Orakei Wharf to give the waterfront crowd a closer look and then sagged away across to the other side of the harbour to salute the Devonport Yacht Club. People were jostling for vantage points around Marsden Wharf as we dropped sail and motored in.

If Blake's XI had had any doubts about what they were involved in, they were gone now. *Ceramco* and her crew were celebrities. We'd won respect and silenced the critics. The real business was yet to begin but the 'Porcelain Rocketship' — a name given the boat by our *Condor* mates back in the UK in a congratulatory telegram to Hobart — had made a spectacular lift-off.

Milford Sound makes a magnificent backdrop for a triumphant return.

4. THE RACE AND OPPOSITION

They that go down to the sea in ships, that do business in great waters;
These see the works of the Lord, and his wonders in the deep.
— Psalm 107 : 23-24

THE WHITBREAD ROUND the World event is variously regarded as a marathon endurance test, one of the last of the great adventures, or outright masochism. In its brief existence, the 27,000-mile circumnavigation has probably been all of those. But now it has come of age as a race, attracting racing talent as opposed to ocean wallopers, and demanding the latest in materials, gear and techniques.

The first Whitbread, in 1973-74, was a gamble for the organisers, the Royal Naval Sailing Association. The logistics were forbidding. Nobody knew whether it was feasible to race modern yachts hard through the high latitudes of the Southern Ocean. But there were plenty of adventurous souls prepared to try. On 18 September 1973, a fleet of 17 yachts from six nations went to the start line off Southsea Castle. The course was from Portsmouth to Cape Town, Cape Town to Sydney, Sydney to Rio de Janeiro and Rio to Portsmouth. Fourteen of those 17 starters made the finish. Tragically, three lives were lost during the eight-month journey. Dominique Guillet, off *33 Export*, and Paul Waterhouse, off *Tauranga*, disappeared overboard when huge, freak waves in the southern Indian Ocean threatened to overwhelm even the biggest and best-found yachts in the fleet. The

Whitbread contingent licked their wounds in Sydney then set out for Cape Horn. They struck more rugged weather, this time off the southern tip of New Zealand, and the race claimed its third victim. Bernie Hoskins, off *Great Britain II*, went over the side and wasn't seen again.

Inevitably, there was criticism of the event and of the organisers, amid predictions that this would be the first and last Whitbread. But the RNSA could hardly be blamed for what had taken place at sea. The race was, and is, subject to stringent safety requirements. Thereafter, the responsibility lies with skippers and crews.

That inaugural event was won by Mexican industrialist Ramon Carlin in a stock, fibreglass Swan 65 *Sayula*. The fastest boat around the world was the 77ft Alan Gurney design *Great Britain II*, skippered by Transatlantic rower Chay Blyth with a crew of paratroopers, in a time of 144 days 10 hours 43 minutes 44 seconds. The experience left everyone with indelible memories of freezing winds, huge, breaking seas, icebergs and snow. Nobody would forget that the Southern Ocean had claimed three lives. But it would not stop people doing it again.

For the 1977-78 race, there was a course change. Auckland replaced Sydney as the south Pacific port of call. This time 15 yachts, again from six nations, faced the starter, on 27 August 1977. They were better prepared, benefiting from the lessons learnt in 1973-74. Nobody was lost, and the damage in the fleet was only minor. *Great Britain II*, skippered this time by a good friend of mine, Rob James, had a close call however. During the Cape Town-Auckland leg, the lazy spinnaker brace looped itself around the waist of crewman Nick Dunlop and around the leg of skipper James. The brace snapped tight, threatened to crush Dunlop and leave Rob a cripple. They were saved from permanent injury by some smart crew work, but the reminder of ever-present danger was there for everyone in the fleet.

On *Heath's Condor*, during the same leg, the reminder was even closer to home. We were tidying up after a gybe, running at 10 knots in 25 knots of wind, when the lazy brace tautened under crewman Bill Abram and whipped him overboard. He was in the icy-cold ocean for 10 minutes before we managed to get back to him and haul him aboard. We were lucky. Apart from a cut hand and being very cold, Bill was alright. But it had been too close for comfort.

That second race was won by Conny van Rietschoten with the meticulously prepared *Flyer*, an S&S special on the Swan 65 theme. *Great Britain II* was again the gun boat, this time taking 134 days 12 hours 22 minutes 47 seconds — nearly 10 days faster than in 1973-74.

The performance improvement was evident right through the 1977-78 fleet. *Sayula* had taken 152 days 09 hours 11 minutes and averaged 7.5 knots when she won the first Whitbread. *Flyer* averaged 8.3 knots and did the journey in 136 days 05 hours 28 minutes. The 55-footer *Adventure* went around in 162 days 19 hours 06 minutes in the first race. In 1977-78 she did the journey in 158 days 14 hours 12 minutes.

The 1981-82 race was always going to be more competitive again, featuring for the first time boats designed for the job — efficient all-rounders with a hefty emphasis on downwind control and speed.

We'd shipped *Ceramco* to Philadelphia, on the eastern seaboard of the United States, on the Columbus Line's impressive container vessel *Columbus New Zealand*. Pippa and I went with her to see to maintenance during the voyage. In Philadelphia we were joined by Newt, Vonny, Lui, OC and Molly for the delivery sail across the Atlantic to *Ceramco*'s English base on the Hamble River near Southampton.

As we eased the boat into her Hamble berth on May 27 we got a first look at some of our opposition. There was *Flyer*, preparing for the Seahorse Maxi Series on the Solent in July, an event we also would use, with the Fastnet Classic, for final tune-up work. The new Dutch hope was impressive, a 76ft German Frers design developed from the maxi racer *Bumblebee*. I'd heard that Conny had delayed his decision on the overall length of his newcomer until details on *Ceramco* were revealed. He had then gone all the way to a full-on maxi, intent on adding line honours around the world to his 1977-78 handicap win.

In the weeks that followed, the rest of the crew arrived by various routes and we tackled the dozens of jobs which still had to be done before the Whitbread start on August 29. These were memorable days, the *Ceramco* team becoming locals in the highly hospitable village of Hamble and starring in the local carnival. Newt and Molly claimed a *Guinness Book of Records* mark for egg throwing while a Gundry-led team was triumphant in the wheelbarrow event which entailed shoving carts up the village high street and downing a pint in four selected pubs en route.

We weren't as successful in the Seahorse series, but we learnt a lot more about *Ceramco* and her requirements as we played with trim, rig tensions and sheeting angles, using the cream of the world's maxi ocean racers fleet — *Kialoa, Condor II, Xargo IV* — as yardsticks. The Seahorse fleet involved four Round the World boats — *Ceramco, Flyer, FCF Challenger* and *Licor 43*. The conclusion was that only *Flyer* would pose a threat in the Whitbread. *Ceramco* was the fastest reaching boat, including *Kialoa* and *Condor*. But *Flyer* looked extra quick flat running and, with her big masthead rig, was a potent light airs performer. She would take some holding in the Doldrums. We gained a lot from the four-race series though. With designer Bruce Farr aboard as well as sailmaker Jim Lidgard, we improved *Ceramco*'s upwind performance significantly, and we were much more aware of where she did, and didn't, like weight.

The days were now flying by and, by the time we'd finished a non-event, drift of a Fastnet Classic and made our way back to the Hamble, arriving on August 17, the Whitbread start was less then two weeks away. There was still much to be done, including a bottom paint job, stores and spares to be loaded and a full gear check and overhaul.

We motored around to the Camper and Nicholson yard, race headquarters at Gosport, on August 22 for the final countdown, and the work went on, the pace quickening as start time drew closer. There were a host of old friendships to renew and faces to remember from the previous Whitbreads. There were also numerous official details to attend to as race chairman, Rear Admiral Charles Williams and his RNSA team brought their preparations to a head. The marina acquired an atmosphere and anticipation. This was it — 24 hours to go to the start gun. Very soon all the years of planning, all the hopes and ambitions, would be put to the test. But there was still time for a final check of the opposition to isolate the boats and the crews to watch for.

Flyer had to rank the boat to beat — for line and handicap honours. Conny was sticking to the story that his aim was to be first around, but I believed otherwise. He was after the double. If my theory about being fast enough to stay with the weather systems for longer was correct, and the conditions were right, the bigger boats had the ability to sail away and leave the small boats to their own race astern.

Ceramco *in action in the Seahorse Maxi series on the Solent.*

Conny had done some modifications since the Seahorse series, deepening *Flyer*'s keel and adding 1650lbs of lead ballast. The determined Dutchman was sparing nothing in a typically methodical and efficient campaign which, it was rumoured, had already cost him $NZ3.5 million. I couldn't see the point in his keel changes though. The lead had all gone on the bottom of *Flyer*'s keel which would only increase her pitching moment in a seaway. The boat's performance characteristics must also change so, in some ways, they would be starting from scratch again. There would be something wrong though if *Flyer* wasn't first to Cape Town.

Ready to take on the world.

36

Kriter IX

Charles Heidsieck III

Flyer

Outward Bound

FCF Challenger

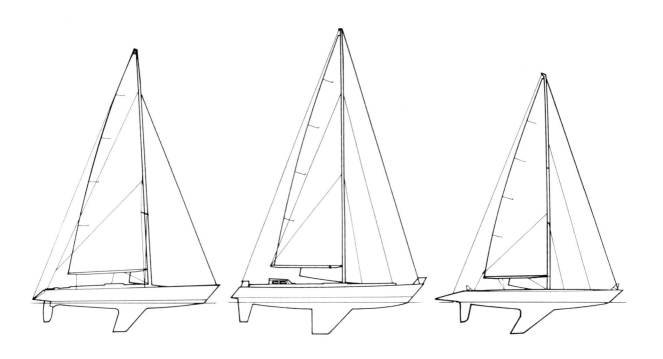

Ceramco New Zealand   Kriter IX   Charles Heidsieck III

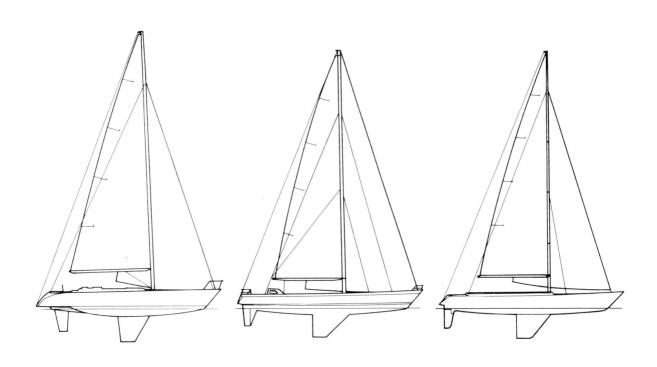

Outward Bound   Flyer   FCF Challenger

1981-82 WHITBREAD ROUND THE WORLD RACE FLEET

Boat	LOA	LWL	Beam	Draft	Displacement	Rating	Rig	Construction	Colour	Designer	Skipper	Country
Alaska Eagle	65ft 2in	53ft	16ft 4in	10ft 6in	55,500lb	50.4ft	Sloop	Aluminium	White	S&S	Skip Novak	U.S.A.
Berge Viking	57ft	45ft	15ft	9ft 1in	47,600lb	42.4ft	Sloop	GRP	Red	S&S	Peder Lunde	Norway
Bubblegum	42ft 9in	34ft 4in	12ft 6in	7ft 3in	21,000lb	33ft	Sloop	GRP	Light blue	Peterson	Ian McGowan-Fyfe	Britain
Ceramco New Zealand	68ft 6in	55ft 1in	17ft 1in	10ft 8in	42,593lb	62.9ft	Sloop	Aluminium	Dark blue	Farr	Peter Blake	New Zealand
Charles Heidsieck III	66ft 6in	53ft 8in	16ft 6in	10ft 8in	44,128lb	54.6ft	Sloop	Aluminium	Black	Vaton	Alain Gabbay	France
Croky	43ft 9in	35ft 4in	12ft 5in	8ft	24,640lb	33.7ft	Sloop	Timber	White	Vankeirsbilck	Gustaaf Versluys	Belgium
Disque D'Or	58ft 3in	45ft 1in	16ft 5in	9ft	31,252lb	46ft	Sloop	Aluminium	White	Farr	Pierre Fehlmann	Switzerland
Euromarche	72ft 9in	59ft	17ft 3in	11ft 1in	71,680lb	60.8ft	Ketch	Aluminium	Black	Mauric	Eric Tabarly	France
European University Belgium	46ft	32ft 3in	13ft 3in	7ft 6in	25,500lb	34.4ft	Sloop	Aluminium	Red	Frers	Jean Blondiau	Belgium
33 Export	57ft 8in	45ft 9in	15ft 9in	9ft	34,280lb	45.5ft	Sloop	Aluminium	Yellow	Briand	Thomas Phillipe/Phillipe Schaff	France
FCF Challenger	80ft 6in	68ft	20ft 6in	12ft 6in	76,160lb	69.6ft	Sloop	Fibreglass	Blue	Peterson	Leslie Williams	Britain
Flyer	76ft	65ft	18ft	11ft 8in	67,000lb	67.8ft	Sloop	Aluminium	White, red trim	Frers	Cornelis van Rietschoten	Holland
Gauloises III	62ft 9in	55ft 7in	16ft 4in	9ft 9in	47,000lb	51.6ft	Sloop	Aluminium	Light blue	Holland	Eric Loizeau	France
Ilgagomma	50ft	41ft 6in	15ft 8in	6ft 6in		40ft	Cutter	Aluminium	White	Carozzo	Roberto Vianello	Italy
Kriter IX	62ft 3in	52ft	16ft 2in	10ft	43,000lb	52.1ft	Sloop	Aluminium	Dark blue	Frers	Andre Viant	France
La Barca Laboratoria	63ft 7in	51ft 5in	16ft 9in	9ft 4in	42,920lb	51ft	Sloop	Aluminium	White	Giorgetti/Magrini	Claudio Stampi	Italy
Licor 43	60ft	48ft 8in	16ft 8in	9ft 4in	66,043lb	51.4ft	Sloop	Aluminium	Red	Bazan	Joaquin Coello	Spain
Mor Bihan	48ft 7in	41ft 9in	15ft 5in	8ft 2in	28,180lb	37.2ft	Sloop	Fibreglass	White	Joubert/Nivelt	Phillipe Poupon/Eugene Riguidel	France
Outward Bound	50ft 8in	37ft	15ft 3in	8ft 6in	24,000lb	40ft	Sloop	GRP	White	Davidson	Digby Taylor	New Zealand
Rolly Go	51ft 3in	42ft 2in	14ft 4in	8ft 5in	26,208lb	39.6ft	Sloop	Kevlar/Balsa	Grey	Frers	Giorgio Falck	Italy
Save Venice	64ft 9in	55ft 7in	17ft 5in	10ft 8in	44,800lb	39.6ft	Sloop	Aluminium	White	Scattolin	Dio Malingri	Italy
Scandinavian	57ft	45ft	15ft	9ft 1in	49,000lb	41.9ft	Ketch	GRP	Dark blue	S&S	Reino Engqvist	Sweden
Skopbank of Finland	50ft 9in	49ft 9in	15ft 2in	8ft 10in	34,944lb	38ft	Cutter	Fibreglass	White	C&C	Ken Gahmberg	Finland
Swedish Entry	60ft 7in	52ft 1in	17ft 7in	9ft 8in	44,091lb	48ft	Sloop	GRP	White	Norlin	Pedder Silverhieim	Sweden
Traite de Rome	51ft 2in	36ft 10in	13ft 10in	7ft 7in	28,500lb	34.6ft	Sloop	Aluminium	Blue	S&S	Antonio Chioatto	E.E.C.
United Friendly	77ft 2in	68ft 2in	18ft 5in	9ft	73,024lb	68ft	Schooner	Wood	Dark blue	Gurney	Chay Blyth	Britain
Vivanapoli	56ft 9in	46ft 3in	16ft 8in	9ft 7in	44,800lb	42.1ft	Sloop	Fibreglass	Blue	Simeone	Beppe Panada	Italy
Walross III Berlin	52ft 7in	40ft 8in	14ft 1in	8ft	43,456lb	36.8ft	Sloop	GRP	White	S&S	Olaf Michel	Germany
Xargo III	64ft 6in	47ft	16ft 4in	9ft 2in	57,344lb	44.4ft	Ketch	GRP	Green	S&S	Peter Kuttel	Sth. Africa

Challenger was the biggest boat in the fleet but Les Williams had been struggling for money. The gear didn't look good, nor did the sails. She might be a force when she was let loose in the Southern Ocean but, again she didn't give the impression that she was easy to handle. With luck (for us that is), they wouldn't be able to sail her efficiently for any length of time.

The French entries *Charles Heidsieck III* and *Kriter IX*, with *Flyer*, looked the greatest threats. *Charles Heidsieck* rated quite high for her length, but she was meticulously prepared and would be driven very hard by Alain Gabbay and his crew who had been nicknamed the 'Marseilles Mafia'. They all came from the south of France and had been sailing together for years, including 12,000 miles working up in *Charles Heidsieck.* Gabbay skippered *33 Export* in the last race and won the Cape Town-Auckland leg. He knew what he was doing and how to get results.

Kriter was the Frers boat that Conny was reported to be interested in until *Ceramco* came along at 68ft overall. She was a pedigree design with good gear and a good crew skippered by the likeable and highly capable Andre Viant. If this race was decided by the first and last legs, with their likelihood of lots of light upwind sailing, *Kriter* could be the boat to beat.

In the small boat range, our compatriot *Outward Bound* had to be the pick. Digby Taylor and his crew had already done a lot of racing miles in their Davidson design as well as having sailed *Outward Bound* from New Zealand to Britain, experiencing 70 and 80-knot winds on the way. They had done their homework and knew their boat — and this was going to be important.

Ceramco had to give *Outward Bound* close on 6½ days on handicap to Cape Town. That was about 35 miles a day. In some conditions that wouldn't present a problem, but in others it would be a struggle. The smaller yachts could be right in the picture on the first and last legs but they'd have trouble matching the pace of *Ceramco* and *Flyer* across the Southern Ocean.

There obviously were others in the fleet, dark horses that we could only guess about. We would soon know. All we could be sure of is that we had done as much as possible to enchance our chances. *Ceramco* was an improved boat for doing the Seahorse races, pointing five degrees higher and sailing half a knot faster upwind. We'd also filled in some gaps in the sail wardrobe with a ½oz kite and 1.7oz ghosting genoa for the Doldrums, plus a reaching staysail to give us more horsepower under the genoa.

We were convinced the boat had the potential to do 350 miles a day in the Southern Ocean. If we could hang on to *Flyer* in the first and last legs, and if she could match our performance downwind in the heavy stuff, this was going to be some race.

5. ALL FALL DOWN

The Ship was cheered, the Harbour cleared —
Merrily did we drop
Below the Kirk, below the Hill,
Below the Light-house top.
— *Samuel Taylor Coleridge,* The Rime of the Ancient Mariner

SATURDAY, 29 AUGUST 1981: Portsmouth. Time to go. The months, years of planning and preparation had all been directed at this typically cool and misty English morning. The Round the World race start was only hours away as Pippa and I left Emsworth and headed for the Camper and Nicholson marinas at Gosport.

The final hours before a long distance ocean race are the hardest. All the work is done, the boat and crew are ready to go. It's time to say goodbye to the people you love. You want the moments to last, but the adrenalin is pumping. The countdown is well advanced and your mind is already racing.

The start was chaotic. By the time we reached *Ceramco*, the Camper and Nicholson marinas were a hive of activity, despite the early hour, jammed with relatives, friends and well-wishers. The comparatively narrow stretch of water between Gosport and Portsmouth was crowded with spectator craft. Through the mist outside the entrance to Portsmouth harbour we could see a massive spectator fleet gathering.

Many of the boats were still loading stores. The pile of gear on the dock alongside the Italian entry *La Barca Laboratorio* had to be seen to be believed, yet 'The Barking Lavatory' was already floating below her marks. *Ceramco* was a scene of comparative quiet. We'd finished preparing yesterday. Only Vonny was busy, finding homes for the last-minute fresh food supplies. Everyone else was relaxed, chatting and signing autographs and saying their goodbyes.

Departure hour — 1000 hours for us. Because of a damaged propeller shaft, we'd have to sail *Ceramco* away from the dock and out of the harbour to the start area. It was going to be an interesting manoeuvre with only catspaws for wind and the harbour already churned up by the growing spectator fleet.

We'd bent the prop shaft on the way back to Portsmouth after the Fastnet race. The weather had been flat calm and, to keep to schedule, we'd motored all the way from Plymouth, back up the English Channel to our base on the Hamble River near the entrance to Southampton Water. As we'd neared the Solent, Lui (Richard White) had come on deck to tell us the fresh water tasted salty. Of course, he was told to use the fresh water pump and not the salt water one, but a pot of tea soon afterwards confirmed Lui's suspicions — there was sea water in the fresh water tanks. It was a problem we didn't need with just two weeks to the race start, and there was only one solution. *Ceramco* was slipped at Moody's Yard on the Hamble River. To our dismay, we found the propeller strut was broken, plus there were cracks extending diagonally up into the aluminium hull bottom. The sea water had entered the fresh water tanks through these cracks.

After several attempts at cutting and rewelding, we made the strut strong enough for light motoring but the plates still leaked slightly so the fresh water tanks in that part of the hull were unusable. We didn't have time to tackle that problem. It would have to wait until we got to Auckland where *Ceramco* would be slipped at the McMullen and Wing yard where she was built. Meanwhile, we couldn't lug two tanks of salt water around the world. *Ceramco* had to be kept light to perform well. Our solution was to cut holes in the tank tops and fill the tanks with polyurethane expanding foam.

We were fortunate that the desalination plant I had ordered two months earlier had arrived and been installed by the agents during the last week. Our project had been running short of money by this stage so I had bought this piece of equipment myself — as a birthday present to Pippa. I still don't know whether she was that impressed, even if her 'present' had cost $10,000. The 'water machine' was to prove invaluable however.

We kept the changes hush-hush but there was little we could do about loading sufficient 20-litre plastic containers aboard to enable us to carry the minimum 50 litres of fresh water per man for the start of the race.

I felt completely happy about the new set-up. It had been our intention, since deciding to buy a desalinator, to use as much of the stored water as quickly as possible after the start of a leg to lighten ship. We'd keep only enough to get us to a nearby port if the 'water machine' failed. The only difference now was that if we had to motor we'd probably end up with salt water in the two bottom tanks again and that would make the yacht heavier. Motoring would have to be kept to a minimum.

As the boys let go our dock lines, the mainsail already hoisted and flapping in the light easterly breeze, we waved farewell to the big support team ashore. Chris Edwards, a good friend of mine, was there to see us off. His friendly nature, I'm sure, helped to keep the tears at bay as I said goodbye to Pippa. We hadn't been apart since our wedding in the summer of 1979 and my heart was heavy as I watched her make her way back up the marina, never once looking around.

We had no real problems out in the harbour. As soon as we were clear of the dock, the big Mylar genoa was hoisted and *Ceramco* came alive as we tacked towards the harbour entrance pushing a strong, flood tide with Lui in the bow to warn off any spectator craft that got too close.

We picked up more breeze as we cleared the narrow entrance to be greeted by the ferryboat *Solent Scene* which had been charted for the day by the Ceramco group of companies and which was loaded with supporters and emblazoned with two huge banners which exclaimed 'C'mon Kiwis'. I could see Pippa on board, looking much happier than she had been earlier, clutching a glass of champagne and generally being quite boisterous. My parents were there too, having flown in from New Zealand for the start along with a host of crew families and friends. Tom Clark let rip with one of his well-known yodels and Alan Topham called encouragement over the ferry's loudspeaker system. It seemed that everyone involved in the project was there for the big occasion and I spotted my partner in crime, Alan Sefton, doing his best to lower the champagne stocks in between taking pictures and recording the event for the *Auckland Star*.

Portsmouth is the oldest naval base in England with a colourful history that spans hundreds of years. I'm sure Nelson, one of the port's most famous sons, would have been impressed with the armada that was assembled but at the same time horrified by the cross-channel ferry that tore through the start area at speed, tooting furiously and scattering the gathering of mostly weekend sailors.

The start area, with a line between Spit Sand Fort and Southsea Castle, was only a mile from the harbour entrance so we were there in plenty of time. I used that time for my usual pre-race crew chat. We dropped the headsail and sat down with a hot drink to discuss the situation. I find this helps to calm pre-race nerves and gives me the opportunity to discuss things like tactics, water usage at sea, personal and ship cleanliness. I also asked the crew not to yell at or abuse spectator craft that would inevitably get in our way before we cleared the Solent. It was all part of the fun.

The wind had increased to a moderate easterly as the 1200 hours start time approached. A dead beat to windward to Bembridge Ledge — the only mark of the course to Cape Town. The sea was really churned up but the start line was kept clear of spectator craft by a flotilla of patrol boats. I wondered how long they would keep things under control.

Half an hour to go, the tension mounted. With the No. 1 heavy genoa and full mainsail, we sorted out our starting position, trying to decide whether we should be on the Southsea shore, near the castle, or down the line towards the fort. The crew was now very quiet, actions and reactions were automatic. The only thought was to be away first.

At the 10-minute gun we decided on a port tack start at the leeward end of the line near the fort. Five minutes to go and everything looked good. I was on the helm, Staggy called tactics and times, OC trimmed the main, Vonny was on runner backstays, Lui on bow lookout, Simon, the Doc, Don and Molly were on the grinders with Jaws and Newt tailing, Chappy called sail trim.

The gun — noon precisely and we were away with 7600 miles to go to Cape Town. Prime position on port tack and going like a rocket across the bows of *Kriter, Gauloises* and *Berge Viking* as we headed down the Solent towards Horse Sand Fort and the open sea. It looked as though we would lay the fort but then another cross-channel ferry came through and seemed to suck up all the wind for miles around. We have to tack and *Flyer,* with her big masthead rig charges through. Everything had been going great but now we were surrounded by spectator craft and being hurt badly by their wash. I got a little stroppy and, none too politely, asked one of the bigger motor yachts to windward of us to 'stuff off' — prompting some withering looks from several of my crew who remembered my recent request for no abuse.

Just after the start, on port tack and away with clear air.

We had to weave our way clear, with *Flyer* sneaking ahead, and, after two more tacks, rounded Bembridge Ledge, to the east of the Isle of Wight, and headed out into the English Channel. *Flyer* was in front of us; *Kriter*, *Charles Heidsieck* and *Challenger* were immediately astern. The rest of the fleet was a long way back. The pattern for the race was already established.

Solent Scene came with us all the way to the Bembridge mark, everyone yelling encouragement and clearly enjoying themselves. But then she peeled away and, with a couple of farewell toots, headed back to Portsmouth. We were on our own as we hoisted the .85oz spinnaker, set a staysail and came on to a south-westerly course down the channel and settled into our watch system and onboard routine.

Watch systems vary from yacht to yacht. *Ceramco's* crew was split into two watches with myself and Vonny floating. We worked two watches of six hours during the day (0800hrs to 1400hrs and 1400hrs to 2000hrs) and three watches of four hours during the night (2000hrs to 2400hrs, 0000hrs to 0400hrs and 0400hrs to 0800hrs). With only two watch teams, this system meant a change every second day and gave the watch below the chance of a good sleep period. The watches were labelled A and Z, under watch leaders Keith Chapman (Chappy) and Geoff Stagg (Staggy). Chappy's A watch for the first leg comprised Don (England), Molly (Richard Mac), Newt (John Newton) and Lui (Richard White). In the Z watch, Staggy had Simon (Gundry), Doc (Trevor Agnew), OC (Owen Rutter) and Jaws (Don Wright). Vonny wouldn't stand a deck watch but was always available for sail changes if required. His duties as cook would be arduous enough, particularly in rough weather. My position as skipper and navigator would keep me from getting bored. I was also available at any time to discuss tactical or shipboard problems, personal or otherwise, help during sail changes or take a stint at the wheel.

At St Catherine's Point, on the southern shores of the Isle of Wight, we squared away a little and interchanged spinnakers and genoas a few times as the now south-east breeze became light and fluky with the change of the tide. Visibility was poor because of a light sea mist, but at least the weather was fine. No more spectator craft and *Flyer* was out of sight, somewhere ahead in the mist. The sun doubled its size and turned blood red as it sank into the western sky. Very romantic, but I wasn't really in the mood to appreciate it, having hit my head on the main boom during one of the sail changes. The encounter has left me with a ruddy great lump that will remind me to be a little more careful in the days and weeks ahead.

Our first dinner of the trip was excellent, a whole joint of roast pork (which Vonny and Simon had precooked ashore) with all the trimmings, including apple sauce. Everyone gorged themselves, glad to be at sea at last, feeling pretty good and looking forward to some excellent sailing once we get down into the trades. For now, however, the forecast is for light and variable conditions with nothing more than Force 3. We'll just have to work and wait for an improvement.

All on deck and psyched up for the dash out of the Solent.

Day 2: Sunday, August 30. Noon position 48.23N 05.37W
Day's run 222 miles. Course 235 degrees.
Wind SSE 10 to 18 knots. Barometer 1012.

A tremendous amount of shipping about during the night. During Staggy's watch, between 2000hrs and midnight, 17 ships passed us, plus one cruising yacht heading north. The ships were difficult to see, only visible at a quarter mile distance, because of the murk. One came too close for comfort, missing *Ceramco* by only three or four boat lengths as it altered course hard to port and we hardened up under shy spinnaker. Things improved as a westerly swell set in soon after midnight with 20 to 25 knots of wind forcing us to change to the 2.2oz heavy working spinnaker. The wind died in the troughs but built up on the tops and we didn't want to risk blowing out the lighter kite. We'd really started to shift under the 2.2, surfing hard off the tops of the seas, always in reasonably controlled fashion. By dawn we were well down the channel but wearing mainsail and genoa only in a dying southerly. We wanted to make Ushant with a favourable tide. The swell disappeared as quickly as it had come up and *Ceramco* was running as though on rails. Down below at the chart table it was hard to tell that we were at sea at all. During the morning we checked out the generator and ran the desalination plant. Both worked fine. We used quite a lot of fresh water from the tanks, even using it to wash dishes, to try to reduce weight. In a few days' time, we'll be relying on the desalinator with a vengeance.

The island of Ushant came abeam just before noon, but we were 12 miles off and hadn't a hope of seeing it in two-mile visibility. A high-speed French naval patrol vessel came out to take a look at us as we cleared the Ushant shipping lanes. These are strictly regulated zones to control the enormous amount of shipping coming past the north-west corner of France, from the Mediterranean to Europe and from European ports to the Mediterranean and Panama. Our Satnav showed us to be in the clear, which was just as well because zone infringements result in heavy fines. Luckily we had the tide in our favour. It was running at three to four knots if our check on a handy fishing buoy was anything to go by.

Our course now is to the south-west towards Cape Finisterre on the southern side of the Bay of Biscay. We creep along for most of the afternoon under the light spinnaker, making only a few knots. The surface of the sea is glassy calm as we head slightly to the west of the rhumbline (a straight-line course on the chart) from Ushant to Finisterre, working up to keep the kite full. A few dolphins about plus one Froggy fishing boat, otherwise we've got the ocean to ourselves.

The 1800hrs fleet radio sched puts *Flyer* two miles astern of us in company with *Challenger.* We try calling Digby Taylor on *Outward Bound* but no reply, so tackle dinner instead. Roast beef, roast potatoes, cauliflower, carrots and peas followed by apple pie and cream and some strange-looking custard. Newt compliments Vonny on a terrific meal and prompts the retort: 'Well, it can only get worse.'

Day 3: Monday, August 31. Noon position 46.24N 07.52W
Day's run 150 miles. Course 170 degrees.
Wind SW 20 to 25 knots. Barometer 1016.

The breeze has been up and down, meaning lots of headsail changes as we've tacked into a south-south-westerly of fluctuating strength. We've had the odd shower or two, but conditions have been reasonably pleasant and slightly warmer. The barometer has been extremely steady at 1018 millibars. The maps from our weatherfax machine (which receives and prints out weather map transmissions from various land stations) show little chance of strong winds. In fact the North Atlantic looks extremely quiet and lacks any dominant features just now. The weather maps which are the most use at this stage are those received from Bracknell, in England, and Madrid, in Spain, but with the current picture they're little help. It's a case of heading for the mark (in this case Finisterre) and keeping our fingers crossed. I had a bit of a start today when the weatherfax stylus broke. This leg of the race is going to be won or lost on the course one takes. The weather information aids we have, particularly the weatherfax machine in conjunction with the barograph and barometer, are vital to the decision making. Fortunately Gordon Holmes, of Southern Communications in Auckland, had done his homework on the spares for the weatherfax. We had a dozen extra styli and a second drive belt.

It is compulsory that we sent our position to the Race Office in Portsmouth twice a week, giving latitude, longitude, date and time. We cranked up the generator tonight to do just that. Today was also *Ceramco's* turn for alarm watch duty. All yachts have to be equipped with watch alarm receivers. These special radio receivers tuned to the 2182 Khz emergency frequency. They let off a high-pitched screamer alarm if they pick up a signal on that frequency. We have a roster to ensure that at least one race boat has its watch alarm receiver operational on any given day. This will be the fleet's means of raising the alarm if something goes wrong and help is needed, especially when we head south from Cape Town into the Southern Ocean, away from shipping lanes and all the alarm routes. In the Atlantic, the alarm receivers are not quite as important as the aircraft distress beacons we carry. These should summon help much more quickly. But it will be the reverse situation down off the edge of the Antarctic pack ice.

This evening we are laying just to the west of Cape Finisterre, approximately 150 miles away. We've had *Flyer* in sight all day, racing boat for boat, tack for tack with *Challenger's* mast top just in sight about seven miles astern. *Flyer* has climbed out to weather of us a bit, but we're delighted with *Ceramco's* performance to windward in these conditions. We fully expected *Flyer* to do a horizon job on us. The fact that we're matching her is a considerable morale booster and the crew has been right on its toes, making sure *Flyer* doesn't give us the slip. We had a chat to Conny on VHF this evening and decided not to give the rest of the fleet our positions. On the 1800hrs sched, Pierre Fehlmann on *Disque D'Or* got a little upset that neither *Flyer* nor *Ceramco* talked, but that is all part of the psyching game. *Disque D'Or* is 60 miles astern tonight and *Rollygo* 100 miles back. That's not bad for two days out. It looks as though they've run into a calm patch. While *Flyer, Ceramco* and *Challenger* have gone slightly west, some of the others have gone east into the Bay of Biscay. This could prove their undoing as the latest forecasts are for a high pressure system forming in the bay.

We had a big clean-out today and, even though *Ceramco* is heeling over at a 25-degree angle, everything is in its correct place. With only 12 people aboard, *Ceramco* seems an empty yacht. To date we've always raced with extras. We took 16 to Hobart and 17 in the Fastnet. Now I keep looking around for people.

We're all eating too much. Breakfast this morning was porridge with brown sugar followed by a slice of smoked ham, fried eggs with baked beans on toast and a cup of tea or coffee. Lunch comprised smoked ham, cheese, pickles, lettuce and Long Life bread (it tastes one month old when new and one month old after six months). Dinner tonight was pork chops, mashed potatoes and vegetables. Everyone is eating as much chocolate as they like but fruit is rationed to one apple, one orange and one banana a day.

The ship's routine requires the crew to wash the dishes for the cook although Vonny has to keep the galley clean and scrub his own pots and pans. This saves the crew moaning and groaning about burnt cooking containers. It is the duty of the watch coming below at 0800hrs to wash the breakfast dishes, tidy the cabin and thoroughly clean and disinfect the toilet before climbing into their bunks for the rest of the morning to either sleep or read. The watch coming off at 1400hrs for lunch have to wash the luncheon dishes before retiring for the afternoon. The routine is the same after dinner.

We have an ample supply of books on board, many of them provided by Spud Spedding, our UK racing navigator. I've already finished one book which is extraordinary for me. But I haven't had much sleep as yet. The race has been uninspiring but we've been churning out dozens of weather maps and plotting the positions of the opposition, trying to ascertain which is the best side of the course to be on. So far things have gone reasonably well, but it can all turn to rubbish very quickly if we make a mistake.

Blake's 'office' in the navigatorium.

Vonny at work – preparing drinks for the deck watch.   A galley tete-a-tete for Staggy (left) and Molly.

Day 4: Tuesday, September 1. Noon position 43.43N 08.48W
Day's run 167 miles. Course 250 degrees.
Wind S 10 to 12 knots. Barometer 1018.

By 1000hrs we were only 25 miles north-west of La Coruna on the Spanish coast after a quiet night of light, fickle breezes. We sent the radar reflector aloft when we ran into a real pea-souper just before dawn. We had been hearing ship's engines all around us and feeling the occasional wash. When the fog lifted suddenly seven large ships were close by, plus one fishing boat, all barrelling along. It made us wonder how close they'd been when the fog hid everything.

No sign of *Flyer* at all today. We can only assume she has wriggled away from us. The forecast is for more variables. There has not been much of that even of late and the weather maps promise little change. Not too encouraging but, on the brighter side, it is certainly getting warmer. The log reads: 'Chappy has become the founder member of the CNZ Sun Club — not a pretty sight, OC is on his third 360 turn on the helm.' Pippa's birthday present is working well — made 35 litres of fresh water this morning for washing and galley use. Cape Finisterre seems so close, yet so far away. Once we turn the corner and head off down the coast of Portugal we have to make the decision whether to go offshore or stay in on the coast and try to pick daytime sea breezes and night-time land breezes which the pilot books say are present at this time of the year. One can't call the race electrifying to this stage but it certainly is comfortable. No problems with seasickness and we're all getting plenty of sleep, charging our batteries for more testing times to come.

Becalmed near Porto Santo.

Day 5: Wednesday, September 2. Noon position 42.42N 09.57W
     Day's run 85 miles. Course 230 degrees.
     Wind variable. Barometer 1022.

Finally got moving yesterday evening, sliding past Cape Volarno towards Finisterre under our lightweight spinnaker. But it didn't last long. By 2200hrs it was flat calm again and it remained like that for two hours before a south-easterly started to fill in just after midnight. The 0100hrs log entry reads: '1.75oz Mylar (genoa) strikes again. Porcelain rocketship fuel.' We were moving in a 4 to 8-knot breeze which veered through the south to the south-west, but then died. Not much of the coast was discernible through the haze and smoke from fires on the shore and then we were in fog all morning. There's been a lot of shipping inshore of us although we haven't seen anything, only heard it and smelt heavy concentrations of diesel. Early this morning we did a couple of circles in no wind at all, just trying to get some sort of weigh on. It was so damp that every time the sails shook in the light swell they showered the deck below with heavy drops of moisture — heavy enough to make us wear wet weather gear.

The weather maps only show that the Atlantic met situation is arse about face with a large, shallow low occupying the position normally associated with a high. We can't really complain though. The majority of the fleet are stuck in the Bay of Biscay and a lot worse off than we are. We must push down the coast of Portugal as fast as possible. If we can make a break now it could be a big one that will split the fleet and decide the leg. We're using harbour racing tactics, shifting crew weight all the time to keep *Ceramco* trimmed properly. The catch phrase on board is 'Wriggle, wriggle, wriggle'.

The impressive thing for me right now is the way the crew has settled quickly into the racing routine. There's nothing special about heading for Cape Town, the leg is just another race and the two watches are performing extremely well under the competent guidance and enthusiasm of Staggy and Chappy. It's a happy team — and that's important.

Kirsten Maersk, a 250,000-ton oil tanker, passed close by on her way to the UK, and wished us a pleasant trip. We also saw an enormous whale travelling north. Jaws identified it as a sperm but Molly, our on-board marine biologist of rather dubious reputation, reckoned it was a humpback whale. Vonny came on deck after the whale disappeared, removed his rather odd yellow underwear, flung it over the side and pranced around the deck in the nick. Newt declared him to be a 'little nymphette' but Vonny is anything but one of those. Next he decided on a salt water bath because the weather was so good. Our cook is definitely not a pretty sight, covered in Badedas, bending over the side to fill his bucket and displaying an awesomely spotty bum. The crew on deck just fell about laughing when he completed his toilet by sitting in the bucket to wash the more delicate parts of his anatomy.

I spent a few minutes checking the deviation of both steering compasses by sighting across the sun. By then using the tables to calculate what the correct reading should have been, it was easy to work out the errors. Today we have 2 degrees east deviation on the port compass and 3 degrees east on the starboard compass, hardly enough to worry about. The Satnav (satellite navigator which fixes our position by communicating with special navigational satellites put up by the Americans) makes position finding extremely easy. I've only used the sextant, so far, to check the Satnav in the initial stages of our journey.

Late this afternoon we picked up a light west-south-westerly and, under a brilliantly blue sky and with slight seas, we were able to lay course to the south.

From the evening chat show, it seems Conny has made a break of 40 miles on us, which is a bit of a bummer. But with conditions the way they are we could easily reverse that situation in the next day or so. This sort of sailing must be a strange initiation for the crew of Les Williams' 80-footer *Challenger*, many of whom have paid £7000 for the privilege of doing the race. They must feel that ocean racing is a piece of cake. I hope it doesn't fool them. *Outward Bound*, we learned this morning, is doing well — only 112 miles behind us and ahead of some pretty hot machines. Digby and his crew must be quite pleased with themselves. We talked to Chay Blyth on *United Friendly* and they've had a slight problem with a leak that developed on the first night out. But everyone on board is doing fine, sampling nine different brands of whisky. The smaller, slower yachts are 240 miles behind tonight. They all sound in good spirits even though it must be a bit demoralising to plot the positions of the bigger yachts and see how far in front we already are.

Because of the long nights with no moon, our Eveready torches have been taking a hammering. We've got a good stock of batteries, but even these are being depleted. In light and variable winds, and with almost constant fog, we're using the torches all the time to trim sails at night. The big Sanyo rechargeable light that Gray Mathias presented us with in Auckland is proving invaluable. We recharge it from the ship's batteries during the day. Then, for any really bright light needed for sorting out tangled halyards or to warn off shipping which is coming too close, we've got the 24-volt searchlight given to me by John van der Syp.

Day 7: Friday, September 4. Noon position 37.07N 15.29W
Day's run 222 miles. Course 230 degrees.
Wind NNE 10 knots. Barometer 1019.

Had a marvellous run all day yesterday, picking up a north-westerly that freshened and stayed with us. We've been tramping along under 1.5oz spinnaker, big staysail and full main. It seems the high pressure system has moved into the Azores area and a low has formed on the coast of Spain and Portugal down towards Gibraltar. In between the two systems is a northerly flow. We heard Digby talking to his PR people in New Zealand. The position he gave put *Outward Bound* still off La Coruna — where we were two days ago. That means we are now 200 miles ahead.

The breeze has not lasted though. By this morning it was light and waffling again. We changed up to the lightest spinnaker and hardened up a bit to the west to maintain speed in a rather sloppy sea. The sea condition, I'm sure, was due to the number of underwater peaks (sea mounts) in the immediate vicinity. The depths hereabouts vary between 5000 metres and 20 metres.

At noon today we'd logged 1053 miles since the start six days ago — an average of 175 miles a day, not bad considering the frustrating conditions. It has been interesting to watch the mood variations as the weather changes. If conditions are quiet, so are the crew. If the going is boisterous or rough, the crew jump around more, and yell and laugh. No matter what the weather does though, it's difficult to contain Chappy for long. He tends to let out yelps, screams and funny laughs, and rushes madly around the deck. Mock battles are common and Don seems to be suffering from a cracked rib after being pummelled into the galley servery this morning.

Chappy's afternoon watch, in boiling heat, turned into a limerick session, not all of the rhymes are particularly clean. Of course, there was a lot of laughter — much to the annoyance of Staggy's watch which was down below trying to get some sleep. The two watches are totally different in personality and approach. Staggy is full on, hard driving and demanding. Chappy is the butt of a lot of his own humour. But they end up with the same results and the boat is kept moving at maximum all the time.

I talked to Peter Montgomery in Auckland and, because of the interest back home, have agreed to increase the calls to Radio New Zealand to twice a week during these early stages of the race. Depending on the amount of traffic using Portishead Radio, it takes anything from five minutes to four hours to get a call through. If you're behind the *QE II* which has 20 or so calls booked, it's hardly worth waiting around.

51

There's little we can do except wait — and take a cooling dip.

As we're nearing the end of the first week at sea, we've had a good sort through the boat and ditched quite a bit of food that was excess to our requirements. We operate six weekly bins, the idea being to use all the food in bin No. 1 by the end of week No. 1, and then start on bin No. 2. This is a good way of monitoring consumption. If all the butter or milk is finished by Wednesday we have to go without those items until the next bin comes into use.

It's quite amazing how much rubbish there is in the ocean, even so far from land (we're 400 miles off the Portuguese coast and 300 miles north of Madeira). We've seen a cargo sling and nets, plastic bags and all sorts of human trash. Quite disturbing to see how badly man is littering his environment.

Lui was hoisted up the mainsail in the bosun's chair this afternoon to remove the third reef line and block from the leach of the sail. The weather is so settled, we have decided to try and improve the set of the sail by reducing the (for now) unnecessary weight on the leach. The effort must have been too much for Lui because late this evening he slipped on the rail and lost one of his Docksider shoes over the side.

The boat is very quiet tonight, matching the mood of the evening. I guess the dinner of large sirloin steaks, cabbage, mashed potatoes followed by steam pudding has made everyone feel replete. The breeze has headed us and Staggy's watch has just changed down from the light spinnaker to a light genoa.

Flyer is 20 miles ahead of us so we have closed in again. Our present course will take us outside the islands of Madeira, although that could change depending on the wind. Nobody seems to have much of that commodity, if the fleet chat show was anything to go by. The back markers have really bogged down. Some of them are more than 400 miles astern trying to run down the coast of Portugal on daytime sea breezes. We haven't done much better today and some yachts have closed in on us, but we're more or less holding our own. We can be thankful for an excellent selection of sails for the conditions. The new .5oz spinnaker is a real beauty, as is the new 1.75oz Mylar genoa for when the wind is only brushing catspaws on to an otherwise glassy sea. All we need now is yachtie's luck — all the breaks our way and none for anyone else.

The trades at last — and a bird's eye view of Ceramco *kicking her heels.*

Day 8: Saturday, September 5. Noon position 35.24N 17.06W
      Day's run 127 miles. Course 235 degrees.
      Wind S 10 knots. Barometer 1019.

Another light and character-forming day. The morning lacked distinction except for a wash in fresh water. Molly serviced the winches while I caught up on the official Whitbread logs. Lui got a backgammon school going as the crew is starting to relax together rather than spend so much time in their bunks. The repartee is developing. Simon was heard to mutter 'Christ' when he got a slight bump on the head from the boom last night. Vonny commented: 'Never mind, if it had hit your leg or something vital you could have been hurt.' Simon got his own back this morning when Don was looking for a small, empty container for some grease. 'Why not use Vonny's head,' Simon suggested.

The cat and mouse game with Conny continues, neither of us giving much away. We've been letting the *Flyer* people think we are further behind than we in fact are. On tonight's chat show, Conny asked if we had much breeze. My reply was: '⅞ths of ⁹⁄₁₀ths of FA, and I'm thinking of going for a swim.'

We picked up a nice south-westerly this afternoon and even spotted a few whitehorses as we changed down to the No. 2 genoa, all of us feeling happy with some breeze at last, and hoping it would last.

Day 9: Sunday, September 6. Noon position 33.14N 16.27W
      Day's run 140 miles. Course 180 degrees.
      Wind zero. Barometer 1021.

The wind stayed all night, turning more southerly, making our course straight for Madeira which is now rearing up in our path ahead. By dawn however we were back to a light genoa in 4 to 5 knots of WSW. Madeira stands nearly 2000 metres high and causes a huge wind shadow, so we want to keep reasonably well clear. Just now it looks like we'll end up going between Madeira and the island of Porto Santo to the north-east. That's if we go anywhere. The afternoon's log entries, in the wind column, read 'FA' then 'SFA' then a series of ticks below that remark until 2200 hours — 10 hours of absolutely nothing.

There's a stomach bug going around the boat. OC was first to get it and now Lui's been confined to his bunk. The Doc has given him a pill and told everyone to be particularly careful about washing, especially hands. I've been feeling down all day. The light and variable conditions we've had for more than eight days since the start have been enough to tax anyone. We haven't seen a hint of trade winds, apart from one short blast off Portugal, and it has been a real grind. Tiredness is my problem and even a short sleep this morning after breakfast hasn't helped. But we must keep driving. Even yards down the track in this stuff can be vital when the situation changes, as it must.

Staggy complained today of strange tasting toothpaste. We found he'd been brushing with sun cream, so he won't have to worry about sunburnt teeth for a while. Simon and the Doc, with little to do on deck, got involved in a deep discussion on anything and everything. They each picked their most evocative phrase in the English language. Simon's was 'A summer afternoon', the Doc's 'loving tranquillity'. Then they chose two books to take with them if they were marooned on a desert island. Simon's were *The Oxford Book of English Poetry* and John Steinbeck's *The Grapes of Wrath.* The Doc chose *Beastly Beatitudes* and *The Works of William Shakespeare.* The Doc later intimated that Simon regards him as 'a communist mole'.

Most of the crew are putting on weight. The light, calm conditions and Vonny's ample meals are to blame, but the afternoon teas aren't helping. Today we had demolished large amounts of Judy Glanville's (Pippa's mum) flapjacks — a kind of bran and honey biscuit — and one of the large fruit cakes baked for us by the ladies of the Devonport Yacht Club back home. All this as we flopped along under mainsail only in absolutely airless conditions.

The watch on deck went over the side for a swim and it was amazing how hard they had to work to keep up with *Ceramco*, even at flopspeed. The mood was good and extended to an exercise session comprising sit-ups and chin-ups. Then Vonny, Jaws, Newt and Molly staged a mock tennis match around the deck — doubles. Vonny was hitting 'slammers' from up on the bow, calling nets and faults.

Strange, but bird and sea life has ceased to exist, close as we are to Porto Santo. We could see smoke drifting off the hills from near a silver mine situated just below one of the higher peaks.

All I've gleaned from the weather maps in the last couple of days is the position of Hurricane Emily, north-east of the Caribbean, and a low approaching Scotland — all of which is about as much use to us as a hole in the head. But I got a bit of a boost from the chat show to find that although some of the boats astern have carried a breeze down behind us and *Flyer* is easing away (90 miles ahead according to Conny's position), we're still doing well and some of the smaller yachts are becalmed 500 miles astern off Lisbon.

Day 10: Monday, September 7. Noon position 31.21N 16.26W
Day's run 117 miles. Course 185 degrees.
Wind E 12 knots. Barometer 1019.

The easterly filled in just before midnight, prompting a log entry of: 'Moving at long last' and a rush of sail changes between the Mylar genoa and the light kite. We slid on past Madeira, heading south towards the Canaries. What a pleasant change. The boat cooled down as the breeze filled in to 10 knots and *Ceramco* made a good eight knots, bang on course. We were shadowed for quite a while by a Portuguese gun boat which must have picked us up on radar. Finally, just before dawn, she powered up to us, played a spotlight on the boat for nearly half an hour, before deciding we were harmless.

We made good time all through the day with the wind flicking SE then back to the east and then into the NE. Lui did a little work around the deck after dinner, was promptly sick again and was ordered back to bed. Don, Newt and the Doc have joined the sick list and it looks like the bug is going to work its way through the whole crew. I got a good, long sleep last night — probably because of the relief of having a reasonable breeze for a change.

Day 11: Tuesday, September 8. Noon Position 28.28N 15.40W
Day's run 180 miles. Course 220 degrees.
Wind NE 6 to 10 knots. Barometer 1019.

We flopped past the Selvagen Islands at dusk yesterday, heading for the passage between the islands of Tenerife and Gran Canaria in the Canary group. The Selvagens are uninhabited, except for the odd rabbit and sheep, and are visited only infrequently by fishermen. My feeling of improvement hadn't lasted long. I spent most of last night in my bunk again with a head that felt like it was full of cotton wool. I had the most vivid dreams involving *Disque D'Or* skipper Pierre

Fehlmann giving me vast quantities of champagne until I was so drunk I couldn't stand. When I woke, I felt as though I had been out on a big bash. I guess it must be a mild dose of the bug.

This morning saw us 40 miles north of Tenerife, but we couldn't see a thing. Visibility was atrocious even though it was a sunny day again. By noon we were in the gap midway between the 3700-metre-high Tenerife and the 1950-metre-high Gran Canaria. The funnelling effect on the north-easterly that was blowing produced a strong tail wind and *Ceramco* was surfing fast under big spinnaker, shooter and full main. We sighted the occasional hydrofoil ferry plying back and forth and a number of large ships bound from the South Atlantic to Europe. But we could see nothing of Tenerife through the haze, even though we were only 10 miles offshore. Thank goodness for the reliability of Satnav.

I steered for most of the afternoon as we left the Canaries astern. Chappy had joined the sick parade and retired to his bunk. It was probably poetic justice in his case. He'd been telling everyone the sickness was psychological and wouldn't affect an iron man like him. Now he's got it too and his frequent visits to the heads haven't been psychological at all. Newt couldn't resist the temptation to stand outside the heads while Chappy was yodelling and ask him how he was enjoying his psychological meal.

The Doc thinks the source of the problem may be the water in the tanks. So we've drained them, refilled them with fresh water from the desalination plant and changed the filters. That should help. Newt, anyway, is feeling better. He was heard to ask the Doc today: 'Hey, Trev, do farts have lumps in them.'

It seems *Kriter* and *Berge Viking* have made quite a breakthrough to the east of us and tonight are very close. *Gauloises* is also somewhere in the vicinity. To prevent the smaller boats astern gaining an advantage from knowing where the holes are, we've decided to stop talking on the chat show. *Flyer* and *Challenger* have already adopted this line, so the feeling must be general.

Molly would prefer a Wellington southerly.

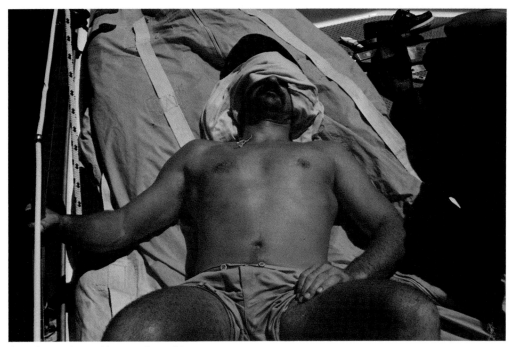
Into the tropics, so Newt works on his tan.

Vonny has made quite a comeback in the galley department. He didn't bring any cigarettes on this leg in an attempt to kick the habit, but he's been quite out of sorts at times and, at others, positively grumpy. Now he's eating toffees as a substitute and, in the last few days, with the help of Jaws (of course) has demolished most of a very large bag of Mackintosh's. We've already decided to make a point of having several hundred cigarettes on board for the next leg just in case he has a relapse. Breakfast this morning was last night's chilli con carne on thickly buttered toast. I missed the morning tea fruit cake but certainly enjoyed the lunch of stuffed sausages with salad. Dinner tonight was stew with fresh cabbage and mounds of mashed potatoes. Went down marvellously. The custard that followed for dessert was somewhat interesting in texture. Simon reckoned it was like the sea conditions — lumpy.

How long this fresh running will last is anyone's guess. So far the leg has been a smaller boat benefit, although not everyone has done well. Tonight, *33 Export* is 400 miles astern. *Outward Bound* is 350 miles behind, having covered only 70 miles in the last 24 hours compared to our 180 miles. They must be feeling extremely frustrated.

For now, we've got 20 to 25 knots from the north-east and *Ceramco* is creaming along, square running into the path of a half moon that lights up the stripes in the kite against a cloudless sky. Down below, most of the crew have dispensed with sleeping bags, using only the liners made from sheet material.

I'm missing Pippa a lot just now. She'd certainly enjoy this kind of sailing and I'd love to have her here. But, later on when we're in the Southern Ocean, I'll be glad she's ashore. It seems a shame to do this race and not be able to stop off at the places one passes by. Madeira looked magnificent, the Selvagens isolated but intriguing, the Canaries spectacular (what we saw of them). Some of the crew say they'll return to see those places, but I doubt if they will.

Day 13: Thursday, September 10. Noon Position 20.45N 18.41W
   Day's run 250 miles. Course 250 degrees.
   Wind NE 10 knots. Barometer 1016.

Two great days of sailing with *Ceramco* hitting 250 miles noon to noon on both of them. The north-east trades are finally doing their stuff and *Ceramco* hers — shooting off the tops of the seas at more than 20 knots, under complete control. In the 24 hours up to 0800hrs today we'd covered 282 miles which is a *Ceramco* best. Vonny has evolved his own system of checking progress. When his sink gurgles, he knows we're doing better than 20 knots. If the oven bangs too often it's time to put a reef in. If things fly off the swinging shelf it's time to put a couple of reefs in. If the detergent bottle is compressed, the barometer must be rising. When he can walk around the boat without any problem when we are hard on, we haven't got enough sail on. Simon wonders whether Brookes and Gatehouse know about this system.

A couple of flying fish came aboard during the night, one just missing OC's throat before hitting the compass and landing on the cockpit floor. I had it grilled for breakfast and we're hopefully anticipating more such visitors.

The winds died for a while during this morning so we changed to a 1.5oz lighter spinnaker, putting a slight tear in it in the process. So we went back up to the 2.2oz while Lui quickly repaired the damage by pegging the sail on Vonny's breadboard, sealing the edges with a 12-volt hot-knife and then applying a patch with the sewing machine.

I spoke to Peter Montgomery for 13 minutes and sent a telegram to the All Blacks saying 'Good luck for the 3rd test (against South Africa). Will be listening to you from West African coast.' We learned from Pippa that the new *Condor* had broken her mast in Sardinia. We're keeping our fingers crossed for ours.

Day 14: Friday, September 11. Noon position 18.54N 19.35W
   Day's run 122 miles. Course 220 degrees.
   Wind SE 5 knots. Barometer 1015.

It was too good to last. Yesterday afternoon developed into a sloppy sail with the wind all over the place, one minute from the north, the next from the east. The spinnaker was up and down like the proverbial knickers of the lady of the night. We just about went around the bend, even tacked a couple of times with the kite up, wrapped around the mast and spinnaker net. Then the breeze died altogether, leaving us to slop and crash about in a big sea with only the mainsail set. The spinnaker was a waste of time in this stuff, so we hoisted the No. 1 genoa and toddled off down the rhumbline in winds from all points of the compass. We managed only 30 miles from midnight to 0600hrs today and, all in all, did quite well to hit 122 miles noon to noon. The situation prompted a log entry of 'Doldrums?!!!?' but we were still quite a way north to strike them yet.

Over the last few days visibility has been poor, due to a fine red dust coming off the deserts to the east of us. This morning all the sails were marked from where they'd been rubbing against the shrouds and where the headsails had been slatting against the spurs. The deck underneath the spinnaker poles was covered in the dust which had turned to sludge in the night's damp. Watches during this period could be described as painful and tiring.

The breeze picked up again, from the SE, this afternoon bringing with it the swallows. By tonight the population on board was up to 10, with two extras of different pedigree. They are becoming quite friendly, eight of them resting on the checkstay at the mast, two on the bow and another on the wheel with the helmsman, twittering and tweeting to each other (the birds that is, not the helmsman). The problem is they dive down below and make a nuisance of themselves and, of course, they'll probably die. Birds that come aboard yachts or ships have generally been blown off their migration track by unusual weather or lost their way because of lack of leadership. Most won't, as a rule, accept food or water (pigeons are an exception).

Heaven help us if we are in the Doldrums already, at such a latitude. The annoying thing is that tonight's chat show revealed *Bubblegum* and *Outward Bound* to be careering down behind us in north-easterly trades, really closing the gap.

What might have happened is that the lack of normal weather in the Northern Hemisphere has allowed conditions in the Southern Hemisphere to push the Intertropical Convergence Zone (the Doldrums) well north of its usual position. The Doldrums are a low pressure belt of variable winds where the north-easterly trades above the equator meet the south-easterly trades from below the equator. At the ITCZ, these trade winds mix and rise vertically before travelling back towards the poles as the jetstreams in the upper atmosphere. Thunderheads, squalls, calms and very heavy rain are likely to be experienced in the belt which is particularly frustrating for people trying to get through in sailing vessels.

If we are in them, they are nearly 600 miles north of where they should be and, if they move south with us, we're in real trouble.

The temperature has soared and it's sweltering on deck and below. Water consumption has increased dramatically. We're now consuming more than five litres a man a day. Yachts without desalination plants must be finding life very difficult, especially when we've had no rain to replenish supplies. We've been sweating so much that the Doc has prescribed salt tablets, two to be taken after every meal, to combat salt loss. Without these tablets one feels lethargic and gets extremely thirsty.

As I write this, I've got a swallow hopping about on my head while another is trying to scramble into the back of OC's clothing locker on the port side. I hope it doesn't die there.

The icebox ran out yesterday so Vonny has just finished cooking all the thawed-out sausages. Tomorrow they'll be used for his version of Toad in the Hole. The crew reckon that his recipe for this is on page six of his five-page cookbook. It all means that from tonight we're on to dehydrated and tinned foods, the freeze dried meats from Alliance Freezing and the tinned meat from Butlands Industries which were specially prepared for this venture.

The talk on deck centres on a variety of topics, much of it about ice cold drinks and girls in Cape Town. Simon has been psyching those of the crew who have not yet been across the equator and they are getting quite nervous about the forthcoming ceremony.

For the last few hours we've been on course doing 6 knots. We reckon we must be in the hunt for the *Guinness Book of Records* for the greatest number of miles sailed without reefing. So far we've raced 2500 miles from north to south across a very differing range of weather patterns in which one would normally expect to have to reef quite frequently. So far we haven't had one reef in, haven't been down below the No. 3 genoa nor used a spinnaker smaller than the heavy, full-sized job. Most of the time we've been using our lightest sails. The leg is turning out much harder mentally than physically. The thing now is to keep pushing as hard as possible without becoming too frustrated.

Sitting on deck after dinner, enjoying the comparative cool up there, we were treated to a magnificent dolphin display. They were leaping right out of the water, coming up on their tails and some doing spirals in the air before crashing back into the sea. One remained right alongside and turned on a superb performance that had everyone clapping and cheering. The dolphin seemed to know he was appreciated because he kept coming back for curtain calls. With the swallows all active at the same time, chirping loudly and flying in and out of the rigging, Vonny reckoned we were on 'Blake's Ark'.

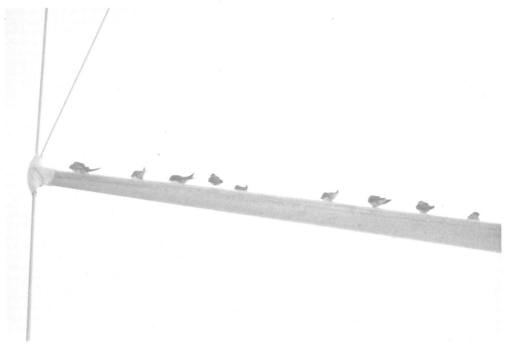

Straphanging on the spreaders.

Day 16: Sunday, September 13. Noon position 13.32N 20.33W
        Day's run 174 miles. Course 240 degrees.
        Wind S 10 to 15 knots. Barometer 1015.

What a mixture of conditions. Yesterday produced a roaring blast under the heavy 2.2oz spinnaker and flapping mainsail, dragging the main boom in the tide at times as we thundered along on the front of some heavy-looking squalls coming off the African coast some 300 miles to the east, towering thunderheads with localised rain beneath them and plenty of squirts. We heard later that *Berge Viking* had been in 50 knots of wind for half an hour, blown a spinnaker to shreds, then spent the next few hours totally becalmed. We'd done only 154 miles to noon yesterday so we were glad to get a wriggle on, particularly after receiving the news that the All Blacks had 'thrashed' the Springboks 25-22. The log read: 'Our Black Beauties rooted them.'

Last night was the best of the trip so far — an inky black sky and a brilliant, nearly full moon with millions of stars. With a gentle ESE ruffling the surface of the water we snuck along quite nicely, right on course for the south, past the Cape Verde islands, which we didn't see. We were joined by a large flock of swallows on their southern migration, most of them wanting to make their home down

Above left: The cook takes his first bath of the trip while (above right) Newt and Molly answer the 'pig' call.

below. They finally ended up in the forepeak and the streaks of swallow guano on the sails wasn't appreciated. To be on the chart covering the Cape Verde islands to Cape Town was quite a boost, but we are clearly in the Doldrums and they are moving south with us. We seem to have been in and out three times so far and unable to get clear as the belt moves slowly south with us.

The desalinator electronics failed yesterday so I spent all last night checking, without success, through the system. After a stop for morning coffee, I reassembled the unit, by-passed the electronics and rigged for manual operation. The system is now purely mechanical so keeping up the supply of fresh water will be slightly more involved, but we're still in business.

The heat has started to rot the cabbages but, as the centres are still okay, Vonny has been lopping off the outsides and using only the good parts. Dried mince is now on the menu, last night converted into a spaghetti bolognese dish which went down rather well. It's amazing what can be achieved with the addition of a few fresh onions, potatoes and a tangy sauce. Our supply of apples is nearly exhausted and the oranges are gone, but the grapefruit are lasting well and should keep for the next few weeks if we limit consumption.

Pippa told me by radio telephone that *Flyer* had reported losing 200 litres of fresh water when a tank split. They're down to five cupsful of water a man a day which must be quite hard on them. I generally drink more than that before lunch and we're still able to use 50 litres a day for washing as well. Thank goodness for the desalinator.

Chappy experimented with cold tea today, using tea leaves and cold water mixed in a powdered milk shaker. He adds a little sugar then leaves it in the sun for a while, telling the rest of the crew what a magnificent drink it is. We're not so sure, as he seems to have trouble drinking it himself.

The barometer has climbed back up from 1012 to 1016 which would indicate that we've pulled away from the ITCZ once more. After a lot of deliberation, we're going to sail the windward route to Cape Town, to the east of the South Atlantic high pressure system — once we're out of these damned Doldrums that is. This means a dead beat of 3000 miles down between St Helena and Ascension Islands, skirting inside (hopefully) the High, picking up the westerlies and so on to the Cape. The alternative is to go the downward route, to the west of the South Atlantic High in a curve out towards South America. This is the route followed by the Clipper ships and promises tail winds for most of the journey. It involves travelling 17 per cent further so the speed maintained must be higher. To go the downwind route is, to me, a gamble and the chances of losing out look too great. So the windward route it has to be.

61

Simon has grown a beard and reckons it looks 'real sharp'. Jaws is endeavouring to sprout one too but has managed only a covering of fluff so far. Molly is lucky. He doesn't have to shave at all. Being able to shave in fresh water is a real luxury, as is being able to finish off a full bath with fresh stuff. I gave myself the full treatment yesterday, using Badedas which lathers well in salt water, then throwing buckets of sea water over myself before finishing it off with fresh water. Eat your heart out Conny.

Cape Town, at noon, was 3567 miles ahead on the great circle course. The distance to sail, because of tacking and because of the South Atlantic High, is approximately 4500 miles.

It has been a brilliantly hot and sunny afternoon with a brisk southerly wind for a change. The sun is still 500 miles south of us but at noon was nearly overhead, meaning little shade on deck at the hottest time of the day. Hats are a must, as are boat shoes. The deck gets hot enough to fry an egg on. I had to stand in a bucket of water while steering for several hours during the afternoon.

Day 17: Monday, September 14. Noon position 11.14N 20.39W
        Day's run 140 miles. Course 235 degrees.
        Wind N 10 knots. Barometer 1017.

Eleven degrees of latitude and 660 miles north of the equator at noon — and the ruddy Doldrums have caught us again. The wind went back into the north during the morning and died. This start-stop sailing is becoming a pain, but the sched this evening showed us to be moving ahead of the small boats again. For most of the day we have been pitching into quite a steep southerly swell, a good sign as it means that the promised southerlies or south-easterlies can't be far away.

When we are on the second leg, from Cape Town to Auckland, and into freezing gales, snow and ice, we'll realise just how easy we've been having it. Frustrating yes, but *Ceramco* has been fairly level most of the time and there's been plenty of fresh water to rinse off at the end of a hot day. Life really hasn't been too bad. Crew reaction has varied. Chappy is somewhat niggly at the moment. After being woken up for his watch, he tends to rant and rave on deck. But he will calm down as soon as we enter the trades. No problems with his performance even though I think he is missing home quite a bit. Staggy is pushing hard all the time, has certainly mellowed and is a fine leader. Lui is just as easy going as always. The Doc confesses to loving every minute of it and continues to be totally enthusiastic all the time, which is a good influence on the rest of the crew. Simon is a tower of strength, keeping the boys in place and making sure the boat is clean and tidy, on deck and particularly below. Jaws is quite amazing. I have no worries about him at all, at any time. He keeps a continual check on the rig for chafe or damage and is living up to his reputation as an eater. He finishes off what others don't want and then can be found in the galley looking for leftovers. Vonny has recently been noticed having two meals at every sitting. He eats with the crew below about to go on deck and then again with the crew coming down off watch. He and Jaws consume vast amounts of toffee between meals as well. Don England is the same as always, excellent value all the time, happy to tackle jobs up the mast in uncomfortable conditions or down below if it's a blocked loo. Sometimes he looks a bit green, but he remains cheerful. OC has been a powerhouse and, while he has his stroppy periods, he fits well into the team. Newt is definitely the comedian aboard and, as humour keeps everyone going, is in his element. Molly is one of the most even-tempered individuals you'll ever meet. He's put on quite a lot of weight and has come in for a deal of ribbing because of it, but he gives as good as he gets and is really enjoying the run.

Day 19: Wednesday, September 16. Noon position 6.29N 19.08W
       Day's run 144 miles. Course 190 degrees.
       Wind WSW 20 knots. Barometer 1016.

Still the Doldrums stalk us. Our runs for the last six days have been 122 miles, 154 miles, 174 miles, 140 miles, 157 miles and now 144 miles, nothing startling. We are still waiting for the south-east trades having recently been on every possible point of sailing. *Kriter, Charles Heidsieck* and *Challenger* are close behind tonight, *Flyer* only 40 miles ahead. *Outward Bound's* last known position was off Boa Vista in the Cape Verde islands, approximately 350 miles astern of us. Sailing has been waffly in the extreme. We had one spell with no headsail or spinnaker, just sitting there under mainsail, flopping around in nothing. But it has been raining hard with big, lumpy seas in southerlies of about 25 knots all afternoon. The temperature has dropped right down and most of the hatches and leeward ports have been closed. We're heeling to 25 degrees and have had to reef. This could be it.

At noon today our position put us at 6½ degrees north latitude, 390 miles north of the equator. We've been in the Doldrums for the last 870 miles. But the forecast from Whitehall tonight gave the ITCZ as being situated at 5 degrees north yesterday. With luck we are about clear of them.

We've been having one squall after the other with blasts from all directions. One minute we've been reaching, the next beating, and the next running. The seas are steep and confused. It's like being in a giant washing machine. It's been impossible to keep dry, but at least the rain is warm. The reef operation came after 3000 miles of sailing from England. Two battens broke in the process, but we have several spare sets on board. The barometer has dropped to 1012 and tonight it's still raining cats and dogs with winds of up to 30 knots. The crew on deck are soaked to the skin, but down below it's nice and dry. The plastic protection screens have been in place all day to deep the damp from the navigation electronics and the night screens at the hatches have been used to stop the spray coming down below off the end of the main boom. I've lost count of the sail changes today — probably 12 headsail changes and five mainsail reefs since that first one — and those in the morning watch alone. The rain is hammering on the deck so hard that, even though the boat is well insulated, it sounds like thunder. Then there's a roaring from the cockpit drains which pass through the navigation area.

Simon's been on deck, walking around in the rain pretending he has a dog with him, whistling and calling the bloody thing. The crew has decided to go along with it and is now complaining that the damned animal has peed everywhere. What next Doctor? Vonny's been asked to save the scraps but I don't think Simon's dog would appreciate the remains of tonight's meal — a magnificent shepherd's pie (sic). It was magnificent until Vonny, while adding pepper to the mashed potatoes, dropped the container into the spuds. The top came off and the whole lot went in. Vonny, being Vonny, didn't bat an eyelid and simply mashed it all up without telling anyone. There were a few quick sprints for drinks of water and the cook copped more than a bit of hot comment.

Day 22: Saturday, September 19. Noon position 00.55N 11.06W
Day's run 220 miles. Course 230 degrees.
Wind SSE 25 knots. Barometer 1015.

The 17th saw us still battered by heavy rain and strong gusts from the west and south-west. Then, just on dawn, we noticed the edge of a very heavy cloud formation to the south. Beyond it lay a clear sky with stars visible. It was as though someone had taken an enormous knife and drawn it across the sky from east to west, like slicing pastry, then thrown the southern piece away. At 5 degrees north we suddenly came out of the Doldrums into steady southerly winds, having entered the belt at 21 degrees north, 960 miles and eight days earlier. On a steady starboard tack with reefed mainsail and Nos 3, 4 or 5 genoas, we settled down on a south-easterly heading into the Gulf of Guinea. What a change to be sailing fast — 9½ to 10 knots to windward was almost a forgotten dream. The run to noon that day was 172 miles. We boosted that to 215 to noon yesterday and to 230 miles to noon today. Conny made contact last night and seems to be only 50 miles ahead. *Challenger* is behind in third place for the line.

Lui went aloft today to refasten the No. 3 leach reefing block and wire into position — an unenviable task in rough seas with *Ceramco* slamming on occasions. Jaws rigged up some control tackle to stop Lui being thrown away from the sail some 10 metres above the deck. Lui completed the task without problems, which says a lot for his constitution and for the control of the deck party.

The concertina job the small boats had done on us was now working in reverse — the big boats were pulling away again, into the trades while the opposition still struggled in the Doldrums. Today is Simon's 30th birthday. The rum came out as Staggy's watch, with Simon, came below at midnight. A mug each was sent up to Chappy's watch on deck. From the coughing and spluttering, I'm not sure how they enjoyed it, but Simon certainly did. He was going quite well by the end of the session, but when it came to waking him for his 0400hrs stint, they needed a boat hook to lever him from his bunk.

Just after noon today we tacked on to port, deciding we'd gone far enough into the Gulf of Guinea and that it was time to head straight down the Atlantic towards our goal. Morale has soared now that progress is so good, the equator is so close and Cape Town is beckoning. I've been having my cotton wool head trouble again, feeling well but very lethargic. I suppose I should take a pill and get a good night's sleep but I don't like doing that on any kind of regular basis. Maybe

it's just the constant angle of heel we're now on and the banging and crashing into uncomfortable seas. All the crew have been sleeping a lot more since we entered the trades.

Ceramco's performance to date has been excellent. She's been sailing extremely well in conditions which weren't a priority in the design brief to the Farr office. We'd like to be ahead of *Flyer* right now, but there's still time. As for now, we're heading away from Monrovia, in Liberia, the 1 degree north latitude being a bit of a psychological barrier for me. That's where we dropped the rig in *Heath's Condor* in the last race, in the same conditions as today. We're on port tack in 20 to 25 knots from the SSE and tramping south.

Day 23: Sunday, September 20. Noon position 02.00S 13.00W
        Day's run 210 miles. Course 215 degrees.
        Wind SSE 20 to 25 knots. Barometer 1014.

South of the equator and averaging 9 knots hard on the wind in a moderate sea. The log notes: 'Crossed the equator and my beard is still on my face despite pre-crossing threats. John Newton.' Then: 'Molly and Newt gave mild resistance during the night to the early hour equator ceremony, when they were officially, and forcibly, admitted to Neptune's kingdom — with egg and flour treatment.' And then: 'I now regret my above comment viz a viz the line crossing. I met my Armageddon at 0230hrs in the morning, scantily clad, with an egg in the eye and flour in the mouth. Newt.'

Those who hadn't crossed the line before were ceremoniously hauled on deck, resisting or not, lashed to the liferaft cover and given the treatment. Crimes were read out, a predictable verdict of 'Guilty' reached, then punishment measured out by Simon and Jaws.

Soon afterwards we were bombarded by a school of flying fish, many of which ended up on board. OC cooked two which were devoured by he and Molly as a pre-breakfast snack. The log noted: 'Bee-Yoo-Tif-Ul!!' and then: 'No. 4 and one slab in main, great sailing.'

Day 24: Monday, September 21. Noon position 05.27S 14.09W
        Day's run 207 miles. Course 195 degrees.
        Wind SE 23 to 28 knots. Barometer 1016.

Ceramco forges south into settled trade winds. The seas are lumpy but moderate, the skies clear. Last night I spoke to Warwick White in Auckland to report progress, then Jim Lidgard to arrange some sail alterations in Cape Town, and finally Pippa to discuss her journey to South Africa and find out the latest from race headquarters.

We were rocketing along under No. 4 genoa, sometimes No. 3, reefing in and out as the wind strength varied through the morning. I went below soon after noon to plot the day's run. We were 100 miles to the north of Ascension Island. Suddenly there was an almighty bang and crash from up top. *Ceramco* came upright and slowed. I leapt for the hatch, yelling for the off-watch crew as I went. I didn't need to look to know what had happened. We'd broken the mast.

6. NO GOOD CALLING FOR MUM

The Sun came up upon the left,
Out of the Sea came he :
And he shone bright, and on the right
Went down into the sea.
— *Samuel Taylor Coleridge*, The Rime of the Ancient Mariner

I DASHED UP on deck. What a mess. The whole top half of the mast was over the side but still attached by internal halyards and wiring systems, plus the mainsail and jib and the headstay. Another section, probably 20ft long, was bent over and dangling down to the gunwhale. We were left with a 16ft stump still in place.

It appeared that the port lower intermediate shroud had broken where it bent over the lower spreader. The mast didn't have a chance and folded at the middle and bottom spreaders. But diagnosis had to wait. The top section of the alloy mast, with all its attachments, was under the boat with the wind blowing *Ceramco* down on to it.

There were some shocked and glum faces about, but nobody hesitated. Fenders were put over the side to prevent hull damage by the section in the water. We used the motor — first making sure there were no lines under the propeller — to reverse the boat around until the spar and entanglements were to windward with *Ceramco* streaming to leeward of their danger. Then we used blocks and tackles to slowly winch the mast section back on board.

With everything back on deck — we salvaged the lot — we had only three bent stanchions to show for all the trouble. But we were 2455 miles from Cape Town,

67

as the crow flies, with only a 16ft stump of a mast from which to hang a bare minimum of sail.

To get us moving again, while we took stock of the situation, we set the trisail and No. 6 jib on the stump and quickly were making 4 to 5 knots in the right direction. That was something. But it was daunting to think how far we had to go — most of it to windward if we contemplated the direct route.

Get it all back on board then we'll decide what to do next.   *Everything salvaged, but what a mess.*

We'd been lucky though. I shuddered when I thought what could have happened if someone had been to leeward, changing sheets or preparing for a headsail change, when it all came down.

The rest of the afternoon was spent cleaning up the mess, de-rigging the pieces of the spar and lashing them to the deck. There was little else we could do until the morning. The trisail and small jib were doing their best, set sideways on the mast stub which was in fact the lower portion of the mast up to the bottom spreader point. It still had the lower shrouds attached so we were secure enough for the moment.

The boat was unnaturally quiet, gloom and doom below and the mood wasn't helped by the necessity to let the outside world know what had happened. This, fortunately, posed no technical problem. Our big Sailor 958 radio worked through two whip aerials mounted on the stern. Things would have been a bit more difficult had we used the backstay as an aerial.

My first call was to Pippa back in England. She burst into tears. Next I called Martin Foster in Auckland. My news was greeted by a stunned silence. Then it was the turn of Peter Montgomery of Radio New Zealand and Alan Sefton of the *Auckland Star*. These two had done so much for our project, they had a right to be the first media people to know. I had already informed the rest of the fleet on the chat show and sent a telex to the RNSA telling them we'd lost the mast but were continuing to Cape Town under jury rig.

Those chores out of the way, I assembled the crew and outlined our options. The direct route to Cape Town was out. *Ceramco* was in no condition to go sailing to windward. If we found we couldn't sail effectively, we could put in to

The tidying up continues, with morale low.   Everything shipshape and we're ready to get some sail on again.

Ascension Island, take on diesel, sail on as far as we could and then start the motor. This went down like the proverbial lead balloon.

We could turn back and head for Monrovia, 800 miles to the north and have a new mast waiting there. But that would mean the end of the race for us. We would never get to Cape Town in time for the restart to Auckland. I'd been to Monrovia before, when *Condor of Bermuda* lost her mast on the first leg of the 1977-78 Whitbread. We encountered all sorts of problems and, anyway, *Condor* had been 400 miles closer when we had to make our decision on that occasion.

Our best solution was to continue on to Cape Town by the downwind route, around the back (to the west) of the South Atlantic high pressure systems, making as much speed as possible and having everything waiting for us to replace the rig when we got there.

We were right in the middle of the Atlantic anyway. The African coast, to the east, was to windward against trade winds which were blowing reasonably fresh compared to normal. We didn't really have much of a decision to make. But I got a big thrill from the crew reaction to this discussion. There was no question of pulling out to motor to Cape Town. We were still racing, albeit with our wings clipped. It would be up to good old Kiwi ingenuity to find ways of setting as much sail as possible to speed our journey. We'd be sailing anything from 1000 to 2000 miles further. But the trades had been blowing reasonably fresh and, with a few breaks, we could still make reasonable time.

In our favour was the way the mast had broken. We had a top section of about 50ft with all the attachments intact. If we could hoist this into place alongside the 16ft bottom section, and hold it in position, there were all sorts of possibilities. We could still make it to Cape Town before some of the backmarkers.

I tried to wrap up the discussion on a light note with: 'Now if anyone wants to get demoralized, come and see me and we'll get demoralized together.' There were no takers.

Left to my own thoughts, I reflected on our misfortune. Our estimates put *Flyer* 105 miles to the east of us. We'd been level pegging it down the South Atlantic and really beginning to look good on handicap. We felt, strategically, we were in a good situation. But...

Then there is the mast itself, slim in section and heavily tapered at the top. It caused a lot of comment when it was stepped in Auckland and there were any number of waterfront experts prepared to bet it would come down. Well, it had — but through no fault in the spar or its engineering. The problem was a rigging failure. It wouldn't have mattered what size mast we'd had — we could have been using a telegraph pole. When that particular piece of the rigging failed, whatever we'd been using would have come down.

We'd had no problems with the spar in 16,000 miles of sailing. It had stood up like a tree trunk, even when we'd been caught napping by a 60-knot squall leaving Auckland for the 1980 Sydney-Hobart. On that occasion we gybed all-standing with no runners on and finished up kicking on our side with the mast in the water. If it was going to go through any fault in its section size, design or engineering, it would have been then.

But there was little point in recriminations. Better now to devote all our thinking energy to getting out of this dilemma in the best possible shape, remembering always that there is still more than three-quarters of the race to run and a lot can happen to the opposition in more than 20,000 miles, particularly in the Southern Ocean where *Ceramco* has been designed and built to excel. Hopefully, we've now used up our ration of bad luck.

For now, we're going back to what they used in Nelson's day. If we can rig the boat the way we intend, and get the same winds we've been having, we'll be doing 7 to 8 knots again. We won't be as hard on the wind as we'd like, but we will be able to steer a pretty good course and reach Cape Town not too far behind the others.

Day 25: Tuesday, September 22. Noon position 6.12S 14.54W
      Day's run 64 miles. Course 230 degrees.
      Wind SSE 10 knots. Barometer 1017.

Not one of the great nights. Everyone retired to their own thoughts, very sad about what had happened. They weren't worried for themselves. They were concerned that they might be letting down a lot of people back home who had shown so much faith in the project. But by dawn we were ready to bounce back and the work to be done diverted everyone's attentions to things productive.

We managed 40 miles overnight in a south-westerly direction. Not a lot, but at least we were moving and in the right direction. Vonny turned on a hearty breakfast before we began the job of hoisting the 50ft top section into place. Most people slept reasonably well despite a lot of tossing and turning. As they emerged from their bunks though there was a fair amount of uncertainty, people mentally pinching themselves hoping it had all been a bad dream. A quick look on deck quickly dispelled those hopes.

There was a 7 to 8ft swell running and quite a lollop so the job of hoisting the 50ft top section wasn't going to be easy. We started by maoeuvring the spar forward until it was over the pulpit and right out in front of the boat. The base of the section had been trimmed off with a hacksaw, filed up neatly and was resting just in front of the stub of the bottom section which was still in position in the boat.

As a pad for the top section, which would of course be deck-stepped, we'd requisitioned Vonny's kauri breadboard from the galley. The cook wasn't too happy at losing such a beautiful part of his set-up, but relented as it was to be put to essential use. The breadboard was fixed in place, in front of the stub, by bolting alloy strips to it and through the deck. We then created a system of ropes and wire around the base of the top section to prevent it shooting backwards when we performed the actual lift.

Next we rigged the stub as a fulcrum with a wire run over the top of it to the hounds of what would be our new mast, up over the pulpit then back over the top of the stub to the mainsheet winch in the helmsman's cockpit. We were almost ready, but as a precaution against the sea that was running, we rigged control lines so that we could keep a tight grip on everything when we started the hoist.

It was quite an operation with a few anxious moments, but slowly the top section was ground to the vertical, in position in front of the stub. Chappy went up and lashed the 'new' spar to the top of the stub while Jaws wired up the bottom. We then pulled it all tight with blocks and tackle and made sure it would remain in position by adding bands of wire and big bulldog clips. Midway up the stub, we bound the two sections together with hefty wire and again tightened this up with blocks and tackle. To make sure the bottom of the new mast couldn't go anywhere, we block-and-tackled it out to the sidedecks.

We had already rigged forestay and backstay — spare halyards and kite braces — from the top of the mast. Now we added shrouds from the mast top and from the hounds, using a jockey pole as a spreader on the port side to improve the load angle on the main shroud on what would be the weather (windward) side of the boat. As we tensioned it all, the new mast seemed to be standing well, so we rigged an inner forestay and prepared to try some sail.

Using light cord, we lashed the No. 6 headsail — through its eyelets — to the forestay and hoisted it. Next came the storm jib, set on the inner forestay (all the stays connected through blocks to the big grinder winches aft). Immediately, the boat steadied down. We had power on and *Ceramco* felt like she was a going concern again, her speed potential albeit reduced. The trisail came next, hoisted to the top of the mast (with no ties on the luff) and sheeted to the quarter. The speedo shot up to 7.5 to 8 knots. We felt pretty pleased with ourselves. It was now noon on September 22 — 24 hours since that ominous crack which had threatened complete disaster. We'd covered only 64 miles, what was to be the worst run of the leg. But it wasn't too bad I guess when one considered that the previous worst run had been 85 miles, noon to noon, in the Doldrums.

The work was far from finished however. Now we had to strengthen the rig to, make sure it would stay there and take the loads. The top of the mast was already tending to wiggle around quite a lot.

It's not a lot, but we're moving again and heading in the right direction.

The bipod mizzen in place, and Ceramco *is a ketch.*

Day 27: Thursday, September 24. Noon position 11.27S 18.47W
Day's run 209 miles. Course 230 degrees.
Wind SE 15 knots. Barometer 1019.

We may look a bit like a Chinese laundry, but we can't complain about the results of our efforts — 198 miles to noon yesterday and then 209 miles to noon today. I think the euphoria has got to the Doc. The log last night read: 'Dr Trevor Agnew just saw a racehorse run across a paddock. I think all those pills are getting to him.' The writing was Simon's. Someone else added: 'I'm surprised you think.' The humour is back.

The south-easter increased to 20 to 25 knots soon after we'd set our cutter rig and *Ceramco*, although a little twitchy, picked up her skirts. Yesterday we rigged one of the heavy wire-running backstays as an extra forestay (run through a big block on the bow and back on a double purchase to a grinder winch). Today we used the other heavy runner in the same fashion as a new backstay, through a block on the quarter, on to a winch and ground in tight. With traditional-type runners from the hounds to cockpit winches, the whole set-up now looks absolutely sturdy. There's a slight kink in the mast, which happened when the top section went over the side, but it's of no real concern.

It looks as though we'll have this breeze for the next 1000 miles or so. The course we've chosen should give us the majority of wind on the beam or from aft

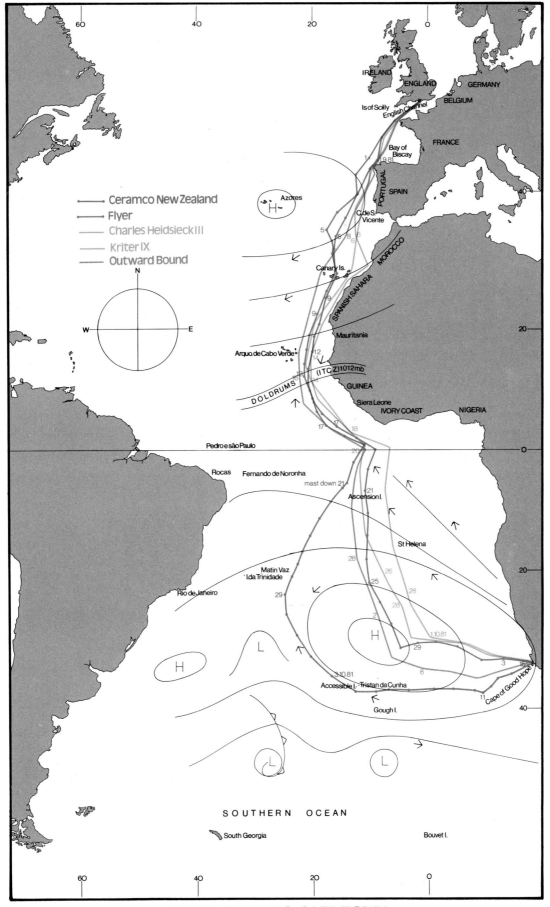

PORTSMOUTH TO CAPE TOWN

of the beam and we already know we can really cover the ground if that's the case. But there's 3700 miles to go on our loop to Cape Town. How can we make the boat go faster still?

We've already worked out a system to use a fully hoisted mainsail, even if it does have four reefs in it. With the electric drill, we bored holes up the luff of the sail at every seam position (about 3ft apart) and inserted long ties cut from foredeck headsail lashings. Then we rolled the sail into a sausage and hoisted it until the headboard was in its correct position at the top of the mast. OC then went aloft and came down the mast securing luff ties around the spar and undoing the ties on the 'sausage' so that the sail gradually came free as he descended. The bottom part of the sail was secured to the main boom and, when the last luff tie was in place, the fourth reef was put in so that we were in the traditional 'four reefs in the main' configuration. We have a problem in that the sail can't be hoisted or lowered and, if we strike a severe squall, we'll have to brail the sail by pulling some lines around the leech and back to the mast. But, if the worst comes to the worst, we have a spare halyard on which to send someone aloft in the bosun's chair to quickly cut all the lashings and drop the sail on deck.

Day 28: Friday, September 25. Noon position 14.18S 20.25W
Day's run 196 miles. Course 225 degrees.
Wind SE 10 to 15 knots. Barometer 1019.

Since dropping the rig we've covered 667 miles to the SSW. We should be happy with that, but the wind has been dying and we're not finished with our quest for maximum speed.

The pressure from the 'new' mast, once it was all tensioned properly, was making the deck creak and groan quite a bit and it was clear we'd have to do something about an under-deck support. Staggy and Jaws got to work with the second jockey pole. This was cut down to length and jammed under the new mast base, below decks, as a reinforcing strut. We've cut the covers for the generator hatches into four pieces and used them as a pad under the alloy deck. To this pad we've fixed strips of aluminium angle to form a collar into which the 4in diameter, heavy-walled aluminium jockey pole is jammed and pop-rivetted between the main mast step on the keelson and the deck head. While this was hammered and levered into place, we slacked off all the stays and ran the boat downwind, to relieve the pressure on the deck. The finished job looks substantial enough and is doing the trick.

While this was under way, the rest of the crew were implementing our plan to turn *Ceramco* into a ketch. The two spinnaker poles were lashed together at their tops and hoisted into position as a bipod mizzen mast over the helmsman's cockpit, just in front of the wheels. The feet of the poles were mounted on cockpit cushion pads out on the sidedecks against the toerail. A pulley system was rigged for a backstay bridle which runs from one quarter, through the pulley block at the apex of the bipod and back down to the other quarter of the stern, then on to a winch. A forestay and halyard completed the job. We couldn't wait to test it. First the new spinnaker staysail was set sideways with the luff at the top, but it was much too long on the hoist (even some of the sails we consider small are proving to, in fact, be quite large). Next came the trisail with the leech as the luff, the luff as the foot and the foot as the leech. This was sheeted to a block on the rail — and it worked like a charm. Boat speed jumped up more than a knot and *Ceramco* steadied down considerably.

Necessity is quite definitely the mother of invention. We must look something akin to a rigged tuna trawler right now but who cares. Spirits on board have soared and we're not done yet. The next job we must tackle is to devise ways of rigging more blocks and tackle so that we can free a winch or two and improve our set-up.

The support team in Auckland hasn't been idle either. Martin Foster has had a team talk with everyone involved in rigging the boat — A. Foster & Co (who supplied the extrusion), Terry Gillespie (our rigger), Graeme Woodroffe (the Navtec rigging agent in New Zealand) and Jimmy Lidgard (our sailmaker). I spoke to them all by radio telephone, for a total of 51 minutes, giving them a full description of what happened, plus a long list of what we would need when we reached Cape Town. Everything will be ready. Now it's up to us to get *Ceramco* there as quickly as possible so that we have enough time to rerig the boat, fix up our sail wardrobe and prepare for the Southern Ocean. There won't be much shore time for the crew in South Africa, but they won't mind that. I couldn't have a better bunch of people to sail with. Their reaction to everything has been magnificent, totally constructive. The feeling is one of 'let's get this mother to Cape Town, stick a new mast in her, and then we'll show them across the bottom of the world to New Zealand'.

Radio time is building up. On the 23rd, I had 21 minutes' talking to Pippa in the UK while Don England put in a call to his mum and fiancee Alison in NZ. I had regular scheds with Alan Sefton and Peter Montgomery who, by all accounts, were keeping New Zealand fully informed of the events 8000-odd miles away in the South Atlantic. This time I had to catch up with them at Antoine's restaurant in Parnell where we'd had a fabulous dinner just before *Ceramco* left Auckland and where now, they claimed, they had a business meeting. As it transpired, they taped the conversation with the whole restaurant listening in, and then had to lend the tape to the kitchen staff. We always find it remarkable that there is so much interest and support back home and this is no small factor in the crew's determination to fight back.

Day 29: Saturday, September 26. Noon position 16.54S 21.43W
       Day's run 176 miles. Course 225 degrees.
       Wind SE 8 to 10 knots. Barometer 1020.

We've completely settled into the new routine as *Ceramco* is committed to her new course. The plan is to continue on this heading for another 870 miles before beginning to curve off south and then come around in an arc to the south-east and then east at about latitude 38S or 39S, fetching up close to Tristan da Cunha. That gives us 3200 miles to go to Cape Town on the course we have chosen. But that's the longest distance we'll have to travel. If we can cut the corner a bit, we'll reduce the amount of ground to cover.

We struck a bit of a light patch last night but the breeze filled in again from the same favourable direction and *Ceramco* finished up with another highly respectable run, everything considered. It's been quite cloudy with rain about. It's getting colder as we move south and the nights are drawing in. We already need sweaters to go on deck and pretty soon we'll want more than that. The water temperature is down too, and we've found this has a noticeable affect on the output of our desalination plant. Output is down, gallon for gallon.

With little or no trimming to do on deck, I've changed the watch system. We only need two people on watch so now we are working a two hours on, eight

Chappy tightens the lashings,
sail goes on and we're a going concern again.

Top section lashed to the stump with sail on.

hours off system. A full inventory of what we have on board has left us with no qualms about supplies. The desalinator will take care of our fresh water requirements and we have enough diesel to run the generator and/or main motor to charge the batteries with enough left over to fire the heaters to keep the boat comfortable down below.

We're really stepping out across the chart. Ascension Island is now more than 600 miles astern and we're getting well down towards the Trinidade and Martin Vaz islands, situated some 550 miles to the east of Rio de Janeiro. We should pass about 300 miles to the east of them as we arc down to the south-west.

The boat feels nicely settled with her bipod mizzen. The extra weight aloft and the increased sail area have taken the sting out of the rather violent motion we had before and got rid of the lee helm we were experiencing.

Finally got rid of the last of the swallows, which by now were getting a little high. They'd found every nook and cranny in which to hide and die, there was nothing we could do about it, and we've been tracking them down one by one, by smell. The only real sea life sighted has been a large whale shark which, at first, we thought was a floating log — until it did a couple of circuits of the boat.

We've been at sea for a month and logged 5000 miles from England. At this stage we're not sure which other boats, if any, are taking the downwind route. One thing is certain, there won't be many yachts further down the track than us even now. Our hope was to average between 7.5 and 8 knots. But we've been doing better than that, hitting speeds up to 11 knots. Once through this lighter patch — that should be in about three days as we slice through the back of the high pressure system — we will be close to the Roaring Forties where we should really pick up speed. If we strike it really fresh down there we'll drop down to the trisail and storm jib, which would be the standard rig for cruising in that type of weather. There should be little loss in efficiency. The big hope now is that the high moves east and slows down the boats that are going the direct route — *Flyer, Charles Heidsieck, Kriter*, etc. It's probably too much to hope for, but we face east and bow every now and then, just in case. *Flyer* has given a Cape Town ETA of October 7. We figure we should be there on October 15, sooner if we are lucky. There are limits on how fast we can go though.

A few more sail combinations have been tried. The storm spinnaker set okay except it was a bit too long on the hoist and kept dipping the foot in the water. Dropped that and hoisted the 1.5oz shooter in normal fashion. It was far too long, so we rehoisted it on its side. That worked quite well for a while but the sail was hard to control and folded when we came up to course, with a significant drop in boat speed.

We finished up back with the twin-headsail rig, of the opinion that the 1.5oz shooter, cut down to fit, was the answer to our needs. OC unpicked several of the bottom panels and is in the process of fitting temporary tack and clew patches. In this new form, the sail should make an excellent reaching genoa which could also be poled out as a single luff spinnaker.

Day 30: Sunday, September 27. Noon position 18.48S 22.32W
       Day's run 127 miles. Course 200 degrees.
       Wind SE/E light. Barometer 1021.

Struggling in light airs since just after midnight. The log this afternoon read: 'Flat calm for most of the watch. The Doc, at the helm, can cure excess wind but not bring it on.' This was followed by: 'Rubbish, he hasn't fixed Gundry.'

It has been interesting to note the various reactions to our situation. For a while, people were walking around with blank looks on their faces. Sometimes they have been difficult to motivate, but most of them are over it by now.

Triple-slotting the jury way.

Vonny has reorganised all the food menus so that we can last another month to six weeks at sea should we come unstuck around the back of the high. We'll feel the pinch after about 3½ weeks but we won't starve. The weather maps show the high to be moving around a fair bit. Yesterday it was directly ahead of us. We're hoping it will have shifted to the east by the time we're another 1000 miles further south. Just in case it hasn't, we've rationed the food slightly. Some of the guys think this is a bit of a joke, they haven't faced a situation like this before. But I'm determined the rationing will be observed. This way we will eat to an acceptable standard for longer. We're going to need regular sustenance when we're further south and it gets really cold. Nobody can call the rationing strict. Breakfast this morning, for instance, comprised a mound of beans and stew left over from last night, plus a half of fresh grapefruit apiece. Lunch was sliced roast lamb and peas (freeze dried) with a couple of pieces of toast.

Chappy talked to his wife Vicky in Auckland last night and learned that she'd broken her nose playing basketball. He thought that was a huge joke. I chatted to Pippa who was in bed with the flu. She's due to leave for South Africa on Wednesday for a brief stay with Chris and Maria Henwood, in Johannesburg, before going to Cape Town to organise things for our arrival. Chris is an old friend of mine from my *Ocean Spirit* days and also the first Whitbread race. Our replacement mast is on its way from Auckland to London, en route to Cape Town. It is being transported free by British Airways, a most generous decision on their part. I've learned also that *New Zealand Yachting* magazine and the *Auckland Star* have organised a limited edition of two pen and ink drawings by well-known New Zealand artist Dave Barker, showing *Ceramco* under jury rig in the South Atlantic. These are to be sold for $20 a set with all the proceeds going towards rerigging the boat. I may have got it wrong, but I thought Alan Sefton said it was to be called the 'Ceramco Erection Fund'. Peter Montgomery has interviewed everyone on board for the Radio NZ sports shows this weekend, the general public at home apparently appreciating the fact that *Ceramco* isn't finished, that she's sailing again and doing rather well too. We get a considerable boost from all of this. The folks at home can move mountains when they decide a project is worth backing.

We gleaned from tonight's chat show that *Flyer* is between 600 and 700 miles from the finish. *Challenger* reported a strange and costly experience. They'd passed close by what they thought was a man-overboard light with someone alongside it. Thinking it was crew from another race yacht, they did an emergency gybe to get back to the light. It turned out to be a large fishing float, broken free from God knows where. Les Williams wasn't too happy about the fact that *Challenger* had damaged her mainsail track and headboard during the gybe, but he'd done the seamanlike thing and was to be commended for it.

Newt, reading the *South African Pilot*, has just broken up this taping session with the exclamation: 'Jeez, it doesn't pay to be a male if you live in the West Cameroons. Their main export product is ground nuts!!'

Day 31: Monday, September 28. Noon position 20.51S 23.30W
       Day's run 140 miles. Course 235 degrees.
       Wind SE 15 to 20. Barometer 1022.

The wind finally filtered in from the south-east again at 2000hrs last night. It was up and down until 0400hrs today when it settled at 12 to 15 knots and then built to 20 knots. We've just got to grin and bear the lighter stuff because there's nothing more we can do.

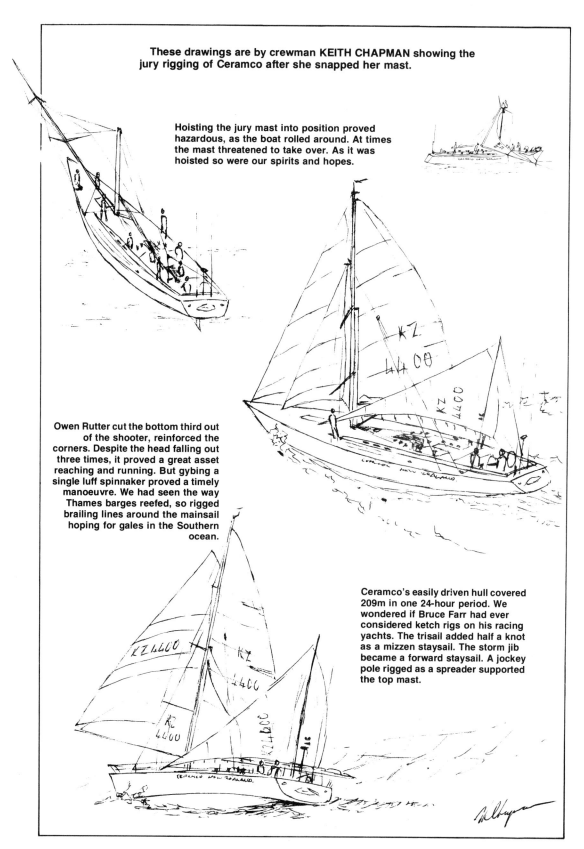

These drawings are by crewman KEITH CHAPMAN showing the jury rigging of Ceramco after she snapped her mast.

Hoisting the jury mast into position proved hazardous, as the boat rolled around. At times the mast threatened to take over. As it was hoisted so were our spirits and hopes.

Owen Rutter cut the bottom third out of the shooter, reinforced the corners. Despite the head falling out three times, it proved a great asset reaching and running. But gybing a single luff spinnaker proved a timely manoeuvre. We had seen the way Thames barges reefed, so rigged brailing lines around the mainsail hoping for gales in the Southern ocean.

Ceramco's easily driven hull covered 209m in one 24-hour period. We wondered if Bruce Farr had ever considered ketch rigs on his racing yachts. The trisail added half a knot as a mizzen staysail. The storm jib became a forward staysail. A jockey pole rigged as a spreader supported the top mast.

OC finished modifying the 1.5oz shooter — immediately dubbed the Sooty Sail (someone reckoned OC's complexion had become suspiciously dark). The sail now has a luff length of about 47ft and is much like what the sailmakers refer to as an MPS (Multi Purpose Spinnaker) developed for cruising yachts and flown without a spinnaker pole. It works well with the wind just ahead of the beam and gives us an extra 1.5 knots of boatspeed. With that from the top of the mast and sheeted to one of the genoa tracks on the rail, plus the four-reefed main, trisail and mizzen staysail, we've been doing 6 knots in light airs.

The boats out to the east have been getting quite a bit more wind than us and the front-markers appear to be stretching out on the main bunch and tailenders. From what we can make out, *Flyer* has a good jump on *Challenger. Charles Heidsieck* and *Kriter* are vying for third place on line. This does little for our frame of mind. In different circumstances, we would be right up there with *Flyer,* in a position to win on handicap not to mention give her a real tussle for the gun. We're still 750 miles ahead of some of the slower boats, like *Traite de Rome* which has reported experiencing a 5 to 8-knot southerly, less wind than we had back there.

The baragraph Pippa gave me as a going away present is ticking away under the chart table. I should really have mounted it on some foam as it really is an impressive piece of equipment. The way it is, the motion of the boat in rough weather tends to move the needle up and down, producing rather a broad line. It's good to have this back-up for the barometer even though both instruments have recorded an almost constant pressure reading since we left Portsmouth. The baragraph line moves up and down a little, but no more than 10 millibars for the whole trip to date. I can't remember a more stable pressure situation in the South Atlantic.

An enthusiastic navigation school has developed on board. Molly, still having a bit of trouble with his sights, is acting as tutor to Newt and Don. Chappy's in on it too. My little plastic sextant is ideal for them to learn with. It's much lighter than the Plath, which I don't let anyone else use anyway. The Plath is my number one back-up for the Satnav. We could turn the Satnav off and go celestial, but the Satnav is such a useful aid and requires little power. It gives us an instant position, day or night — handy in case of an emergency. The Satnav has its own aerial mounted on the stern of the boat and so was unaffected by the dismasting. Not so the reliable little Kenwood communication receiver which provides the signal for the Ratheon weatherfax machine which produces all those invaluable met situation maps. Its aerial was the main topmast backstay. Luckily, we have two whip aerials on the stern, one of them for the big Sailor main transceiver through which we talk to everyone, the other for the Simrad RW 105 automatic alarm receiver. The latter stays on all the time listening for the emergency alarm on 2182 Khz. To retain the Kenwood facility, I've unplugged the communications receiver from the backstay and plugged it into the second whip aerial in place of the Simrad. It means that on Mondays, when it's *Ceramco's* turn to have the Simrad on to listen for any problems in the fleet, we have to be without the Kenwood and so the weatherfax. But that's no real hassle.

The whole set-up, and our ability to remain almost totally functional electronically, is a tribute to the work of Gordon Holmes and his team at Southern Communications in Auckland. We've even got a back-up for the VHF. Its aerial is still at the top of the mast but the wiring was wrecked during the drop. If we need the set however, we've got a spare aerial taped to the underside of the deck near the mast and all we have to do is hold it aloft or tape it to the shrouds. It could prove handy if the main set goes out. We have a final back-up of the liferaft radio on which, at night, we could talk to the fleet on 6 megs.

With a lot of time to kill, my thoughts continually focus on Pippa, back in England but soon to fly to South Africa. I'm now absolutely certain I made the right choice of partner and it's nice to know she feels the same. If I ever do this race again Pippa will have to be there too.

We're now a long way south of where we dropped the rig and I've calculated that, by the time we reach Cape Town, we'll have covered nearly 4000 miles under jury rig which probably hasn't been done before in an ocean race or cruise. I can understand why.

We picked up the football results from home, via Peter Montgomery, along with the news that a crewman has been lifted off by helicopter from a boat in the Ponsonby Yacht Club's spring regatta after getting bashed on the head by the main boom. We are always highly conscious of this sort of possibility while working about the deck on *Ceramco*. It happens so easily. The difference in our situation is we are a long way from anywhere and, as Tom Clark said at *Ceramco*'s launching, when you're 2000 miles from land — which is about where we are right now — it's no good calling for mum. The fact that we have our own doctor on board with equipment to handle just about any emergency, takes a load off my mind. The Doc reckons the only thing he'd fear tackling is brain surgery because he'd have trouble finding a brain.

Day 32: Tuesday, September 29. Noon position 23.39S 24.43W
      Day's run 178 miles. Course 220 degrees.
      Wind SE 10 to 12 knots. Barometer 1021.

Euromarche gave her position to noon yesterday as 27.34S 12.21W, so Tabarly's gone down the middle of the track. We were sure he'd have come the downwind route that *Ceramco*'s taking. *Flyer* and *Challenger* didn't let on where they were but let it slip that they were still enjoying fresh winds. *Xargo*, not quite as far to the east as *Flyer* and *Challenger*, had run into 30 to 40-knot south-easterlies. *La Barca Laboratorio* dropped her mast yesterday and is heading for Recife on the north-eastern coast of Brazil. The weather maps we're getting today don't tie up with the conditions we're experiencing, and the forecast from Portishead gives another version again. The maps at this stage are from Pretoria, in South Africa. It's confusing, to say the least, but we'll just have to keep going in a south-westerly direction, starting to curve slightly to the south, hoping that the wind will soon go east or north-east. A high has developed below us and moved quickly away to the east so we should start to get something off the back of that. We saw our first wandering albatross this afternoon, a young one with a wing span of between 6ft and 8ft. He was with us all afternoon, sweeping around the boat in a beautiful exhibition of controlled flying, interested obviously in what we might throw over the side in the way of food. He must have got a shock, as we were dumping very little. We're already low on biscuits — down to two packets a man. It was decided to give everyone their allocation now and let them do their own rationing for the rest of the trip, however long it might take. Simon laid all the packets out and ran the allocation like a raffle. He'd divided the packets into pairs of various combinations and numbered them, putting a corresponding number into one of Vonny's mixing bowls which was the 'hat'. Everyone then drew a number and collected his 'prize'. I ended up with two packets of chocolate

Deciding on a mizzen staysail.

wheaten, which was rather nice. Newt wasn't at all happy with his lot. A chocolate fanatic, he'd got one of wheaten and one of malt. He promptly did a swap with Vonny then tucked himself away to devour a whole packet of his favourites like a kid let loose in a sweet shop. It's going to be interesting to see what happens when he runs out altogether. We were going to do the same with other goodies, such as peanuts, but decided it would be a bit silly to have everyone with open packets of peanuts in their lockers. Instead we rationed ourselves to one packet a day. In hindsight and from a comfortable chair ashore, little things such as these may seem trivial. But after weeks at sea, with another couple of weeks still to go, the simple pleasures taken for granted ashore assume great importance.

With all this leisurely stuff going on, it is going to be quite a shock to the system when we are racing seriously again. Under our present jury rig, it would take a gale to make the boat heel and one could get quite used to this more comfortable way of going about the oceans, even though *Ceramco*'s motion in her present form is quite quick and tiring.

It's nice to have the Southern Cross directly ahead of the bow in the evenings. Makes you feel closer to home. In a straight line, we are 2300 miles from Cape Town. We expect to sail 2700 miles to get there. In eight days since we dropped the rig we have sailed 1288 miles, averaging 161 miles a day. Not too bad. *Flyer* and *Challenger* are in gale force headwinds, *Challenger* having difficulty reefing and unreefing because of her damaged mainsail headboard and track. They're having to send someone aloft with a hammer and chisel every time they want to shorten sail or shake a reef out. *Kriter* has reported water in her diesel. She's running her electronics off a tiny, petrol emergency generator. The fleet leaders are clearly doing better than the boats astern which have struck more southerly conditions. Out where we are, away to the west, the opposition isn't doing much to us. *Gauloises*, in the last three days, has gained only 20 miles on *Ceramco*.

Up and running, and making the spray fly.

The baragraph trace has to be seen to be believed, it's so constant. Maybe there was a mix-up when they came to name the Atlantic and the Pacific oceans. Right now we could be sailing on Lake Taupo, it's that flat. The highs are lower down in the South Atlantic than normal but they are moving through to the east quite quickly and, thank goodness, they appear to be gradually shifting north. If they do, we may only have to go down as far as 30 South before flattening out our curve and heading straight for Cape Town. If the highs don't shift, we could end up going down past 40 South.

The humour persists. Vonny and Simon have acquired an imaginary collection of livestock on board. Simon is talking of raising the lifelines to keep his deer in the park and there's been a search mounted for the Doc's racehorse. Vonny's usual meal-time call of 'Here pig, pig, pig' changed today after a timely warning from the Doc that he might not be able to roll over in his bunk one of these mornings, because of the large carving knife stuck in his ribs. This morning, before breakfast, he woke everyone with a smacky, wet kiss on the cheek so he's switched to 'I say chaps, dinner is served'. The initial response is good, but I can't see it lasting. Vonny claims he calls 'pig, pig, pig' because he cooks swill.

Staggy proclaimed today: 'In 15 years of ocean racing I have never learned anything about navigation. I think this is my chance to do something about that.' Newt agreed, with: 'Good idea. Pass me the Satnav manual, then I'll know which buttons to punch.'

Day 34: Thursday, October 1. Noon position 29.49S 22.41W
Day's run 215 miles. Course 180 degrees.
Wind NE 25 knots. Barometer 1025.

Vonny began the day with: 'I say chaps, your delicious breakfast is ready.' Nobody took any notice.

The breeze kicked back in early yesterday, from the south-east, and built slowly while backing east and now north-east to 20 to 25 knots. Our noon run yesterday was 180 miles, which put a smile back on our faces. The waves have been too big and choppy for the amount of wind, so somewhere not too far away there must have been quite a fresh breeze. It must have been varying in direction a lot as the sea has been coming at us from all directions, quite steep and giving *Ceramco* an uncomfortably quick motion. We've changed course slightly and are heading SSE. It's a boost not to be going SW any more. The South Atlantic High has moved well to the east and the latest forecast is for another high to form at 33S 8W — at 1029 millibars. This should extend a ridge across to another high which is fractionally to the east and north of Cape Town. Hopefully this will slow down *Flyer* and company. The only trap for us could be a bit of a gap towards Rio where we expect another high to form reasonably quickly. The faster we get down south, and make a bit of easting, the better.

Jaws, Chappy and Staggy have attached one of the medium-length spreaders, off the unused middle section of the mast, to the starboard side of our jury rig so that we can rig a shroud on that side for when we start tacking or gybing. We don't want to have to swap the jockey pole from side to side. This means the only stay we'll have to change over is the main standing backstay. This is led to a block on the port quarter and back to a handy-billy on the side deck, with a four-part purchase before it goes to the mainsheet traveller winch. If we tack or gybe, this whole arrangement will have to be duplicated on the starboard side. One of the spinnaker topper halyards has been rigged to support the mast while the backstay is switched across and we've also got the runners. It sounds a bit 'Michael Rodent' but it should all work. Jaws has also been up the mast to attach another block, on wire strops, to the masthead to enable us to rig a spinnaker brace as a shroud for the newly fitted starboard spreader. We're beginning to run short of blocks by now.

The equipment we chose carefully for this race is all getting a lot of use, none more so than the industrial size pop-rivet gun, which takes $\frac{3}{16}$in or $\frac{1}{4}$in Monel rivets, and the big bolt cutters which double as a talurit machine. This is a versatile unit with interchangeable jaws. It has coped easily with all the halyard and stay shortening involved in our complicated jury rig and has been worth its weight in gold.

It's amazing how much extra speed we're getting from our 'Sooty Sail', and it steadies the boat down considerably. It must also be pushing a flow of air through behind the mainsail which otherwise is a bit stalled out.

My 33rd birthday today. I'd intended to celebrate properly with a bottle of rum at midnight, but slept on through and had to make do with a packet of biscuits when I finally woke up.

We've been going for 33 days so far, so it looks like this leg is going to be the longest I've spent at sea. The current mark is 42 days. That's how long this leg took us in *Burton Cutter* in the 1973-74 Whitbread race.

The requirements for Cape Town have all been communicated to the support team in Auckland — a new mast of course, a new tube for the starboard jockey pole (which has been cut down to support the deck), wet weather gear replacements from Dorlon for the guys who work the foredeck (coats and trousers without zips), new No. 2 and No. 3 battens (glass or timber) from Jim Lidgard, a lot more Teflon tape from 3M, new styli for the weatherfax machine (from Gordon Holmes), and a new roller for the Merryman genoa cars (from Chris McMullen). Terry Gillespie and Jim Lidgard will meet us in Cape Town to rerig the boat and attend to the sails. They're going to have a fair amount of excess baggage.

The crew has been busy with a host of jobs, some of them necessary, others not. The idea is to keep everyone busy. Newt has been down the stern locker again greasing the rudder stock, which tends to get a little tight after a number of days at sea, especially when the speed is up. Jaws and Staggy finished off the starboard spreader which has been quite an operation. Chappy has been evolving a system to brail the mainsail to the mast in case the breeze really gets up. If we have to replace the main with the trisail, we'll need to reduce sail area while undoing the luff ties, so the sail doesn't flop around our ears or damage the mast. It looks as though we'll take a line from the hounds, around the leech of the mainsail and back to the top of the mast stub, then around the leech again and down to the mainsail tack. This will be left loose until it is needed but could then be quickly hauled in by three or four guys, pulling the whole sail forward to the mast and taking a lot of grunt out of it. Molly has checked all the torches and batteries while Don has been doing what maintenance is possible on the winches. Most of them are in use holding up the mast. Simon has lashed the spinnaker pole bipod legs to the deck toerail. If we get a 90-degree knockdown, we don't want to lost the whole lot over the side. He's also reattached the port safety wire, which runs along the deck from bow to cockpit, for harness clips. This was removed when we were dismantling the broken rig. There's also been a complete check on personal safety gear to ensure that harnesses and clips are in good order. We're praying for a blow to hasten progress so we've got to be fully prepared for one.

Day 35: Friday, October 2. Noon position 32.58S 20.12W.
Day's run 227 miles. Course 165 degrees.
Wind NNE 20 to 25 knots. Barometer 1022.

This is more like it. For most of the night we were doing between 9 and 12 knots, rocketing along under the red and white 'Sooty Sail', storm jib (as staysail), four-reefed main and trisail (as mizzen staysail). We're well out of the tropics, down below the latitude of Montevideo, and curving around the back of the high pressure system on a course that will take us close to Tristan da Cunha which is 500 miles to the SE of us. We've covered 1910 miles since losing the rig 11 days ago, averaging 173 miles a day. *Flyer* and *Challenger* are again being coy about their positions but Conny must be getting close by now.

As we've come around the western side of the high, the isobars have squashed up between the high and a low pressure system to the west of us. The wind has followed us around so that it is still on the beam and we are maintaining best possible speed for the shape we're in. *Ceramco* has been surfing to 14 knots but the conditions are keeping the pressure on Lui and OC. The head blew out of the 'Sooty Sail' again this morning, another trip up the mast for Lui and more repair work for OC. But we're really jumping across the chart and Cape Town has become a destination, not just a name on a map. All going well, we could be there in seven to nine days. We try to forget that *Flyer* could make it in two or three. That's where *Ceramco* should be.

Vonny decided to make me a belated birthday cake, a sponge, but missed badly in the 'rise' department. His concoction finished up as a thick biscuit, quite tasty. The bits that did rise he smothered in jam and an icing of cream and coconut, topped with chocolate raisins. Went down a treat with my birthday bottle of rum (also belated). We were down to opening cans with kitchen knives. The patented types of tin openers had all gone the way of the gas lighter for the stove. The best opener on a boat has to be the basic job with which you pierce the top and lever around. All the fancier types give up the ghost. There are still some of the Devonport Yacht Club ladies' fruit cakes left. They were baked in Auckland before *Ceramco* was shipped. Remarkable how long they have lasted. There's the odd bit of mould, but that's soon hacked off and, as long as the cake was baked with the right amount of rum, brandy or sherry in it, they still taste perfect.

Ceramco is jumping around quite a lot now as she gets a wriggle on. This, and the fact that the ocean is distinctly cooler, should put a stop to Staggy's toilet habits. Everyone else uses the downstairs loo, but he insists on using the pushpit.

We heard of a marvellous bit of Kiwi ingenuity aboard *Outward Bound* which today is 1400 miles from Cape Town and looking good on handicap. A week ago, they broke their main halyard. They had a light line up the mast to hoist a spare, so it wasn't a problem until two days later when the spare broke. Now they had no way of hoisting the main nor of getting a man to the top of the mast to fit a new halyard. Their solution, in 30 to 35-knot SE winds and big seas, was to hoist Matt Smith up to the hounds on a spinnaker halyard (remembering *Outward Bound* is fractional rigged) and with him the 17ft-long spinnaker pole. He lashed the middle of the pole to the mast as high as he could reach above the hounds then used a line attached to the top of the pole to pull himself up another 5ft or so. His next step was to tighten the lashing on the pole and mast before climbing on up to the top to reave a new main halyard. Quite a performance, even if *Outward Bound* did lose 30 to 40 miles of weather ground while it was being achieved.

Chappy rigs brailing lines so that we can reduce sail in a hurry.

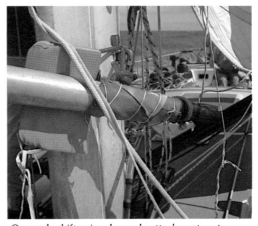

Our makeshift spinnaker pole attachment system.

Day 37: Sunday, October 4. Noon position 37.46S 12.42W
        Day's run 232 miles. Course 145 degrees.
        Wind NE 20 to 25 knots. Barometer 1018.

The damage in the fleet is mounting. *Rollygo* has lost her mast and is struggling on at 5 knots with a stump about the same size (proportionally) as ours. They apparently are short of food and water, just to add to their problems. *Bubblegum*, the smallest boat in the race, has broken her port chainplate which is lifting the deck. Both her steering cables are also broken. She's heading for St Helena Island while attempting repairs. The damage tally is now: *Ceramco*, broken mast; *La Barca Laboratorio*, broken mast; *Rollygo*, broken mast; *Bubblegum*, broken chainplate; *Charles Heidsieck*, broken forestay; *Swedish Entry*, broken forestay; *Save Venice*, broken forestay; *Berge Viking*, broken forestay; *United Friendly*, damaged mainsail track; *Challenger*, damaged mainsail track and badly torn main. And we haven't struck any severe weather as yet.

Our noon run yesterday was the best since the mast came down — 238 miles. We were only just short of that today. Our luck is holding as we barrel along about 25 miles south of Inaccessible Island in the Tristan da Cunha group. The ocean has turned a grey-green colour and we're seeing vast numbers of birds from the huge colonies on Tristan. There's a real Southern Ocean feel about all this. We've been keeping a close watch on the rig, but it's standing like a telegraph pole. If we had our proper rig, we'd probably be averaging 11½ to 12 knots in this stuff. With the jury rig we're averaging 10 knots. Can't complain. From the look of the weather pattern we'll being going down to 40 South as we level out.

The BBC world news last night informed us that *Flyer* is due in Cape Town on October 6. *Charles Heidsieck* looks to be running second and *Kriter* third. Those two must have had a great run to be ahead of *Challenger*.

Ceramco still has 1500 miles to go on a great circle course. That means between 1600 and 1650 on the course we are following. If we average 200 miles a day, we will be in on the 11th or 12th.

The humour continues. The Doc went up top this afternoon to sharpen the lawnmower so that he can cut the front lawn. Simon reckons there are dogs and cattle all over the boat and that he'll definitely have to raise the fence around his deer park. Chappy, meanwhile, hit a magical 16½ knots. The log entry read: 'Pity we were heading for the South Pole.' The Doc managed to fill Newt's boots again. Some people have a knack for dropping big waves on board while others keep everything nice and dry.

The Satnav has been occupying a lot of my thinking. It hasn't been turned off since we left England. It certainly makes the navigator's job easier and it is reassuring to know exactly where you are all the time. But I'm inclined to the view that it takes some of the adventure out of the race. It adds to the safety but detracts from the skill. The weatherfax machine is a different thing altogether. It provides information which then has to be interpreted before decisions are made by the navigator or the skipper. You can ask the Satnav questions and receive answers without any of the traditional navigational drill.

Conny informed the evening chat show that *Flyer* was only two hours from the finish. They could see the lights of Cape Town. I sent him *Ceramco*'s congratulations. He came back with: 'Keep it up. You've done extremely well and we're all proud of you.'

Day 38: Monday, October 5. Noon position 37.43S 09.20W
         Day's run 171 miles. Course 130 degrees.
         Wind NNW 8 to 12 knots. Barometer 1022.

Flyer got the gun at 2157hrs GMT on October 4. *Charles Heidsieck, Kriter* and *Challenger* are expected today. We still have 1300 miles to travel, and we've slowed down with the wind going NNW and then NW and dropping to 8 knots. The wind change meant we had to drop the bipod mizzen and then gybe for the first time in 17 days and for the first time with the jury rig. Three more gybes followed that one so we're back on port. Chappy devised a system to rig the trisail from the top of the mast to the end of the main boom, most of which was doing nothing with four reefs in. This filled up the gap between the mainsail area and it made an appreciable difference while the wind was dead astern. Our noon position put us about 200 miles north of the iceberg limit. We still had one bottle of rum left and planned to polish it off when we crossed the Greenwich Meridian of zero degrees longitude, which isn't too far ahead.

From the chat show we learned that boats such as *Gauloises, Xargo, United Friendly* and *Euromarche* were all within 500 miles of us, ahead. We found this staggering considering the on-off sailing we'd been experiencing. *Gauloises'* position puts her only 450 miles ahead of *Ceramco*. She was that far in front a week ago.

Tonight we sent a message back to John Adshead and his New Zealand soccer team, telling them to give Kuwait heaps in the World Cup qualifier. Then we settled down to nursing *Ceramco* through light and variable winds that shifted through the west and into the south.

Day 40: Wednesday, October 7. Noon position 37.32S 03.23W
         Day's run 172 miles. Course 120 degrees.
         Wind N 18 to 20 knots. Barometer 1020.

The days are starting to drag and it doesn't help to know that boats are already in Cape Town, their crews celebrating ashore. Yesterday's noon run was 104, the worst since the day after we dropped the mast. The breeze went back into the NW early yesterday morning but was only between 5 and 10 knots all day. It started to perk up just before midnight, flicking around the north but pushing us along at a good clip again. The log notes: 'Only 103 miles to the rum bottle.' Newt and the Doc claim they have become the harbingers of good breeze. They went through their usual routine before taking over at midnight: 'Time to go Doc.' 'Okay John, let's get up there, square away the topsails to the breeze.' 'Yeah, and get her leaping from wave top to wave top.' 'And piss down the track to Cape Town.' This was all greeted by derisory snorts and abuse from the rest of the crew but, sure enough, soon after they went on deck the breeze kicked in and they had *Ceramco* doing 8 knots again.

Charles Heidsieck, on the evening sched, reported she was 25 miles from the finish in a fresh southerly. She'd lost her forestay bottle screw earlier in the leg and didn't have a replacement. They 'borrowed' one from the main shrouds but this meant transferring the remaining shroud screw to the new weather side every time she tacked. *Kriter* is expected to be third across the line and it's going to be close between those two on handicap. Pippa came on the chat show, talking from *Flyer* which was beginning to look good for the line-handicap double. My good wife had sounded down in the dumps when I'd spoken to her earlier in the day, but now she sounded quite a bit better and informed me she was going out for a rip-roaring dinner.

Day 41: Thursday, October 8. Noon position 37.21S 01.01E
     Day's run 210 miles. Course 115 degrees.
     Wind NNW 15 knots. Barometer 1017.

The morning became a countdown to 'The Rum Line', the breeze a steady 15-knot north-north-westerly. Clearly Staggy's watch had been hoping to crack the bottle, but the 0800hrs log entry read: 'Didn't quite make it — seven miles to go.' We were back in business with a 200-plus run. Send it down Huey.

Day 42: Friday, October 9. Noon position 37.20S 4.28E
     Day's run 165 miles. Course 115 degrees.
     Wind NW 8 to 12 knots. Barometer 1021.

Huey's an unreliable son of whatever. The breeze died again overnight and held us back to 165 miles. Still, that's not too bad. It's just that we're impatient to finish this ordeal, get to Cape Town and restore *Ceramco* to her racing best. After a little drink that is. God knows how the booze will affect us when we finally do make it to the bar of the Royal Cape Yacht Club. Everyone on board has vowed to 'hit it hard' the first 48 hours in. I can't blame them but, with only the odd tot of rum over the last six weeks, the outcome should be interesting to say the least. The crew is in remarkably good spirits considering the length of time we've been at sea and the problems we've had. The watch pairings provided some intriguing comparisons. The Doc and Newt spend half their watches relating lengthy and involved tales which tend to send Newt to sleep. The Doc's alternative is opera, which isn't exactly Newt's taste in music. Don and Lui go up top with Sonny Walkman sets to while away the hours crooning to tapes, sometimes the same tapes, other times different.

Staggy and Owen sit up there making high-pitched squeaking noises, pointing around and squealing, like two-year-olds, 'Mooon, waater' and so on. This was the only act which, I know, got on the nerves of our easy-going doctor.

Simon and Molly are different again. Simon spent his watches reciting poetry, favouring Banjo Patterson heavily, or crooning (much to the despair of anyone in earshot). Molly got around in his long woollen underwear which had a large number of holes in the crutch area. Heaven only knows why as nobody else had this problem. He is still wearing the same jumper and shirt that he had on at the equator. When Molly can stop Simon's singing, the conversation invariably centers on rugby.

Jaws and Chappy while away the hours discussing yachts and designing 90ft versions of the famous old Mullet boats indigenous to Auckland's Waitemata and Manukau harbours, developed to fish the tidal estuaries for mullet. Chappy does most of the talking. Jaws' mouth is usually involved in his favourite pastime — eating.

The boat is immaculately clean, the result of the constant work parties organised to kill time. We still had headsails stowed along either passageway in the centre of the ship though. We'd tried putting them forward but ended up thumping and crashing through the seas, the boat too wet because of the bow down trim. She's a touch bow down anyway since the dismasting, because of all the rigging which is now lashed down for'ard.

Ceramco is an incredibly dry boat below. Most yachts have water sloshing around. On *Condor,* in the 1977-78 race, if we were on one tack for any length of time we'd have to wear sea boots in the galley. We get a bit of water in the sump, from the rudder stock (the gland needs repacking) and if we are running hard we get a half pint of water below if we take a wave on board. But this simply runs through the channelling and down into the central bilge which we pump out two or three times a day.

Flyer apparently needs a bottom paint in Cape Town. I don't envy Conny that job on a big, rusty dry-dock unit. *Ceramco* will only need a diver for a bottom clean. He'll need to watch out for seals which are prolific in Cape Town harbour. Then again, if it's Jaws who does the job, the seals will have to watch out for him.

There must have been quite a blow down in the Southern Ocean below us. We're now in a large, long swell estimated at 150 to 200 metres between crests and probably 5 to 6 metres high. Only 694 miles to go now, not much more than a Sydney-Hobart which we cut out in under three days last December. There are distinct symptoms of channel fever on board as Cape Town looms closer. The boats to the north of us appear to be stuck in a high and only four yachts — *Flyer, Charles Heidsieck, Kriter* and *Challenger* — have finished. It looks like *Kriter, Heidsieck* and *Flyer,* in that order, will be the top three on handicap. I spoke to Pippa and Terry Gillespie in Cape Town tonight. They were aboard *Challenger.* Terry already has things moving on the new spar. There has been a delay with the new rod rigging but British Airways are sorting that out and it should all be in Cape Town by tomorrow.

Day 45: Monday, October 12. Noon position 36.58S 11.04E
        Day's run 88 miles. Course 090 degrees.
        Wind light and variable. Barometer 1015.

We're still out here and, damn it, there's no sign of anything to boost us in. I've been too frustrated to maintain the log even. We're so close — 420 miles to go — yet, in these conditions, so far. We managed a respectable 171 miles to noon on the 10th but then the bottom dropped out of the wind and we struggled to a run of 76 miles to noon yesterday. The total is only marginally better today. I try to comfort myself with reminders that, considering the small amount of effective sail we're able to fly, we're not doing too badly in near flat calm conditions. But it doesn't work. Time is wasting and the meter is running.

The 76-mile run was our worst since leaving England, with the exception of the 24 hours after dropping the rig. Half of those 76 miles must have been due to a favourable current. We must have had ¾ knot up our stern. The barometer's been dropping steadily and a low has developed to the west of Cape Town but nothing's reached us in the way of a decent sailing breeze. We've been flat running, the 'Sooty Sail' out on the pole, in dead light airs — our most vulnerable condition and worst point of sailing.

Heidsieck had a lucky escape as she neared the finish. Their timing was out as they swapped the shroud bottlescrew to the weather side in a tack. The mast all but came down and they limped home with the stick bent 40 degrees. This probably cost *Heidsieck* the handicap lead to *Kriter* which has endured her own problems with a damaged forestay. The *Heidsieck* people are flying a new mast to Cape Town. It will be a rush job without the kind of notice we were able to give our support team in Auckland.

Day 46: Tuesday, October 13: Noon position 35.53S 12.14E
        Day's run 88 miles. Course 080 degrees.
        Wind SW 5 to 10 knots. Barometer 1014.

Another disheartening 24 hours, but there's still some humour left on the boat. After wallowing through this morning in variables, the breeze picked up from the south-west then backed again into the north-west at 10 knots. The log read: 'Moving again, ever so slightly at first but I think we're going forwards.'

Day 47: Wednesday, October 14: Noon position 35.19S 14.35E
    Day's run 118 miles. Course 110 degrees.
    Wind W 8 to 10 knots. Barometer 1015.

Oh, the pain of it. We broke the ton — but it's hard going. The only relief comes from Cape Town still 190 miles away. Jim Lidgard has arrived to help Terry and Pippa with the mast which was now fully assembled and on its way from the local sparmaker's to the yacht club, complete with police escort. When we spoke to the three of them again tonight they'd been out celebrating something or other. They told us they had a welcome party organised with plenty of ice-cold champagne, 40 crayfish and a large number of oysters. I'll swear the boat picked up speed. There wasn't much wind in Cape Town but here's hoping Huey is huffing and puffing for our arrival. We are quite proud of our jury rig and, after all the effort that has gone in, we want to arrive with a bit of dash.

The log reported: 'The Jets (Chappy and Jaws) hit 12 knots?? Jaws was on the helm, we saw it coming from 30 yards. A wave bigger than the rest. A hardened champion, Jaws wiggled the stern and we were away. In our path a container, an iceberg and a whale. Talk about weave. Truly magnificent.' This was followed by a caustic: 'Sounds like the Jets' after burners are expounding forth.'

Day 48: Thursday, October 15. Noon position 34.09S 17.27E
    Day's run 160 miles. Course 105 degrees.
    Wind SSW 18 knots. Barometer 1014.

The boys have been warming up for the party to end all parties. Nobody slept much last night and the Doc was prompted to observe that he thought Vonny's somewhat hypermanic state was due to the proximity of Cape Town and the probability that he would soon be able to attend to his thirst. In mid-afternoon we were buzzed by a light plane which made two trips to enable Pippa, Terry, Jim and photographer Bob Fisher to see *Ceramco*, the Chinese junk. We could see Table Mountain and the Cape of Good Hope in the distance. *Ceramco* must have made quite a sight — a bone in her teeth and trucking along in the 15 to 20-knot south-wester. Good on you Huey. By 4.00 pm we were into Table Bay and picked up *Outward Bound* which had brought the Kiwi contingent out to cheer us on. It was an emotive moment. Finally, at 1828.10 GMT, we crossed the finish line and were the toast of the dock. It had taken *Flyer* 36 days 10 hours 56 minutes 37 seconds to reach this destination. We'd been at sea for 47 days 7 hours 28 minutes and 5 seconds. *Ceramco* had some time to make up across the Southern Oceans, but for now we could relax, content in the knowledge that we'd completed a difficult assignment with a certain degree of ingenuity and determination. And there hadn't been one cross word.

7. ONE DOWN – THREE TO GO

A ship is floating in the harbour now,
A wind is hovering o'er the mountain's brow; ...
— Percy Bysshe Shelley, Epipsychidion

CERAMCO WAS GIVEN a moving reception. We were 18th across the finish line and most of the crews from the yachts already in were on hand to greet us, along with a huge crowd of locals. We tied up to a cacophony of ships' sirens and boat horns.

Pippa had hitched a ride on *Outward Bound* and scrambled aboard *Ceramco* as soon as we crossed the line. It was great to see her. On the dock, loaded down with champagne, crayfish and oysters, were the support team of Terry Gillespie and Jim Lidgard, keeping a wary eye on Bob 'Tooloose la Fish' Fisher who has a certain reputation for eating and drinking and a known liking for oceanic delicacies. The party that ensued was one of the big ones and I still can't remember how and when Pippa managed to get me 'home' to the apartment she'd rented, handy to the city and Duncan Dock where *Ceramco* was moored.

94

There was much to be done in the 16 days before the restart to Auckland but I gave everyone three days off before requiring them back on board to derig the boat and prepare to step the new mast. At the prescribed hour, they were all there with various degrees of hangover — except Molly. He finally made it, most apologetic and looking terrible, to plead for the rest of the day off. I had to agree. He would have been useless in his condition anyway. The boys explained that Molly had been the target of much female attention and, on the second morning in, had arrived back from a nearby park covered in mud and proclaiming: 'I'm in love, I'm in love.' The only problem was, in his hungover state, he couldn't remember what the girl looked like. He spent the rest of the day avoiding phone calls and taking a terrible ribbing from the crew.

Vonny had earnestly warned everyone to take it easy on the grog the first night in — then proceeded to write himself off, and spent the rest of the dark hours calling for Herbert.

Fortunately, Terry, Jim and Pippa had everything organised. The new mast, which had been flown to Cape Town in three pieces by British Airways, was assembled and the new rod rigging sorted and fitted. We weren't taking any chances. This time the shrouds terminated at universal end-fittings on the spreaders to eliminate possible stress areas. The mast itself was an exact duplicate of the original but, as a precaution, we'd beefed up the size of the lower intermediate shrouds. There had been plenty of time for post-mortems and to examine the broken rig and it seemed clear to us that the mast itself was fine. The problem had been the rod which had fractured at a stress point caused by the way it was passed through the end of the spreaders. Just like a piece of wire bent back and fore, the rod had finally broken and, lacking support, the mast had collapsed.

While most of the crew, under Terry's direction, tackled the work still to be done on the spar, OC and Lui went away to a local loft, with Jim, to repair the mainsail, restore the 'Sooty Sail' to its original dimensions and attend to general sail maintenance.

Vonny, meanwhile, organised his food supplies. We'd done most of the general maintenance, on deck and below, to keep busy while struggling towards Cape Town, so now could concentrate on the items of major importance.

In no time at all, the new rig was ready to step. We had one anxious moment as the crane lifted the stump of the old rig out of the boat. The heavy alloy section slipped and dropped straight down on the deck. Fortunately nobody was in the way and the deck was plenty strong enough. The remains of the first rig was piled in a tangled heap on the dock and the new mast went in with a minimum of bother. It remained only to adjust tensions, await delivery of the refurbished sail wardrobe and we could go out into Table Bay for trials.

The Royal Cape Yacht Club had done a commendable job on its shore set-up. The fleet wanted for nothing in the way of facilities and the hospitality was brilliant.

I think we received extra-special treatment because we were Kiwis. The South Africans were genuinely pleased to see us, particularly in the wake of the Springbok rugby tour of New Zealand. We'd been pressured, by the HART (Halt All Racist Tours) movement back home to withdraw from the race because the fleet included the South African entry *Xargo III*. I tore up HART's telegrams and threw them away. Why should we be singled out when all the big nations — the United States, Britain, France, Germany, Italy and so on — were involved. Nobody was condoning apartheid, nor were they interested in the political

A garden party on board was our way of saying thank you to Cape Town.

situation. We were entered in a boat race, the multi-national crew on *Xargo* were a great bunch of people and, like us, were intent only on the race in which the elements were the main opposition anyway.

The fleet trickled in through the settled weather that was dominating the southern tip of Africa. There was a wait of 2 days 23 hours after *Ceramco* until the 50ft Italian entry *Ilgagomma* crossed the line to be 26th yacht home. Unfortunately, there was no way the fleet could hang around for the Italian 57-footer *Vivanapoli.* She'd run foul of Angolan authorities who claimed she'd breached territorial waters. Beppe Panada and his crew were forced to follow an Angolan gunboat into the port of Luanda even though they insisted they were 45 miles offshore when confronted. In Luanda, an Angolan guard slipped over the side on *Vivanapoli* and shots were fired. Nobody, fortunately, was hit, but *Vivanapoli*'s crew were subjected to a 13-hour interrogation before they were able to contact the Italian ambassador. His advice was to 'play it cool'. An American yacht, arrested in similar circumstances not long before, had been held for six weeks. When the *Vivanapoli* people were finally allowed to return to their yacht, an armed guard would not allow them on board, and they had to sleep on the quayside.

This went on for a week, the Angolans insisting that Panada and his shipmates were spies. What they were supposed to be spying on was never explained, although the South African visas in their passports were the source of much suspicion. Finally, *Vivanapoli* was allowed to leave. She arrived in Cape Town nine days after the restart for Auckland, 35 days after *Flyer* and 24 days behind *Ceramco*.

The leg had gone as we'd expected it would, once the calm weather set in and closed the door behind the leaders. *Kriter* was the corrected time leader from *Charles Heidsieck* and *Flyer* in that order. *Flyer*'s elapsed time of 36 days 10 hours 56 minutes 37 seconds clipped 2 days 10 hours off the record for the leg set by Conny's previous *Flyer* in the 1977-78 race. The three leaders had a big jump on the fourth placed *Berge Viking*. *Outward Bound* had been poised to win the leg only days from the Cape Town finish, but had been trapped by the calm. Digby had to make do with what was still a highly creditable sixth. The calm had hurt *Ceramco* even more. We were down in 26th place on corrected time, 264 hours, or 11 days, behind *Kriter*. That would take a power of making up, but there was still threequarters of this race to go.

Although relatively easy in terms of conditions, the Portsmouth-Cape Town leg had taken its toll of the fleet. The Swan 57 *Scandinavian*, crewed by Scandinavian Airlines personnel, had withdrawn and diverted to the Mediterranean. Nobody knew why. Then there had been three broken masts (*Ceramco*, *La Barca Laboratorio* and *Rollygo*), five broken forestays and four boats with rigging or spar problems. The Southern Ocean would be a lot tougher, and one had to wonder what the casualty rate would be down there.

Pippa and I moved out of our rented apartment to accept the generous hospitalty of B.P. South Africa general manager Ian Simms and his wife. They could not have been kinder and the rest of our stay, all too brief, was unforgettable because of them. The crew had been adopted by a friend of Staggy's brother Andy — a Hobie Cat sailor Harry Foukes who runs a large underwater construction company in South Africa.

Harry treated us royally and, the night before our departure for Auckland, invited the whole team to his home on the Atlantic slopes of Table Mountain. It was a magnificent set-up and we had the most enjoyable relaxing evening making full use of his swimming pool and spa. Molly was otherwise engaged. Fancying himself as something of a squash player, he'd bet Harry 100 rands he could beat him. Harry generously offered Molly a point a game. The 'match', for want of a better word, was played in Harry's own glass-backed court near the barbecue and pool. While the rest of us lounged around and sipped ice-cold drinks, Molly sweated his way to ignominious defeat against an opponent who was one of the top players in South Africa. The *Ceramco* representative didn't win one point.

Another Harry, this time the surname was Braun, was particularly kind to us and helped make the stay so memorable. Nothing was too much trouble for he and his wife and they made a lasting impression when, right out of the blue just before we were about to leave the dock, he came down to present us all with a large beach towel each. We would never forget these wonderfully hospitable folk.

But departure time was drawing near and we were itching to tackle the Southern Ocean. One of our final chores was to scrub the bottom and spruce up the topsides which were black with oil. Cape Town harbour is a repair facility for all the shipping that rounds the Cape of Good Hope. A ship can go into dock on a Friday and emerge on Monday completely repainted by teams using towers with multiple spray units powered by powerful pumps. Unfortunately, they are not as pollution conscious as they might be and the environment takes a pounding from overspray and oil dumped from bilges. The rise and fall in the smallish harbour is only 4ft to 5ft, so most of the muck is trapped. From the top of Table Mountain, you could look down at what really is an impressive, U-shaped and man-made harbour and see the perpetual grey-brown colour of the harbour itself licking out into the beautiful blue of Table Bay.

We took *Ceramco* out into the bay for a final clean, Jaws and Molly doing the honours, going over the side in diving gear. There were a lot of seals around but the word must have been out about Jaws. None of them ventured too close. The bottom was in excellent condition and the only problem was with goose barnacles, a marine growth, rather like a pipi on a stalk, which likes to block up any openings in the hull. We were careful to ensure that all inlets and outlets were clear and that there was nothing attached to *Ceramco*'s bottom that might slow her down. We had a date with New Zealand, and would be in a hurry to be there on time.

PORTSMOUTH-CAPE TOWN

	Elapsed Times			Corrected Times	
	Boat	Hrs/Min/Sec		Boat	Rating	Hrs/Min/Sec
1.	Flyer	874.56.37	1.	Kriter 9	52.1ft	840.38.39
2.	Charles Heidsieck III	926.37.20	2.	Charles Heidsieck III	54.6ft	852.35.20
3.	Kriter 9	929.22.45	3.	Flyer	67.8ft	867.06.51
4.	FCF Challenger	966.48.35	4.	Berge Viking	42.4ft	899.25.42
5.	Alaska Eagle	1005.19.03	5.	Alaska Eagle	50.4ft	904.18.49
6.	Euromarche	1010.40.30	6.	Outward Bound	40.0ft	906.21.55
7.	Disque D'Or III	1037.25.00	7.	Disque D'Or III	46.0ft	909.05.41
8.	Gauloises III	1047.36.30	8.	Bubblegum	33.0ft	918.42.05
9.	Berge Viking	1054.05.46	9.	Morbihan	37.2ft	927.57.57
10.	Swedish Entry	1056.58.30	10.	Xargo III	44.4ft	929.20.52
11.	Xargo III	1076.33.21	11.	European University	34.4ft	929.24.31
12.	33 Export	1078.15.56	12.	Traite de Rome	34.6ft	935.20.21
13.	United Friendly	1078.46.07	13.	Croky	33.7ft	935.53.55
14.	Outward Bound	1080.03.27	14.	Swedish Entry	48.0ft	942.17.61
15.	Licor 43	1103.20.42	15.	FCF Challenger	69.6ft	944.48.35
16.	Save Venice	1105.14.16	16.	33 Export	45.5ft	946.26.19
17.	Morbihan	1125.35.22	17.	Walrus	36.8ft	946.53.50
18.	Ceramco NZ	1135.28.05	18.	Skopbank of Finland	38.0ft	948.54.15
19.	Skopbank of Finland	1139.29.54	19.	Gauloises 3	51.6ft	955.51.19
20.	Rollygo	1154.31.56	20.	Euromarche	60.8ft	960.09.45
21.	Bubblegum	1156.21.36	21.	Rollygo	39.6ft	977.31.47
22.	European University	1158.42.56	22.	Licor 43	51.4ft	1010.21.55
23.	Walrus III	1161.34.05	23.	Save Venice	54.8ft	1032.20.02
24.	Traite de Rome	1162.45.15	24.	Ilgagomma	40.0ft	1032.52.38
25.	Croky	1166.29.19	25.	United Friendly	68.0ft	1061.07.05
26.	Ilgagomma	1206.34.10	26.	Ceramco NZ	62.9ft	1105.00.49

8. PUSH TO THE LIMIT

The sheets were frozen hard, and they cut the naked hand;
The decks were like a slide, where a seaman scarce could stand.
— Robert Louis Stevenson, Christmas at Sea

THE FLEET WAS down to 26 yachts when, at 3.00 pm local time on October 31, in Table Bay, the gun sounded for the start of the 7010-mile Cape Town to Auckland leg. We were going home. Ahead of us lay some of the roughest and most dangerous waters in the world — the Southern Ocean. Two men lost their lives when swept overboard by huge seas on this leg of the inaugural race in 1973-74.

Everywhere else around the globe, there are land masses to check the sea's progress. But down south, between the Antarctic ice shelf and the southernmost capes of South Africa, Australia, New Zealand and South America, the oceans roll unobstructed all the way around the world. Low pressure systems sweep through these ocean wastes with a frequency and velocity that has led to the various high latitudes being dubbed the Roaring Forties, the Furious Fifties and the Screaming Sixties.

Ceramco New Zealand was conceived, designed and built to excel in these waters, to take full advantage of the strong tail wind and long sea conditions that are to be 'enjoyed' by taking yachts to the edge of the pack ice on a great circle course across the bottom of the world. But we were setting out with a new and untried mast, with a crew that was bound to be a little gun shy after the mishap of the first leg. It was going to take a lot of personal discipline and dedication to push *Ceramco* to the prudent limits in a bid to beat the bigger *Flyer* into the sheltered waters of Auckland's beautiful Hauraki Gulf and Waitemata Harbour.

We were all sorry to bid farewell to those wonderfully hospitable people of Cape Town, but there is a job to be done for our own people in New Zealand.

We tried the No. 1 heavy genoa about 50 minutes before the start, manoeuvring through a large spectator fleet in a fresh west-north-westerly and smooth seas. *Ceramco* was labouring so, remembering that we still hadn't fully tested the mast, we changed down to the No. 2 genoa just before the 10-minute gun. The spar looked to be bending correctly as we took the boat to the line, hardening up on a starboard tack which took us right inshore. We were in reasonable shape as we short tacked our way around the corner to Hout Bay, going in close until the depth gauge showed 10 metres. But the wind slowly died, forcing us to change up again, this time to the full-size heavy Mylar No. 1, getting more and more shape into the mainsail as we carried on along the coast to Duiker Point.

We were beating around headlands against a strong tide. One board to sea cost us dearly. *Flyer, Kriter, Gauloises* and even little *Croky*, staying in on the shore, put one across us and, 15 miles after the start, had a handy lead. But we grabbed it all back, and more, by going inside a group of rocks off Duiker Point. Chappy went as pale as a ghost and was speechless as we sailed through breaking water to reach the inside track. But once in there we had the advantage of a nice breeze and smooth water. We picked up 30 minutes and passed 15 boats.

On past Slangkop Point lighthouse just before nightfall, the breeze started to die and we had plenty of time to appreciate the long, sandy beach of Chapman Bay. The bottom shelves gradually and the 15ft swell, coming in from the Southern Ocean, piled up as it hit the Continental Shelf and got bigger all the time as it ran on into the shallower water. The fleet was in line astern just outside the breakers, having to harden up to head into the curlers, doing only one or two knots in boatspeed. It was a somewhat uncomfortable situation but nobody was giving an inch.

Around the corner the seas were a lot easier and, as we eased away to head south past Albatross Rocks, we could see the Cape of Good Hope light away out on the port beam — one of the most famous capes in the world, and one of the most important lights.

Inshore near Hout Bay.

Inside the rocks and in good shape.

Day 2: Sunday, November 1. Noon position 35.20S 18.24E
     Day's run (21 hours) 90 miles. Course 170 degrees.
     Wind ESE 10 to 12 knots. Barometer 1018.

Late last night we were still in company with *Flyer, Charles Heidsieck, Kriter* and *Disque D'Or* but tacked to sea and came back through to windward of the whole fleet. At dawn we could see 16 yachts, *Ceramco* was still the weather boat. *Flyer* was to leeward and about a quarter of a mile ahead. *Gauloises* was down below us on our beam. The wind was down to three knots at times, but the seas were still big.

By nightfall the wind had backed through the south into the south-east, increasing to 15 to 18 knots. We began to get a wriggle on — as we'd need to if we were going to be home in New Zealand to vote in the general election on November 28.

We're eating well. Dinner last night comprised the chicken casserole cooked for us by Ian Simms' girl, plus apple pie and thick cream. Breakfast today started with superb South African fruit juice, muesli and apricots, then bacon and baked beans on toast. Lunch was Vonny's rice speciality with a nice salad (tomatoes, boiled eggs, fresh spring onions). It's going to be hard when the fresh food runs out in a couple of weeks' time. The icebox is full of fresh meat that should last that long, particularly as we are heading south and away from the warming influence of the Agulhas Current which comes down from the Indian Ocean, around the bottom of South Africa and then waffles up the other side of the continent. We're still plugging against that current at the moment, but once we're down below 37S we should be starting to pick up favourable Southern Ocean currents.

The common theme in conversation around the boat right now is New Zealand. Everyone is conscious of the fact we are taking *Ceramco* home.

The chart I am using notes that in April 1928, many icebergs — some of them 100ft high — were seen around our current position. More big ones were sighted close by in 1853. Fortunately, not many had been seen since and I'm not expecting to encounter ice until we're well below 45 to 50 South. Our course will take us almost due south towards Marion Island. We're digging south early as there is a high pressure system building to the east of us which inevitably will form the Southern Indian Ocean High. Then there's a low coming through from the west at 40S. That's what we're after and the quicker we get down into its path the better. The low means westerlies and south-westerlies — high speed spinnaker stuff.

The log notes: 'Moved ahead of *Gauloises* some more. *Flyer* still holding up while we slip through to leeward, sailing slightly cracked (yacht or crew?).' It's quiet down below. Everyone is getting over the good living ashore in Cape Town. It certainly is a place you can enjoy without having to have a limitless cheque book. The food and wine are both excellent yet inexpensive. The low acidity of the wine meant no hangover. Combined with low price and high quality, it made an attractive proposition.

Cape Town radio passed us a telegram from England. It read: 'Re last leg. Every dod must have its day. From now on, keep it up. Best of luck.' It was signed: 'From No limit on the fun Co. Pty., Devon.' Of course it was from our old friend Andrew 'Spud' Spedding, the mad Devon farmer. Spud has a Dartmoor property owned by HRH Prince Charles, and lives quite close to Dartmoor Prison, which we reckon would be a much more apt place for him to reside. *Ceramco*'s picking up speed, doing 5 to 5½ knots in 8 or 9 knots of wind. We're pulling in *Flyer* and dropping the boats astern.

Day 3: Monday, November 2. Noon position 37.10S 19.58W
       Day's run 134 miles. Course 160 degrees.
       Wind SW 20 knots. Barometer 1016.

A not too clever run, but we more than held our own in the fleet. Between 0100hrs and 0200hrs today the barometer dropped three points, the breeze freshening as it swung NE. We thought we were off. But by 0800hrs it had died and swung west. We waffled through a string of sail changes before the breeze died completely, then came in with a bang at 20 to 25 knots from the SSW.

I was waiting for the afternoon weather map from Pretoria when I noticed a disturbing amount of water in the boat. We'd repacked the bottom rudder bearing in Cape Town but it obviously wasn't bedded down properly. Every time we surfed, the water poured in. Staggy was on the wheel and I asked him to keep the boat level while we sorted out the problem and tightened the nuts on the stern packing. This seemed to work for a while, then we had a lot of water sloshing around the bilge again. The crew pumped manually while the electric pump was started up. The latter sucks up the power and isn't exactly fast, but it's a solid worker. We made no impression on the water level. The sea was coming in as fast as we could pump it out.

By now, Vonny had grabbed a bucket and Staggy was getting more than a little frustrated, having to ease back the speed while he held the boat level. 'What the hell you guys,' he shouted down, 'we're racing up here.' Vonny shot back: 'You may be racing up there, but we're sinking down here.' Then we found the cause of the problem. An exit pipe from one of the sink drains had ruptured, leaving a one-inch diameter hole open to the ocean.

Vonny didn't know it, but the buckets he was emptying into that sink were sluicing right back into the bilge. We shut the outlet valve down and pumped for another 30 minutes before we had things under control. *Challenger* slipped through the weather during all of this, while Staggy was running square so that all the water would empty into the sump. Les Williams must have thought we were all drunk.

Day 4: Tuesday, November 3. Noon position 39.29S 21.57E
       Day's run 168 miles. Course 170 degrees.
       Wind ESE 25 to 30 knots. Barometer 1016.

The wind came in at 0600hrs, after another light night, then really started to honk. As it built, we changed down to the No. 5 jib with three reefs in the main to reach off on a great circle course for the Kerguelen Islands. We drew away from *Challenger*, which was heading more south. *Flyer* was holding up more to the east, *Heidsieck* was astern of our port beam. The Porcelain Rocket ship started to lift off, squirting to 16 knots in lumpy seas which already had that cold green look of the Southern Ocean.

I figured it was time to sort out the aft heater, a compact diesel-burning unit, which hadn't worked at all on the way across the Atlantic to the UK. Lack of draught had to be the problem, so I'd brought along a good length of plastic tubing to extend the flue. With this taped up to the port whip aerial on the stern the outlet was 6ft higher than before and made a most efficient chimney. The heater now works superbly. It looks as though we're going to need it.

Day 5: Wednesday, November 4. Noon position 43.25S 25.10E
         Day's run 230 miles. Course 158 degrees.
         Wind WNW 10 to 12 knots. Barometer 1009.

The plunge south has begun in earnest. We've picked the right way to go, between the high and the low. The boats which decided to head east immediately have had light airs and we've really stacked some time on them. The wind backed into the NE yesterday afternoon and blew hard (25 to 30 knots) until 0400hrs today when it started to moderate. It's in the west tonight and still hasn't settled. But the signs are good.

On the first leg, Conny had a photo of *Ceramco* stuck to the mast below decks with the legend: 'Know your enemy.' If we can help it, he's going to find out just how prophetic he was.

It's getting colder. The night watch crews are donning polar gear, socks and boots and balaclavas, and the odd set of longjohns have appeared.

I've made one change in the watches for this leg, swapping the Doc into Chappy's team and OC into Staggy's. This balances out the heavy weather helmsman for the heavy going we must soon experience.

Day 6: Thursday, November 5. Noon position 45.05S 29.21E
         Day's run 240 miles. Course 165 degrees.
         Wind WNW 25 to 30 knots. Barometer 1001.

The barometer plunged seven points between midnight and 0600hrs. We've been barrelling along under full-sized kites for the last 36 hours and the mileages are building. So is the wind which has swung into the north-west and is now gusting 45 knots. The log entries reflect the anticipation on board. They've gone from 'Truckin along' to 'Truckin along like she was built for' and now 'Don reckons this is better than 120mph on a motor bike.'

The westerly is rising, with OC on the wheel and Newt enjoying the ride.

Better not to look astern.   *No control problems.*

The weatherfax machine is working perfectly. This morning, just before dawn, I tuned into Canberra, more' than 6000 miles away on the eastern seaboard of Australia, and got the most magnificent, clear pictures. It's heartening to know we are going to be able to pick them up whenever we want them. Canberra will take over where Pretoria leaves off and we should have good coverage all the way to New Zealand. It's not the be-all, end-all, but it's a boon to have a visual map in front of you after only having to tune a receiver. It saves having to decode high-speed morse broadcasts, which I'm not capable of doing at the moment anyway.

Challenger had a tape recorder installed in Cape Town which should enable them to record the morse signals at high speed and then play them back at low speed for decoding. But the whole process — decoding, working out what it means and drawing maps — is a four to six-hour exercise. All I have to do is switch on the weatherfax machine, tune it and then switch if off again 15 minutes later when the print-out is finished.

Vonny is back to his gracious best. His meal calls have reverted to 'Here pig, pig, pig' or 'Get up you mongrel bastards'. His dining-room manners wouldn't get him a job in a pie cart, but we can't complain about the food he's dishing up.

As we've cleared the Agulhas Current and dug well into the Roaring Forties, the seas have evened out and the weather pattern is returning to normal with massive westerly, south-westerly and north-westerly winds rolling right around the Antarctic. We're aiming to reach 55 degrees south just below the Kerguelen Islands. The weather pattern will dictate what we do from there.

Day 7: Friday, November 6. Noon position 47.04S 36.26E
      Day's run 316 miles. Course 150 degrees.
      Wind NW 25 to 30 knots. Barometer 999.

A mind-blowing 24-hour run of 316 miles — a Whitbread record, averaging more than 13 knots and verified by log and Satnav. The previous best was *Condor*'s 309 miles in 1978, with the help of the strong Falkland Current up the eastern coast of South America.

The breeze freshened to full gale yesterday afternoon and kept at it all night. *Ceramco* blasted along in front of the gale under the big, heavy spinnaker (2.2oz) and one reef in the main. All yesterday afternoon she averaged better than 15 knots, bursting off the clock to an estimated 35 knots. The seas weren't exactly favourable, they weren't long enough for *Ceramco* to really stretch her legs. But she loved it, tearing down the seas so fast that all the sails were aback. It was like being on a runaway train, except this one was totally under control. Not even a hint of a nosedive. The closest we came was when the boat barrelled off one sea and charged for the next, but the bow just nicked the top off the second wave and kept on going. Jaws, sitting in the forward cockpit and ready to throw the spinnaker brace if we got into trouble, casually turned his back and pulled his wet weather gear hood over his head as the sea was shovelled down the deck.

Last night was extra dark and we had to back her off a bit. It's important to see the waves so that you can place the boat accordingly. But we roared on through the blackness until, just on midnight, we got a wrap. The spinnaker backwinded and rolled itself tightly around the forestay. We should have had a spinnaker net to prevent this, but for some reason we didn't. Jaws had to go aloft to sort it out. With *Ceramco* hitting 16 and 17 knots under double-reefed main only, he hooked the bosun's chair onto a tightened genoa halyard, to prevent being thrown about and injuring himself on a spreader, and went to it. By the time we got him up there, the spinnaker had completely demolished the heavy plastic headfoil and *Ceramco*, without the steadying influence of the kite, was rolling all over the place. The little man with the big appetite was oblivious to it all. He sat 70ft above the heaving, rolling deck for 10 minutes before he managed to unclip the head of the spinnaker and drop it down to the deck.

We untwisted the sail and removed the pieces of demolished headfoil and prepared to rehoist, but the spinnaker net which was going up, to prevent a repeat of the costly mishap, got twisted itself and we had four guys up on the bow for a good 30 minutes sorting it out. They finally had to take it below to get some light on the subject (the steaming light on the mast had, of course, chosen this moment to blow its bulb) before we were ready to hoist. This time it all went smoothly, the net went up without a hitch, followed by the storm spinnaker, and we were off again in 40 knots plus.

Pushing big yachts through nights like this, bursting to speeds of 30 knots or more, is a unique experience. Like everything else one does that involves an element of risk, the initial reaction is one of cautious apprehension. But, as familiarity establishes itself, apprehension becomes exhilaration. Some boats, designed with more upwind than downwind characteristics, are cranky with the wind fresh and from aft of the beam. In these conditions they would be dreadful to sail. But *Ceramco* has proved she's a thoroughbred downwind machine, flashing along at prolonged high speed, providing no reason for anxiety.

The whole boat is organised for speed. The sails have been dragged aft into the navigatorium area, the off-watch crew are using only the bunks near the stern and we're eating all our meals down the back as well. We need to keep the weight as far aft as possible, over *Ceramco*'s wide planing sections and out of the for'ard area. It doesn't make for comfortable living, but comfort is the last thing on our minds.

Jaws has been up the mast again today to replace the steaming light bulb, remove the top sections of the broken headfoil and to get ready to fit the spare foil we carry for just this situation. Chappy's watch is getting some hard-earned rest. They spent much of their 'down time' last night helping to clear the mess on deck as we struggled with the spinnaker wrap and fouled net. The breeze has moderated to 15 to 25 knots, but there's more to come. Tonight we're 25 miles to the SW of Marion Island, which is in the Prince Edward group in the south-west Indian Ocean. A South African scientific team operate a weather station on the island and we have arranged a sched with them on VHF and 2182. So far we haven't raised them, even though we've tried to alert them through Cape Town radio.

Day 8: Saturday, November 7. Noon position 49.04S 42.40E
       Day's run 285 miles. Course 135 degrees.
       Wind NW 40 to 55 knots. Barometer 980.

The gale built to storm proportions. I quote from the Doc's personal log: 'Bloody hell, what a time. Great tumbling, broken seas, screaming wind up our bum, the roaring of waves and the coldness are something very different. Up and down constantly. Nobody's had much sleep over the last 48 hours. The sail changes, from one reef and kite, to two reefs then three reefs, to storm jib then later poled out No. 6, have taken everyone's efforts. Has a few broaches when we tried to set a storm spinnaker, and subsequently tried to set a blast reacher in 50 knots of wind. A bloody lonely place to be in 50 knots.'

The normally eloquent doctor did better a couple of days later when things had quietened down. He wrote: 'I will never forget Guy Fawkes day, 1981, for the excitement of sailing in the gale. Nor will I forget the storm which followed on November 7th. The gale involved a breeze of about 40 knots and lumpy, uneven seas. We carried a large spinnaker and, for many hours, had only a flattened mainsail but later put in one reef. For about 36 hours we ran at unbelievable speeds. When we were ploughing down the waves our bow wave extended back almost to the stern and were often as high as the boom. The yacht would accelerate and her nose would drop as we took off down a big wave into the water ahead until it seemed the bow would go under. Then, as we accelerated, the bow would lift well out. All about us would be the roaring of the sea. The noise and the vibrations within the yacht were overwhelming. None of the off-watch crew could sleep during this period. To improve buoyancy, everything that could be moved was dragged aft until the navigatorium looked like an old junk shop with sacks of cabbages and spare water containers competing for space with the odd sail. On deck, we put a sail in its bag across the stern just inside the lifelines. The three deck crew who were not sailing the boat clipped themselves on and perched on that sail. The other two took a wheel each. One man actually helmed. The other threw his weight on when necessary to avoid a broach.

'On the 7th it was clear we were in the middle of a storm — heaving seas, breaking crests, spume blowing off the tops. *Ceramco* was still surfing down these by-now enormous waves. It was a truly awesome experience. Under much reduced sail we were still maintaining excellent boat speed as the day's run of 285 miles showed. It seemed, in fact, safer when the yacht was travelling fast since, in these circumstances, there was less chance of a breaking wave dumping on us. The screaming rides down the wave fronts carried with them the risk of pitch-poling, but this was never a cause of major concern.'

The barometer had plummeted from 995 to 989 in just two hours to midnight as a prelude to the blow. From 0400hrs to 0800hrs it dived another five points, from 985 to 980.

The reasons we come down this far into these conditions are shorter distance to sail and speed. At 55S, one degree of longitude represents only 35 miles. The same degree of longitude a couple of hundred miles to the north represents 40 miles. Further north again it represents 60 miles. The reduction as you go south or north, from the equator is a result of the earth's curvature as it tucks in towards the poles. The high latitudes also involve a greater frequency of gales and storms with the systems, travelling in a favourable direction for us. The advantages then are obvious. The disadvantages are the severe cold and the fact that you can get on the wrong side of the low pressure systems sweeping through and finish up with

This is what we came for.

gale or storm force headwinds instead of tailwinds. Just how far we go down depends on the latitude at which the systems move through. If we look like running into easterlies we'll move north to stay in tailwinds on top of the lows. The other thing we have to consider is ice. If we strike concentrations which we consider too heavy, we'll ease north again. It isn't particularly cold as yet. The pilot says Marion Island has rain or snow most days of the year but I was walking around a dry deck in carpet slippers as we came past there.

Day 9: Sunday, November 8. Noon position 48.47S 49.24E
      Day's run 260 miles. Course 170 degrees.
      Wind WNW 20 to 25 knots. Barometer 1003.

The performance figures make impressive reading. Despite the slow start from Cape Town, we've still logged 1723 miles in eight days, an average of 215 miles a day. In the last five days we've logged 1331 miles at an average of 266 miles a day. In the last three days we've done 861 miles, averaging 287 miles a day. This has put us 160 miles south of the Iles Crozet and 780 miles to the west of the Kerguelens. It's now a lot colder. The sky has a heavy, brooding look about it and we've had sleet and snow to remind us where we are.

Our little dash has paid dividends. *Flyer* is less than 30 miles ahead. At one stage, after the light stuff earlier on, she'd opened up a lead of 80 miles. We learned from the chat show last night that she broke her main boom during the storm. Conny must be feeling the pressure of having *Ceramco* hard on his stern.

The breeze is down to 20 to 25 knots from the NW, giving us a slight respite. But there could be more strong wind on the way. There's a low coming through at about 52S.

We've been sailing with a west-south-westerly swell which means we've had the swell on the leeward quarter — quite a strange situation. Because we were crashing and banging all over the place this morning, we gybed over to port, using both poles (twin pole gybe). The kite was set to the new pole with the old one still in position all the time. Then we gybed the mainsail and settled everything down before dropping the old pole. We considered this a safer way of doing the gybe, and so it proved in daylight. But we've had problems following the same procedure at night in heavier conditions. If things get really severe, we will have to drop the kite, gybe the main and then rehoist the spinnaker on the new gybe.

The other night, when it was blowing hard, we had problems when the brace on the two-ply 1.5oz spinnaker jumped out of the parrot beak on the pole end. The beak had tripped itself open. The spinnaker skied away and we had to let the brace run in order to pull the sail down to leeward. In the process, the brace unclipped itself from the kite and we lost it. To overcome this problem, we've now rigged a secondary brace on the pole, a spare genoa sheet wrapped around the end of the pole so that if we have to run the brace again in a squall the spare sheet will hold the pole in position and let the brace and lazy sheet whistle through the end fitting. The pole won't damage the head foil either. This system will be particularly useful for the smaller spinnakers. The only way to drop them safely is to let the brace run.

Day 10: Monday, November 9. Noon position 49.04S 54.50E
Day's run 212 miles. Course 130 degrees.
Wind SW 10 to 20 knots. Barometer 996.

We managed a full generator service during the lull — it was giving a few problems and caused us to ration fresh water for a while — but the respite didn't last long. The breeze has backed into the SW and is now gusting 30 knots. We're down to the 2.2oz kite and blasting again through heavy snow.

Safety harnesses and 'shotgun' helmsman were a must.   *Dressed for the cold, the Doc opens his birthday present — a broken, inscribed batten — with Molly for company.*

Day 11: Tuesday, November 10. Noon position 49.53S 61.41E
     Day's run 275 miles. Course 160 degrees.
     Wind SSW 35 to 40 knots. Barometer 1001.

Another big run, but we've had our problems. *Ceramco* ripped off the miles throughout the night under the big kite and full main. The seas weren't big and the boat was at her best, averaging 14 knots with ease. But by morning the sea was up and things were a little trickier. Chappy was caught by a vicious squall. The boat broached violently and lay on her side. The brace was run, the bow came up into the wind and wouldn't fall off again. The kite halyard was run — a mistake as the rope tail was too big for the sheave block at the top of the mast. It jammed. The spinnaker filled astern of the boat then dropped in the sea to act like a bloody great parachute scoop, trying to pull the rig out of the boat. The halyard, by now, was around the leech of the mainsail and under the main boom, the wire putting a couple of tears in the foot of the sail. The brace and sheets on the kite, flailing all around the place, wiped off one whip aerial and badly bent the other. If we weren't quick the mast would join the casualty list. We managed to grind the sheet back aboard and then, after dropping the mainsail to bring the boat to a stop in the water, dragged the kite back on board without wrapping it around the steering gear or propeller. *Ceramco* shook and shuddered, staggered back to her feet and sat there quietly waiting to see what we had in mind for an encore. There were some rather white faces around as we rehoisted the main (two reefs in this time) and stuck up the No. 5 jib to proceed with a touch more caution. A check of the gear showed that, whip aerials apart, we'd been lucky. The small tears in the mainsail and a ripped spinnaker wouldn't take long to repair.

The gloom on board after this lifted slightly when the noon run was noted. We'd ripped off 275 miles in 22 hours (the ship's clocks went forward two hours at 1300hrs yesterday). Clearly, we would have topped 300 again in an uninterrupted 24-hour run.

We carried on with the No. 5 and staysail until 1800hrs when the wind eased enough for the storm kite. It was still snowing hard, the barometer steady at 1005. We had ice building up on the lifelines, up the sides of the mast and over the spreader fittings — plus snow all over the deck. The crew was going to have to tread carefully. By now we'd got our confidence back and had *Ceramco* averaging 12 knots and bursting to 20 knots — closing quickly on the Kerguelen Islands.

One or two of the crew are starting to show signs of tension. Don isn't sleeping and admits to being wound up like a clock spring. Vonny mutters about crazy bastards and makes token gestures of disagreement when Staggy calls for more sail.

We don't know where Conny is but his silence could mean we have got past him. *Challenger* is 100 miles behind while *Outward Bound* is 600 miles astern. At this incredible rate we'll be at the half-way mark in another three days or so.

Day 12: Wednesday, November 11. Noon position 51.05S 69.00E
     Day's run 288 miles. Course 140 degrees.
     Wind NW 20 to 25 knots. Barometer 1008.

Another traumatic day tempered somewhat by a run of 288 miles. We trucked on through the night, and the snow showers, under storm kite with little or no fuss. At these speeds we must have been doing nasty things to the rest of the fleet. Spirits were high and manifested themselves in an intense snow fight after one squall deposited enough on deck to provide the armament.

Just before the 0800hrs watch change the brace jumped out of the parrot beak. We retrieved the spinnaker, set another and repacked the first. Then, at 1000hrs, Staggy lost her in a confused sea. *Ceramco* broached and rolled on to her starboard side. The brace was thrown, the spinnaker ground aboard on its sheet and rehoisted. Four hours later it was 'all hands' again when Staggy lost control for a second time. It was starting to honk, gusting 40 knots and *Ceramco* was roaring down the waves. She started to broach and Chappy, waiting to take over, yelled 'Throw the brace'. Staggy thought he could still hold her and retorted, 'Shut up Chappy — I've got control.' But he hadn't, and down she went. We lay flopping on our starboard side, the kite full of water. The Doc was hanging from the weather lifelines, vertically down across the deck. Newt was standing on the leeward coaming, up to his waist in water. Staggy, still hanging on to the wheel, was standing on Newt's head. The brace was thrown but jammed in the parrot beak. The spinnaker downhaul broke but this didn't help. Water was pouring into the cockpit and almost up to the hatch level. We lay their wallowing until Simon managed to drop down and throw the spinnaker sheet and halyard. *Ceramco* shook herself upright and we carried on gingerly under the poled out No. 5 with three reefs in the main. I had to do some firm talking at this stage, pointing out that to do well on this leg we first had to finish it, and in good shape. It would be worse than ridiculous if we pulled the rig out and had to retire or damaged so much gear and wrecked so many sails we were no longer competitive.

The desire to go for broke was understandable. We'd learned that *Flyer* was 30 miles north and 15 miles east of us. At our lower latitude, the distance to run to Cape Reinga, on the north-western tip of New Zealand's North Island, was the same — 3,400 miles. We were neck and neck. But there were limits to how fast we could go and for how long — limits imposed by screaming winds and rough, confused seas. At the rate we were going, we had to do some serious damage. So far we've been lucky. Three sets of spinnaker braces have been lost, we've cracked a pole end fitting and some snatch blocks, and wiped off the whip aerials. There are spares on board but the supply isn't inexhaustible and we might not always be so lucky.

I've discussed our whip aerial situation with Gordon Holmes at Southern Communications in Auckland. The whip that was only damaged has been taped up and is back in position. But I don't know how long it will last. Gordon tells me the backstay will be no good as a replacement. If our last whip aerial does break we'll have to rig a 27ft length of wire (the same length as the whip) to the top of the mast on the main topping lift, connect it to the radio through the deck insulator. This apparently will work fine as an emergency set-up. Handy to know in circumstances like these.

Euromarche is the closest boat to *Flyer* and ourselves, 100 miles astern. *Kriter* is 230 miles back and *Xargo* more than 300 miles behind. The main bunch is now between 800 and 900 miles astern and there are 1200 miles between us and tail-end-charlie *Ilgagomma*. The smaller yachts have been doing well, averaging 8 knots. But that compares with *Ceramco*'s 11 knots. We've logged 1876 miles in the last seven days — averaging 268 miles a day. At this pace it won't be long before we start arcing up into the familiar waters of the Tasman Sea. Two priorities now are to sort out the brace problem — the leathering on the wire jams in the parrot beak — and decide on the rig which gives us best speed without control problems in really heavy going. *Ceramco* is a dream to sail at high speeds in winds up to 35 or 40 knots. But at 40 knots plus and rough seas, she's skitterish and just like a big dinghy.

111

Here comes the snow.

We're not the only ones with problems though. *Flyer* has blown out a lot of spinnakers and suffering from 'down time'. Her big kites can't be put back together in a hurry. Judging by Conny's voice on the radio, he's under a lot of strain. Pushing a maxi the size and displacement of *Flyer* through these conditions must be a demanding experience. OC and Lui are flat out repairing the sails we've damaged in the last few days, quite a task while also standing their watches and trying to grab some sleep. But so far we haven't blown out one sail, something we can thank Lidgards for. The wardrobe was build extra strong and this is paying off in minimum down time.

Day 13: Thursday, November 12. Noon position 50.18S 76.07E
Day's run 273 miles. Course 145 degrees.
Wind NNW 10 to 15 knots. Barometer 1014.

After settling down with storm kite and three reefs in the main, we rushed on through last night in winds of up to 50 knots. The weather started to moderate around 2100hrs though and now we're enjoying a moderate north-north-westerly. The sun has been out and the crew has been grateful for the respite, taking the opportunity to get some dry air through the interior.

We had a look in the forepeak, closed off by a thickly padded canvas door, the other night and found it to be full of thick fog. That part of the boat isn't insulated and is extra cold when the temperatures dip towards zero. Further aft, protected by insulation, we're quite comfortable, if a bit damp from all the condensation and from the wet sails lying in bags up the aisles. The crew have been using the aft heater to dry their clothes — and most of them are now walking about in socks and gloves with holes in them. Some of the garments burn quite nicely when they are dumped on top of the heater as the boat is chucked around in a sea.

The generator is playing up again. It was running when we did our last major broach and, although we shut if off quickly, I think it's sucked up some sludge from the tank. We've checked the lines and changed the filters again but it still won't go. Newt and I have spent the whole day in the forepeak rigging an old water cannister as a diesel header tank. We can get fuel into this through the lift pumps on the main tanks and so operate a gravity feed system, by-passing the pump on the generator. It's a bit Heath Robinsonish, but it works and we can still make fresh water.

We've shaken out the reefs in the main and have the 2.2oz kite on, pushing on as the barometer starts to plummet again.

Day 14: Friday, November 13. Noon position 50.44S 83.27E
      Day's run 280 miles. Course 150 degrees.
      Wind NNW 30 to 35 knots. Barometer 999.

The beat goes on — 280 miles in 23 hours (we put our clocks forward an hour yesterday). The wind was from the north blowing 15 to 25 knots until just before midnight when it freshened and swung NNW, gusting 35 knots. We switched to the blast reacher with one then two reefs in the main, and *Ceramco* poured on the pace, proving that she does not need to be over-pressed. We've given up totalling

The Flyer *boys were pushing hard, main boom dragging in the water.*

113

the miles logged. The days have now melded into a blaze of speed. We had the Kerguelens as a mental staging point but roared past to the south of them two days ago without a second thought. A pity really as the pilot book paints an interesting word picture of that remote group.

We've levelled off at around 50 South. There's no point going any lower as the weather maps show a series of intense low pressure systems whistling through below us. We don't want to get on the wrong side of those or we'll find ourselves battling 30 to 35-knot headwinds instead of reaching with fresh tailwinds. We intend continuing along at this latitude until we reach 120E longitude. At that point we'll start to arc up into the Tasman.

The damage check today revealed small cracks in the main boom at the internal entry point. They'll need to be watched closely. All but the bottom batten in the mainsail were broken and the slugs had broken off the mainsail headboard car. A two-watch blitz was organised to affect repairs as quickly as possible. We dropped the main just before the change of watch at 1300hrs, replaced the battens and attended to the batten pockets while we were at it. The headboard car was slightly bent so we sewed slug slides onto the top of the sail itself. For good measure we replaced some of the reefing lines. It was cold work, particularly as most of it had to be done with gloves off, but less than 90 minutes later the sail was rehoisted almost as good as new.

On the crew front, everyone is bearing up well. Don is the only one showing signs of strain. He's still wound up and not sleeping. The Doc has given him some Soneryl which should help him to relax and get some rest.

Molly is proving an excellent heavy airs downwind helmsman. At present he's on antibiotics for an infected gum flap over a partially erupted wisdom tooth. This ailment has been the source of some derision among the crew. Molly claimed some success with the females in Cape Town and speculation is rife as to the cause of his problem.

Flyer's position tonight puts her six miles to the east of us and 15 miles to the north. It's a match race, but somewhat different to an America's Cup contest.

Day 15: Saturday November 14. Noon position 51.26S 90.47E
    Day's run 283 miles. Course 155 degrees.
    Wind NW 25 knots. Barometer 988.

The barometer tumbled through the night, from 996 to 988, and the breeze did likewise, dropping to 15 knots for the 0400 to 0700hrs watch period. It has been back up to 25 knots, swinging a bit, but tonight is settled in the NW at 15 knots. We've put sail on accordingly, graduating from the blast reacher and No. 5 to the two-ply 1.5oz spinnaker and then the 2.2oz kite.

The run, in what we now consider only moderate airs, confirms my opinion that *Ceramco* would make a superb Transpac (Los Angeles to Honolulu) boat. She slides along with consummate ease in the conditions for which that race is noted.

We had only one bad moment last night — when it was discovered that the gooseneck pin which holds the main boom to the mast had worked its way out and disappeared. The whole damned thing was about to drop. It would have been lovely if it had done so in the middle of a gybe. We had a spare on board and, with a lot of manhandling, manoeuvred the boom back into position, inserted the new pin and locked it in place.

I've been having trouble getting good weather maps and am spending a lot of time tuning to different stations in South America and Australia trying to produce something I can work with. We're probably close to 4000 miles from Pretoria by now and that's a long way for weather map transmission by anyone's standards. For some reason we're not getting Australia very clearly. These maps are absolutely essential. I need all the information I can get to make decisions on where the lows will pass through and where *Ceramco* should be to take best advantage of them.

The damage through the fleet is mounting. *33 Export* has broken her mast and is heading for the Kerguelen Islands where she hopes to make repairs and then continue to Australia or New Zealand to step a new rig. *Challenger* has broken her main boom and *Alaska Eagle*, some 600 miles astern of us, has reported a crewman with a broken leg.

We're highly conscious of the dangers in these latitudes, pushing hard in rough weather so far from land. The crew wear harnesses at all times on deck except when the weather is particularly quiet. A harness can be a nuisance, but it can also save your life. At the speeds we're travelling, we'd have little or no chance of finding someone who went over the side, even if they survived the shock of immersion in waters only a couple of degrees above freezing.

We are now almost two different families. The watches see little of each other except for a 'hello, goodbye' when they changed over or during a 'all hands' situation. Vonny and I are the exceptions, floating between the two watches. I've been spelling people to allow them to have a good sleep, alternating between the two watches. Vonny is doing a great job cooking under difficult circumstances. He rarely appears on deck now except to poke his head through the hatch, mutter about the weather and complain that his galley telltales reckon we've got too much sail on. Some of the crew reckon 'The Iron Man from Muriwai' — Vonny is a longtime surf lifesaving devotee and Muriwai one of Auckland's best-known surf beaches — is going rusty.

Day 16: Sunday, November 15. Noon position 51.03S 97.48E
    Day's run 260 miles. Course 145 degrees.
    Wind NW 20 knots. Barometer 998.

Another gale — chilling fog and blowing like hell. It came in from the NNW just on midnight and gusted 35 knots for most of the morning. Since then it has moderated to 12 to 20 knots from the NW.

Life has become a routine of cold watches on deck and damp periods below. We're just about half-way having logged 3594 miles from Cape Town with roughly that distance to go to New Zealand's northern capes.

In 15 days at sea we've averaged 240 miles a day and now we can almost see New Zealand on the charts. Not really, for there are few charts that cover this somewhat foresaken part of the world. The one we're using only has a bit of the south-western coast of Australia high up on its right-hand side. The heavy gales have given us consistently high runs, but they have placed heavy demands on boat and crew. The fact that the wind is down doesn't mean rest either. Fluctuations in strength mean lots of sail changes.

Day 17: Monday, November 16. Noon position 51.13S 105.13E
    Day's run 280 miles. Course 130 degrees.
    Wind NW 15 to 20 knots. Barometer 999.

The 280-mile run was more proof of *Ceramco*'s liking for the moderate to fresh.

115

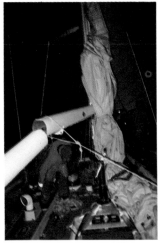

Too hard?   *Goose winged* Flyer *while the main boom is repaired.*

With the wind between 15 and 30 knots, the old girl has been dancing through the Southern Ocean. We're still dicing with *Flyer* which is at the same longitude but 30 miles north of us. *Challenger* is 360 miles behind having hit two whales in 24 hours, damaged her mainsail track and had a fire in the generator. *Outward Bound* is 700 miles astern. Most of the fleet is now so far back we can't pick them up on the chat show.

It was our turn to break the main boom, or at least discover that it was broken. Just before 0900hrs, in 15 to 20 knots of breeze, I suddenly noticed the boom was badly cracked just behind the vang fitting. It was hinging on the plate. We were smoking along at the time under full main, staysail and big spinnaker. Gingerly, we ground the boom inboard with the mainsheet and released the vang. This closed the gap while we decided on a course of action. The log read: 'Bloody big break in the main boom. Broken right through except for the top plate. Super Jaws comes to the rescue.'

We vanged the aft sections of the boom down to the rail so that it couldn't move anywhere and then set about repairing it with T-section aluminium splints which Jaws had brought along just for the occasion. The splints were heavy-gauge 1in x 1½in jobs already drilled for pop-rivetting. The repair job went without a hitch and by late afternoon we were fully operational again.

We removed the hydraulic vang so that no more stress went on the area of the crack and rivetted a couple of temporary vang points further aft on the boom, with a strop between them, to complete the job. With a block from the strop down to the rail and on to a winch, the new system worked well. The boom was less flexible and more controllable and there was no load on the crack point at all. We'd be a bit slower gybing, but that was a small price to pay.

Earlier in the day, Don had had his own boom problem. Chappy's watch was in the process of lowering the kite pole when they dropped it on Don's head, just about knocking him out. He's been a touch stroppy lately and the Doc intimated that the prognosis was an elephant-size tranquilliser or a kite pole on the noggin. The pole treatment was cheaper and just as effective. Don was put to bed with a human-size sleeping pill and we left him to sleep for the remainder of the day.

Day 18: Tuesday, November 17. Noon position 50.11S 111.46E
Day's run 248 miles. Course 115 degrees.
Wind W 18 to 25 knots. Barometer 1005.

If we had picked a time for the boom to break and have to repair it, we couldn't have done better. The breeze shifted into the west soon afterwards and gusted 25

Cape Maria van Diemen — a sight for sore eyes.

Across the top of the Capes and still hard on.

knots. *Ceramco* was trucking again under blast reacher, staysail and reefed main. I've already ordered a new main boom through John Street. It will be ready when we arrive in Auckland. This time it will be one which won't break. I've got my own views on what's needed for hard racing at these latitudes and this time I'm going to insist on what I think should be done, no matter what the Farr office says. The world's yacht designers are going to have to accept that the Whitbread race, especially now that it is highly competitive, imposes extra demands on gear. They'll need to adopt a whole new design and engineering approach to what is required for the Southern Ocean when boats are pushed really hard.

By now we are 'underneath' Australia, and it's a comforting feeling. Coming up is the decision on whether to remain south for a while longer or to loop north and tuck in close to Tasmania. A central Tasman entry appeals to me most, even if it means staying down here for three or four more days. If we get too close to the Tasmania coast, we could end up with light airs. Tactics are now critical. We have to keep *Ceramco* moving at optimum speed, but we also have to keep an eye on the opposition — *Flyer.* We know she's very close. The strength of her radio transmissions confirm that. If we want to beat her to Auckland we'll need to outperform or outsmart her up through the Tasman.

Day 19: Wednesday, November 18. Noon position 49.42S 118.45E
Day's run 279 miles. Course 110 degrees.
Wind NW 30 knots. Barometer 1005.

To celebrate the Doc's 47th birthday, I quote another extract from his log, describing a fairly typical watch in these circumstances.

'2340hrs — woken to prepare to be on deck by midnight. Roll up sleeping bags, clamber into polar gear, balaclava, gloves and wet-weather gear and emerge sleepily up top. It is very cold, blowing 30 to 40 knots, and dark. We are shipping a lot of waves over the weather rail where three of us sit on a sail bag whilst the other two take the twin wheels. The other watch had been pushing hard and, half an hour earlier, had put up the small kite. There is one reef in the main and we are doing a steady 12 to 14 knots. It is very dark and the horizon is only vaguely visible. Those on the weather rail peer ahead for icebergs, the temperature is around 2 degrees C. but the chill factor is considerable. The exposed parts of our faces are lashed with spray.

'We find we can't hold the course of 135 degrees and, after discussion, Chappy asks for the blast reacher. It's dragged from down below, wet and heavy in its bag, taken forward to be positioned for hoist in the headfoil feeder, hoisted and set. We then ease the kite pole forward and release the tack of the spinnaker. Three of us drag the kite in behind the mainsail, the fourth controls the halyard. We follow the kite down the hatch to bag it so that it is ready to use again. It is now 0130hrs. One of us stays below to make coffee, the other two return to the weather rail. We are now holding course and two-sail reaching at high speed through this cold, black, whistling night. There is a lot of weather helm and some discussion about another reef in the mainsail. Chappy thinks we need the power however and that a small genoa staysail, set inside the blast reacher, would help balance the yacht. This sail is dragged up through the forward hatch, clipped on and hoisted. It was a good call by Chappy. The yacht is much more controllable and so more efficient. Now 0230 hours. We sit cold and silent. I can feel my feet going numb. The chill extends up my legs. The mittens I wear protect hand and fingers from the wind, but they are soaking wet and very cold. The breeze increases. Another reef in the main. At 0330hrs we become more animated as the end of our watch approaches. We look forward to shaking off our wet clothes, wiping the face with a damp towel and climbing into a sleeping bag for four hours of relative peace.'

The Doc was provided with a special birthday present — apart from a suitable inscribed piece of broken mainsail batten — when the Aurora Australis lit up the night sky in a spellbinding display. This natural phenomenom of the polar regions is difficult to describe to anyone who has not witnessed its sheer grandeur. The sky lights up with green, shimmering curtains of fire from horizon to horizon. If you've seen the aurora you have been privy to nature at its grandest and most stunning.

We hadn't seen ice yet, except on the mast and lifelines, but *Berge Viking,* down at 55S, had four icebergs in sight when she came in on last night's chat show. *Save Venice,* 200 miles to the east of *Berge Viking* at 55.45S, has been in ice for three days. *Outward Bound* is down there too and, by all accounts, having a tough time of it.

Day 20: Thursday, November 19. Noon position 49.46S 125.53E
Day's run 285 miles. Course 090 degrees.
Wind W 35 knots. Barometer 991.

If we keep this up, we'll make nonsense of the record for the Cape Town -Auckland run. *Xargo,* 900 miles astern, has reported 60-knot westerlies. We can expect some of that tomorrow. Molly spent last night and much of today in his bunk, suffering from a mild dose of frostbite in his feet. He's got the circulation back but the feet are still white numb. The Doc assures him there is nothing to worry about however. Our trusty medic isn't so bright himself. He has a couple of chilblains, one on each cheek, that aren't anything to joke about. Keeping warm is always a problem, especially on deck. *Licor 43* has lost her mast and is heading for Hobart — that's nearly as far for her as it is for us to Auckland. At least she has stern winds to help her along. *Gauloises* has asked us to arrange for a sparmaker to meet her in Auckland. She's having major spinnaker and headsail halyard problems. *Disque D'Or* has made a similar request, but for someone to make her a new main boom. It seems we have been in the Southern Ocean for ever, but in another couple of days we'll be in the Tasman. It's funny, but we used to regard the Hobart - Auckland race (1570 miles) as long. Now it seems like a short sprint to finish the trip.

Day 21: Friday, November 20. Noon position 49.58S 133.04E
Day's run 280 miles (22 hours). Course 075 degrees.
Wind WSW 25 knots. Barometer 1001.

Incredible sailing. We'd have topped 300 miles in a full 24-hour run (the clocks went forward two hours yesterday). It got up to 40 knots from the west last night and rough seas. But at 0100hrs today it swung WSW and moderated to 20 to 30 knots and we've been blasting, alternating between the 2.2oz and 1.5oz spinnakers. We're still holding down around 50S but we must start to curve north-east soon.

Know your enemy — Conny at the helm on Flyer.

Flyer *approaching the Orakei finish.*

An incredible homecoming.

Orakei Wharf becomes a grandstand.

Good to see Pippa.

Day 24: Monday, November 23. Noon position 49.03S 151.39E
        Day's run 235 miles. Course 045 degrees.
        Wind N 20 to 40 knots. Barometer 1020.

Not a very hospitable welcome by the Tasman. For the last 48 hours it has been blowing between 30 and 50 knots. We've been down to three and even four reefs in the main, the No. 5 or No. 6 jibs and now the storm jib, pounding hard in a chaotic sea which very much resembles a tidal race. The log reads: 'Blowing like shit,' and then 'You're not wrong there Clive.' The wind has been NNW and now north just when we want to make some northing into the Tasman proper. Just now we are some 420 miles to the south of Hobart. The weather maps show we are in between a high which is moving south-east out of the Great Australian Bight (absolutely abnormal) and a low coming through astern. The high extends right the way across the Tasman to the south-east of New Zealand. The result is a northerly airstream right down the Tasman and it looks like it's here for a while. Just what we don't need. Our runs for the last three days — 252 miles, 260 miles and 235 miles — reflect the rugged weather and slower sailing as we've been headed by the wind. It looks like a beat to windward coming up but for the present we're sailing slightly free on the port tack, just hanging on to *Flyer* but losing about 10 miles a day to her. Whether we can continue to do so remains to be seen. She's a more powerful windward machine than *Ceramco,* but she owes us 22.6 hours on handicap in Auckland. Whatever happens, if we can't beat her we must finish within that time behind her. It has been a hectic three weeks at high speed in rough weather and from his voice on the radio, Conny is feeling the pressure of having *Ceramco* so close without a let-up.

There have been the odd moments aboard — irritable as well as funny. The other night Simon asked Vonny to help retrieve the spinnaker. Vonny told him to 'get stuffed', that if Staggy's watch wanted to sail the yacht like 'crazy bastards' they could get themselves out of trouble. Vonny argued that every time we broached, *Flyer* gained another mile on us. This led to a rather heated exchange and I later had to have a chat with Vonny about lending a bit more support. He's doing his own job in the galley in difficult circumstances however. We're eating three good, hot meals every day and, because food lasts much longer in these climes, those meals still include fresh meat, vegetables and fruit.

Molly's frostbite now seems to be confined mainly to his right foot which looks disturbingly cold and pale. He has big feet and couldn't buy sea boots big enough to allow him to wear two pairs of socks with comfort. Newt has infected skin lesions on his wrists — someone reckoned he'd tried to slash them but was typically inadequate — while Lui, OC and the Doc have mild burns from the heater flue. The silly so-and-sos grabbed hold of the flue and then wondered what the burning smell was.

One particularly entrancing display of the Southern Lights prompted the following exchange on deck. The Doc: 'What do you think Chappy?' Chappy: 'Well Doc, I've seen some great sights in my time — Colin Meads knocking the lights out of an opposition forward within five minutes of the start of a test in Auckland; Andy Haden doing the same at Eden Park in front of the main stand; and I also remember a great beer can fight among cricket fans at Eden Park. I reckon this is comparable.'

Day 26: Wednesday, November 25. Noon position 46.09S 161.00E
    Day's run 229 miles. Course 025 degrees.
    Wind NW 25 to 30 knots. Barometer 1016.

The pounding continued all through yesterday and we were reduced to one of the lowest runs of the leg — 196 miles in 23 hours — as the breeze flicked NNE and then back to the north. To our relief, late last night it backed into the NW again and we were able to get a wriggle on. *Flyer* is 57 miles closer to Cape Reinga than us but she has dropped down on her previous course. Last night we could just hear *Outward Bound* on the fleet sched. She was still well south at around 55 degrees latitude, being held down there by the weather pattern. Digby reported ice everywhere, to the point where his crew couldn't work the gear. They've seen lots of icebergs too.

Outward Bound's position puts her more than 1500 miles astern along with *Berge Viking, Swedish Entry* and *Save Venice. Ilgagomma* is now 2000 miles behind.

Day 28: Friday, November 27. Noon position 42.45S 168.39E
    Day's run 159 miles. Course 065 degrees.
    Wind NE 15 to 20 knots. Barometer 1016.

The north-westerly lasted until noon yesterday and gave us another 229-mile run. Since then it has been all bad. The wind has been north and then north-east, smack on the nose, and today's run was down to 159 miles, despite the fact we'd worked like demons, changing sails and tacking on the shifts.

Yesterday we had OC up the mainsail leech to replace the broken third batten. It took him an hour and wouldn't have been a pleasant task in the sea that was running. Then Don was hoisted to the masthead to replace a headboard slug. While he was up there an RNZAF Orion aircraft came through on a training run which just happened to take it down our projected course. We were now well over to the eastern side of the Tasman and could almost see the Southern Alps of New Zealand. We talked to the Orion crew on 2182 Khz and she gave us *Flyer's* position, only 63 miles ahead. It was still a race — and going to get closer if we had anything to do with it. Tonight we're working the 100-fathom line out off the coast from Greymouth and Westport. There's a sea breeze forecast and that should give us an ENE slant and enable us to lay course for Cape Reinga. Today was the first time since leaving Cape Town that we've been able to open the hatches and ports and let some air through the boat. If conditions had been kinder, we'd be entering the Hauraki Gulf by now, but here we are still with 700 miles to go. The weather is completely abnormal for this time of the year with high pressure systems developing just south of Australia and spiralling down into the Antarctic. The lows are doing the opposite, crossing the Tasman almost horizontally or bending slightly north as they move eastwards. The danger for both *Ceramco* and *Flyer* is that the boats astern come through with a different breeze and go straight up the Tasman. If they do, all our driving through the Southern Ocean will have been in vain.

Day 29: Saturday, November 28. Noon position 41.18S 170.11E
    Day's run 125 miles. Course 345 degrees.
    Wind NE 18 to 20 knots. Barometer 1016.

We sent Conny an incorrect position last night to see how he would react. He's listening in to the Radio New Zealand broadcasts involving *Ceramco* and has the advantage of knowing where we are without saying anything himself. There's nothing in the rules to prevent this variety of gamesmanship. We are required to furnish an accurate position twice a week to race headquarters in England, which we did faithfully. What we were now attempting was a tactical ploy — trying to suck Conny into thinking we were going out to sea. The distance to Cape Reinga was accurate but we put ourselves further west than we in fact are. If he takes the bait, we'll put ourselves further west again tonight. There's a good head sea running out there. We, meanwhile, will be over to the east going up the western coast of the North Island with a lee from the north-easterly winds. *Flyer* has been covering our every move so far in the long beat up the Tasman. We're not going to catch Conny unless we pull something extra out of the bag.

The two watches have been giving it everything in fluctuating NE winds but there's not much we can do against *Flyer*'s big masthead rig and the extra power she has for this kind of upwind sailing. I don't expect Conny to take the bait, but it's worth a try.

Day 30: Sunday, November 29. Noon position 37.54S 172.01E
       Day's run 216 miles. Course 010 degrees.
       Wind ENE 25 knots. Barometer 1009.

It's working. Conny has gone to sea thinking he's covering *Ceramco*. *Flyer* has been really lumping it, hard on the wind in a 30 to 40-knot north-easterly and punishing seas. We copped it going across the western approaches to Cook Strait and up the Taranaki coast past Cape Egmont. But now we're free-sheeting, with

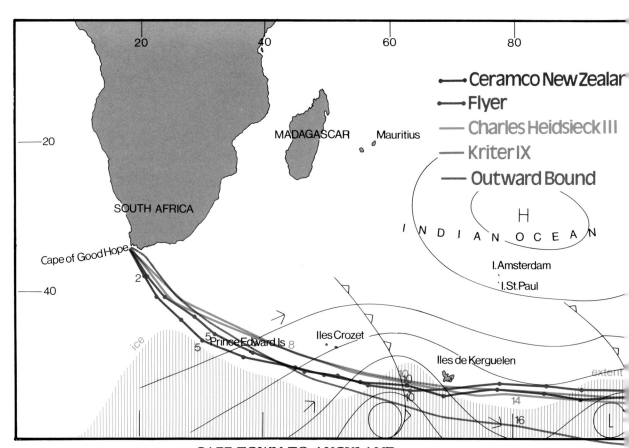

CAPE TOWN TO AUCKLAND

all the wind we want and relatively smooth water, under flattened main and No. 2 genoa. In 12 hours we have picked up 50 miles on *Flyer*, and we're still gaining.

The log last night read: 'The Doc and Bill Rowling lost the election,' referring of course to Labour's demise at the polls, despite Dr Agnew's confident predictions of a Labour victory. The Tasman prevented us from being there to vote.

The humour is running full blast again with Vonny the butt of much of it. He's handling it fine, as well as keeping the food coming. I think he's quite liked spending so much time below. Today, when he stuck his head outside, Newt took him on a familiarisation tour of the deck, pointing out the various features, reckoning he hadn't seen him up top since we left Cape Town. The ability to be on the wrong end of humour, some of it ultra-sharp, as well as dish it out was one of the reasons we'd had so little crew upset despite the cramped and trying circumstances of our recent existence. Most of the guys could accept fun poked at them as well. They had to. Sessions developed where one member of the crew became the target for the day, and he would really catch it. But he knew it was all in good spirit and that his turn at the other end would come. This proved a valuable safety valve.

Some more variations on Vonny's 'Pig, pig' theme. Yesterday he borrowed one of the Doc's opera tapes and piped it through the ship before breakfast. Newt threatened to 'punch his lights out' so he switched hastily to Neil Diamond, which found much more favour.

Don, due to get married during our stopover in Auckland, turned to the Doc and said: 'You must know a bit about sex, being a medical man.' The Doc replied:

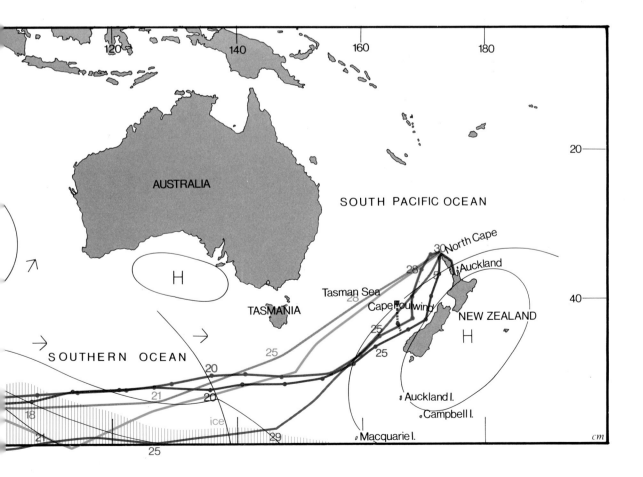

'Yes, what do you need to know?' Newt interjected: 'Don't listen to the Doc. I've got the whole thing down to three minutes — no kissing, no foreplay, just action.' A somewhat taken aback, Don asked why. Newt replied: 'To spend more time in the boozer, you fool.'

Day 31: Monday, November 30. Noon position 34.59S 172.40E
      Day's run 180 miles. Course 035 degrees.
      Wind NNE 25 knots. Barometer 1010.

The best laid schemes of mice and men. It had looked like *Flyer* and *Ceramco* would reach the capes together and then it would have been all on down the Northland coast into Auckland. But the wind backed into the NNE and freed *Flyer* at the vital moment, at the same time heading *Ceramco* and kicking up a nasty sea for us to punch into as we covered the final 60 miles to the capes. *Flyer* slipped around Cape Reinga at 0600hrs today, making slow time across the 20 miles to North Cape in light airs against strong tide. We finally had Reinga abeam at 1830hrs with a good breeze and a big tide running with us. We scampered 'across the top' to North Cape and turned hard right for the final 180-mile stretch down the Northland coast to the Waitemata Harbour.

Day 32: Tuesday, December 1. Noon position Hauraki Gulf

Flyer crossed the Orakei finish line at 0635hrs local time. It was a cool, dank morning but she was given a fine reception. We listened to the live coverage of the moment on radio as we chased down the coast under 2.2oz spinnaker in 15 to 25 knots from the north-east. We knew we were in for a big welcome. We'd picked up the first spectator craft and spotter aircraft soon after dawn, out off Tutukaka some 70 miles from the finish. The entourage grew all the way in. At Tiritiri Matangi Island, guardian to the inner Hauraki Gulf, the escort fleet was joined by RNZN patrol boats and countless small craft. They struggled to keep up as *Ceramco* surged for home, doing 16 knots. Peter Montgomery was doing his thing on Radio New Zealand and it seemed the whole of Auckland was waiting to see us come in.

Off Rangitoto Light, three miles from the finish line, we were confronted by a wall of boats and it looked as though there was no way through the armada. We were running by the lee and not looking forward to the gybe because of the broken main boom and the fact we had only one good kite pole (the end fitting had gone on the other).

It was a wild scene — launches charging out of control down the wakes of others, runabouts fizzing in close to yell to the *Ceramco* crew, many of whom were now close to tears, overcome with emotion. We finally threw caution to the wind, dip-pole gybed half a mile from the finish and swooped across the line at 1450hrs.

We'd missed the record, thanks to an out-of-character Tasman. We'd failed in our long-stated aim to be first into Auckland. But nobody seemed to care. We'd pushed *Flyer* for 7000-odd miles and finished only 8 hours 20 minutes behind. It looked certain we'd win the leg on handicap and the most appreciative and informed yachting public in the world had come out in their tens of thousands to let us know that we hadn't let them down.

9. LAMB CHOP HOSPITALITY

The harbour-bay was clear as glass,
So smoothly it was strewn!
And on the bay the moonlight lay,
And the shadow of the moon.
— *Samuel Taylor Coleridge,* The Rime of the Ancient Mariner

*F*LYER BROKE THE record for the Cape Town-Auckland leg of 30 days 9 hours 3 minutes 30 seconds set by *Heath's Condor* in the 1977-78 race, by just 4 hours 36 minutes. *Ceramco* missed that mark by just 3 hours 47 minutes. Ten days earlier, coming into the Tasman, we'd both looked set to slash *Condor's* time by at least two days. With half the journey done, *Flyer* was running 2 days 10 hours 4 minutes 36 seconds ahead of the record for the race.

The first few days in Auckland were a whirl of invitations and interviews, but our minds were still at sea — logging the progress of the main threats on handicap, *Charles Heidsieck* and *Kriter*. While we had been beating up the Tasman, these two had brought up a new reaching breeze and closed the gap dramatically. We owed *Charles Heidsieck* 43½ hours for the leg and *Kriter* 58 hours. Had we done enough? It would be an injustice if they carried their reaching breeze all the way in and pipped us.

Finally, we could relax and celebrate. The early summer weather settled down to warm days and light winds and the French threat evaporated. *Ceramco* won the leg by 11 hours 46 minutes from *Charles Heidsieck, Flyer* took third place while *Kriter* was fourth.

Ceramco had made dramatic progress up the elapsed time chart. After the two legs, we were sixth — climbing from 16th in Cape Town. But we were still down in 19th place on corrected time. A pity, because off Tasmania I fancied that we were carving big chunks out of everyone but *Flyer.* As it was, the handicap prize looked destined to be fought out by *Kriter, Charles Heidsieck* and *Flyer. Kriter* still led, but *Charles Heidsieck* had closed the gap to 7 hours 37 minutes, with *Flyer* a further 17 hours 17 minutes behind.

The leg had been expensive. *33 Export, Licor 43* and *European University Belgium* had lost their masts. On *33 Export,* co-skipper Thomas Phillipe was lucky. He was in the pulpit, handing the spinnaker, when a backstay block broke and the mast fell forward on top of him. He was pinned under the tangle of spar, rigging and sails but the pulpit had taken the brunt of the punishment and Thomas emerged shaken but unscathed. It was the end of the race for him and his crew though. There were no repair facilities at the Kerguelens and all they could do was wait for a supply ship to take *33 Export* back to Cape Town or to France.

Licor 43, skippered by Joaquin, persisted — reaching Hobart under jury rig, stepping a new mast and continuing on to Auckland — still racing and determined to complete the course.

European University Belgium also headed for Hobart but was caught in a storm which swept her jury rig over the side. Completely crippled, the yacht was swept past to the south of Tasmania. Skipper Jean Blondiau sent out a distress call and the Australians launched an air-sea search. Finally, *European University* was located and taken in tow by a fishing boat to the fishing village of Bicheno on the eastern coast of Tasmania. There, Blondiau affected repairs and finally resumed the journey to Auckland.

They had their problems on *Ilgagomma* too. Skipper Roberto Vianello was suffering from severely frostbitten feet, but he refused to divert to Tasmania for treatment. Despite the considerable pain, he kept *Ilgagomma* on course for Auckland and brought her across the finish line before allowing himself to be whipped away to hospital to have his feet attended to.

Outward Bound was given a marvellous reception, 8½ days behind *Ceramco* and early on a somewhat unpleasant morning. Rangitoto Channel was a mass of riding lights as she ghosted through the last few miles, under spinnaker in light airs. The waterfront roads were packed with cars as was Marsden Wharf as Digby brought *Outward Bound* in to complete a circumnavigation he and his crew had begun eight months earlier when *Outward Bound* set sail on her delivery trip to England.

They'd had their problems deep in the Southern Ocean, going down as far as 55 degrees south and encountering huge seas and bitterly cold temperatures. Their worst moment was when the boat iced up in a sudden vicious cold snap. The deck gear was frozen solid and they'd have been helpless if they'd had to reduce sail in a hurry and had to work flat out with boiling water and chipping implements to keep the boat functional until the temperatures rose again. Still, they'd finished leading small boat again, 11th on corrected time, and were in seventh place overall for the two legs. The *Outward Bound* camp had to be happy with that situation.

We weren't all that enamoured with the situation at Marsden Wharf though. HART demonstrators were making a nuisance of themselves and forcing the authorities to impose stricter security measures than otherwise would have been necessary. Things came to a head the night *Xargo III* arrived. A group estimated at between 50 and 60 demonstrators lined the wharf to hurl verbal abuse at Peter Kuttel and his crew. It was rather sickening. Here was a group of yachtsmen who'd plugged through some of the worst seas in the world to reach Auckland, concerned only with racing their yacht. They deserved better from a country renowned for its hospitality. Fortunately, the overseas contingent in the fleet didn't miss the facts that the protesters were few and mostly teenagers anyway. They viewed it all with good-natured tolerance and did not let the occasional protest upset their stay.

I had no doubt that we should take some comfort from the fact that New Zealand enjoyed a democracy which permitted people to air their views, but I didn't take kindly to being called various insulting names by people barely old enough to know their own minds, or to having those people attempt to force their views and the way they would have the world on others. They would have achieved much more, and earned greater respect, if they'd taken the time to discuss the issue with a group of people who had just come from South Africa. Instead, they wrongly tried to create the impression that anyone who associated with or competed against a group of individuals on a South African boat wasn't welcome in New Zealand, and wound up appearing rather pathetic.

Ceramco meanwhile was out of the water at the McMullen and Wing yard for a variety of maintenance jobs, not the least of which was the repair of the propeller strut and hull cracks. The mast and rigging were x-rayed in a check for potential problems. The new main boom had arrived and was dubbed 'The Southern Ocean Special'. The Farr office wasn't happy with it. They thought it was too heavy and that we should have a duplicate of the original boom made. They argued that a heavier boom would affect the performance of the boat. It did. It improved our control of sail shape, as we quickly established during work-up sessions on the Waitemata, and it gave us a lot more confidence.

There was no rest in Auckland, as we were innundated with requests for our time. So Pippa and I snuck away to the Waitangi Hotel in the Bay of Islands. It rained most of the time but we thoroughly enjoyed our long walks, albeit in wet-weather gear, and the opportunity to discuss things other than boats and the Whitbread race. I needed the break. The crowds down at the dock never let up and the stream of people who wanted to have a look around the boat or just say hello was endless. I knew it was time to take off when I found myself getting a bit short-tempered with a little old lady who had been collecting all the newspaper cuttings on the race and wanted a couple of autograph books signed. I was late for an appointment, it was raining and here she was hammering on the window of the car. I told her I was terribly sorry but was in a rush and would sign the books when I returned. I immediately felt foolish. It was a strain for us all, but the interest of thousands of people just like that elderly woman had made the *Ceramco* project possible. What difference would another couple of minutes have made. If she reads this, I hope she will accept my apologies and understand the situation.

I wasn't exactly ready to return to the hurly-burly of Auckland, but Christmas was approaching fast and there was still much to be done. *Ceramco* went back into the water to have her rig stepped and tuned. The crew had gone their own ways for the first couple of weeks, but now everyone was back on deck to prepare *Ceramco* for Cape Horn, in between the constant round of receptions, parties and barbecues. The facilities at Marsden Wharf were almost non-existent and a poor reflection on Auckland. There would have to be major improvements in this regard if the city was to remain a Whitbread port of call. But nobody could complain about the hospitality. It was boundless. The boats all had individual hosts who took care of things like laundry and transport. The major clubs, the Royal NZ Yacht Squadron, Devonport Yacht Club, the Royal Akarana Yacht Club and Bucklands Beach Yacht Club, put out the welcome mats and major race supporters, such as Ceramco and Healing Industries, pitched in with barbecues which left nobody in doubt as to the quality of New Zealand meat, wine or hosts.

Christmas was almost an anti-climax. By then even the hardiest souls were beginning to shudder at the thought of another glass of something alcoholic. But the crews battled valiantly to stay with the pace. They welcomed the many offers to spend Christmas Day with various families, for those were opportunities to spend a few normal hours a long way from home, with time to reflect that very soon the race would be on again. In less than 24 hours they'd be back to the cramped quarters of a yacht and, if the weather was rough, probably regretting that they'd had such a fine time in lamb chop country.

CAPE TOWN-AUCKLAND

	Elapsed Times			Corrected Times	
	Boat	**Hrs/Min/Sec**		**Boat**	**Hrs/Min/Sec**
1.	Flyer	724.27.30	1.	Ceramco NZ	702.00.14
2.	Ceramco NZ	732.51.14	2.	Charles Heidsieck	713.46.15
3.	Euromarche	772.45.47	3.	Flyer	716.31.44
4.	Charles Heidsieck	788.45.55	4.	Kriter IX	718.05.09
5.	Kriter IX	807.58.22	5.	Euromarche	724.06.19
6.	FCF Challenger	810.15.32	6.	Disque D'Or	729.19.40
7.	Disque D'Or	859.18.56	7.	Xargo III	735.26.51
8.	United Friendly	860.03.14	8.	Berge Viking	748.21.58
9.	Gauloises	862.11.20	9.	Skopbank of Finland	751.19.15
10.	Alaska Eagle	876.24.22	10.	Morbihan	758.28.33
11.	Xargo III	882.54.19	11.	Outward Bound	759.32.02
12.	Berge Viking	905.02.30	12.	Gauloises	769.14.41
13.	Outward Bound	935.28.51	13.	Alaska Eagle	774.22.30
14.	Skopbank of Finland	944.23.21	14.	Rollygo	776.59.40
15.	Swedish Entry	953.23.21	15.	Traite de Rome	795.19.18
16.	Rollygo	956.17.41	16.	Bubblegum	799.31.07
17.	Morbihan	958.39.53	17.	Croky	804.50.20
18.	Save Venice	973.02.53	18.	FCF Challenger	810.15.32
19.	Traite de Rome	1024.46.14	19.	Swedish Entry	837.12.32
20.	Croky	1038.25.20	20.	United Friendly	844.30.05
21.	Bubblegum	1040.15.44	21.	Walross	886.24.08
22.	Walross	1102.49.35	22.	Save Venice	899.11.52
23.	Ilgagomma	1121.29.19	23.	Ilgagomma	945.32.30
24.	Licor 43	1261.31.53	24.	Licor 43	1167.20.40

Did not start: La Barca Laboratorio, Vivanapoli, Scandinavian.
Did not finish: European University Belgium, 33 Export.

	Legs 1 & 2 Elapsed Time			Legs 1 & 2 Corrected Time	
	Boat	**Hrs/Min/Sec**		**Boat**	**Hrs/Min/Sec**
1.	Flyer	1599.24.07	1.	Kriter IX	1558.43.48
2.	Charles Heidsieck	1715.23.15	2.	Charles Heidsieck	1566.21.35
3.	Kriter IX	1737.21.07	3.	Flyer	1583.38.41
4.	FCF Challenger	1755.04.07	4.	Disque D'Or	1638.25.21
5.	Euromarche	1783.26.17	5.	Berge Viking	1647.47.40
6.	Ceramco NZ	1868.19.19	6.	Xargo III	1664.47.43
7.	Alaska Eagle	1881.43.25	7.	Outward Bound	1665.53.57
8.	Disque D'Or	1896.43.56	8.	Alaska Eagle	1678.41.19
9.	Gauloises	1909.47.50	9.	Euromarche	1684.16.04
10.	United Friendly	1938.49.21	10.	Morbihan	1686.26.30
11.	Berge Viking	1959.08.16	11.	Skopland of Finland	1700.13.30
12.	Xargo III	1959.27.40	12.	Bubblegum	1718.13.12
13.	Swedish Entry	2010.21.51	13.	Gauloises	1725.06.00
14.	Outward Bound	2015.32.18	14.	Traite de Rome	1730.39.39
15.	Save Venice	2078.17.09	15.	Croky	1740.44.15
16.	Skopbank of Finland	2083.53.15	16.	Rollygo	1754.31.27
17.	Morbighan	2084.15.15	17.	FCF Challenger	1755.04.07
18.	Rollygo	2110.49.37	18.	Swedish Entry	1779.29.33
19.	Traite de Tome	2187.31.29	19.	Ceramco NZ	1807.01.03
20.	Bubblegum	2196.37.20	20.	Walross	1833.17.58
21.	Croky	2204.54.39	21.	United Friendly	1905.37.10
22.	Walross	2264.23.40	22.	Save Venice	1931.31.54
23.	Ilgagomma	2328.03.29	23.	Ilgagomma	1978.25.08
24.	Licor 43	2364.52.35	24.	Licor 43	2177.42.35

Charge... Ceramco leads the fleet out of Auckland.

10. I CAN SEE YOU

The ship drove fast, loud roar'd the blast,
And southward aye we fled.
— *Samuel Taylor Coleridge,* The Rime of the Ancient Mariner

BOXING DAY DAWNED bright and clear. The Waitemata Harbour lived up to its name (Waitemata is Maori for 'sparkling waters') in the early morning sunshine as Pippa and I drove across the harbour bridge for what would no doubt be the last time for quite a while.

Marsden Wharf was jammed with thousands of well-wishers, every race yacht getting its due share of attention. The race crews will never forget the hospitality they'd experienced in Aotearoa ('The Land of the Long White Cloud'). Outside the entrance to the dock we could see the steady procession of hundreds of pleasure craft making their way down harbour for the start. No sad farewells this time. Pippa gave me a couple of farewell hugs and looked happy enough as she jumped aboard Radio New Zealand's fast launch from which she'd watch the departure. This made a big difference to the way I felt about taking off again.

A few more cakes from the ladies of the Devonport Yacht Club to stow, the last-minute goodbyes, then we slipped our dock lines and eased out into the harbour, happy to be going racing again but sad too that the stopover in our home port had come to an end.

Keep that spinnaker full.

The spectator fleet closes in.

The start was scheduled for 11.00 am from a line stretching eastwards across the harbour entrance from North Head. With an hour to go, we were in the loosely patrolled start area, mainsail up and motoring around to check the breeze and the line. We knew that the eyes of New Zealand — the start was telecast live throughout the country — would be on *Ceramco* and *Outward Bound*. We wanted to make this a good one. The forecast was for a moderate southerly

133

turning to a north-easterly sea breeze during the afternoon. It was going to be an interesting day.

The vantage points around one of the world's most beautiful natural harbours were packed with people and cars. On the water it was 'standing room only' as the spectator fleet swelled to thousands. They came in all shapes and sizes, from surfboats and canoes to large motor yachts and harbour ferries crammed with cheering schoolchildren. We learned later that there were an estimated 300,000 people on or around the harbour to see the fleet leave.

Ten minutes to go. We'd decided to have the .85oz spinnaker set up and ready, but to manoeuvre close to the line under main and genoa only. The wind was south-west, so the first stage of the journey would be a spinnaker reach out of the harbour to round the sail training vessel *Spirit of Adventure* anchored five miles away off Auckland's East Coast Bays. The departure would be in full view of the shore and within range of the television cameras for at least an hour after the gun.

The five-minute gun. Last-minute thoughts break through the tactical concentration. We're soon to be headed for the world's most famous maritime landmark, Cape Horn and, for tax reasons, *Ceramco* would never return.

The gun, with *Ceramco* positioned perfectly at the pin end of the line. There was a roar of appreciation from the huge crowd of spectators as our kite went up immediately and we jumped out of the blocks doing 9 knots and pulling away from the opposition to gain clear air. We got a lot of pleasure out of this — just as we did from seeing *Flyer* caught in the back of the fleet.

The send-off was almost indescribable. The spectator fleet was solid all the way down the course to the *Spirit of Adventure,* which was surrounded by hundreds more craft which had anchored early to claim a grandstand view of the turn. Above us, five photographic helicopters and two light planes made conversation impossible.

Our gybe was perfect and we weaved *Ceramco* through the anchor warps and spectator fleet on to a course to the north-east to Cape Colville, 34 miles away at the tip of the Coromandel Peninsula. Behind us, we could see *Flyer* starting to pick up speed after her poor start, and soon she was chasing up astern. The race was on again. There would be no quarter asked, none given.

The south-westerly died and the fleet ran into a huge, windless hole. We rushed down the spinnaker to replace it with the light Mylar genoa and spent the rest of the afternoon tacking into a light north-easterly.

Flyer, Challenger, Charles Heidsieck and *Euromarche* have worked their way up to windward of us now, just on nightfall, we head into Colville Channel, between the Coromandel Peninsula and Great Barrier Island. The breeze has freshened and we're on our own again, the last of the spectator boats having just shouted their farewells and headed for one of the many friendly anchorages hereabouts.

Day 2: Sunday, December 27. Noon position 37.32S 177.47E
       Day's run 160 miles. Course 092 degrees.
       Wind NE 18 knots. Barometer 1022.

A very dark night, but it didn't deter us from using a bit of local knowledge to gain ground. Deciding it would be best to stay on the coast as we started into the Bay of Plenty, we sailed through the 'Hole in the Wall', a narrow, rocky passage inside the Mercury Islands. *Euromarche* followed our every move. You need large-scale, local charts for this sort of exercise and, of course, we had them.

We spent the whole of the day beating across the Bay of Plenty, past the active offshore volcano White Island, and on to East Cape. It's now 1900hrs and *Ceramco* is passing between East Cape and East Island with *Euromarche* still dogging our tracks. *Flyer* is 10 miles to the south-east. *Challenger* is a speck on the horizon to the north-east. The wind has gone south-east and we've reached what could prove a vital decision. We'll take *Ceramco* on down the eastern coast of the North Island and try for the north-easterly winds forecast for coastal waters in the next 12 hours. This means sailing away from the mark — Cape Horn — but my reading of the situation is that we should get south as quickly as possible, just as we did leaving Cape Town.

Day 3: Monday, December 28. Noon position 39.25S 178.26E
Day's run 148 miles. Course 170 degrees.
Wind SE 15 to 18 knots. Barometer 1027.

Flyer is out of sight, probably having tacked over on to starboard, the tack closest to the course to Cape Horn. We're still on port, 80 miles out to the east of Cape Turnagain. *Euromarche* is still with us despite the light and variable conditions all last night. The breeze finally filled in from the SE, puffing 20 knots, at 0700hrs. It remained in that quarter all afternoon, making me wonder whether my tactics are correct, then, at 1900hrs swung suddenly to the east. With the high country of the Urewera National Park showing purple through the late evening haze astern, we bid 'adieu' to New Zealand and came up on course for Cape Horn, our speed increasing all the time.

Day 4: Tuesday, December 29. Noon position 42.33S 179.45E
Day's run 197 miles. Course 120 degrees.
Wind ENE 15 to 20 knots. Barometer 1028.

With the wind ENE for most of the day, we freed up under full sail, right on track, and went for the doctor. We knew the main opposition was stuck in the high presssure system to the north-east of us and wanted to press home our advantage. *Euromarche* is still hanging on and has looked dangerous out on our port beam. At 1600hrs the wind backed into the NE and we were all smiles. We freed up even more, put a slab in the main and hoisted the genoa staysail. If the wind kept backing it would soon be kite time.

We are saying nothing on the radio. We want to break completely from *Flyer* so the longer Conny's kept in the dark the better. At noon we crossed the 180 degrees meridan, putting us officially back into Monday. But we have decided to keep this Tuesday — it has been a good one. We'll have another one tomorrow.

Day 5: Tuesday, December 29 (2nd time). Noon position 45.30S 175.43W
Day's run 258 miles. Course 105 degrees.
Wind N 20 knots. Barometer 1024.

The crew's eagerness showed in the log entries which, all through the night, read: 'Close to kite time.' Finally, at 0500hrs came the one we wanted: 'No. 3 genoa and staysail down, 2.2oz kite up.' We later added a small staysail and *Ceramco* was up and running. If we'd written the script, it couldn't have been more suitable. At 2100hrs tonight the wind backed further, into the NNW and started puffing 25 knots. *Ceramco* is averaging 11 knots, shooting down long, easy seas. This is what we all came for.

What a way to go.

Every man and his dog.

As a matter of normal maintenance, we tightened the steering cables, taking up the initial stretch. They were new, fitted in Auckland. We also tightened the stern gland as water was flowing in freely. Again, this was new from Auckland and would need occasional attention until it settled down.

Kite on again.

Going south again.

Day 6: Wednesday, December 30. Noon position 48.10S 170.04W
      Day's run 289 miles. Course 100 degrees.
      Wind NNW 25 to 35 knots. Barometer 1008.

The breeze slowly increased until by noon today we had gusts of 35 knots up our tail, the sea building. *Ceramco* is flying with three slabs in the main and the two-ply 2.2oz spinnaker. We worked out from the chat show that *Flyer* is 50 miles astern. The 'head south early' tactics paid off. Now we must concentrate on giving Conny something to chase. *Ceramco* will take some catching in this stuff. New Year's Eve in New Zealand tonight. The log recorded the fact with the 2400hrs entry: 'Happy New Year! May your cesspit never clog.'

Day 7: Thursday, December 31. Noon position 50.25S 163.19W
      Day's run 315 miles. Course 090 degrees.
      Wind N 25 knots. Barometer 1000.

What a way to start 1982 — on New Zealand time that is. The noon run of 315

Snow clouds forming.

was just one mile short of our best on the Cape Town-Auckland run and we achieved it with a lot less fuss. It's been overcast and drizzling all day but this hasn't dampened our spirits. We heard from Peter Montgomery tonight that *Flyer* did 327 miles while we were reaching 315. A magnificent effort by Conny's team. Clearly they are giving the chase everything they've got. It's going to be a great race for first around Cape Horn.

Day 8: Friday, January 1. Noon position 52.37S 157.31W
    Day's run 258 miles. Course 080 degrees.
    Wind NW 20 to 25 knots. Barometer 989.

Vonny has been nursing a king-size hangover all day. We celebrated New Year by sending a couple of rocket flares into pitch-black sky at 2400hrs and then it was rum toddies all round. Simon and the chef finished off the bottle — but Simon was crafty, emptying his mug into Vonny's when he wasn't watching, then pushing the pace. Our intrepid galley man emerged this morning with eyes like the proverbial pee holes in snow.

Chatted with *Charles Heidsieck* and learnt they'd been becalmed all day. That news didn't dampen our spirits either. It's taken longer for the crew to settle down again on this leg, after leaving behind homes, families and friends. Jaws seems to have been the hardest hit in this respect. But now everyone is in full cry, driving yacht and skipper to the limits. They'll need to. *Flyer* has closed to within 25 miles with the breeze dropping and going SW last night. It's been WSW and NW today, blowing 40 knots. Tonight it seems settled in the south-west at a steady 40 knots. *Ceramco* is blasting under the 2.2oz kite with one slab in the main.

We're keeping a watch for ice as we're already as far south as we went on the last leg. There's snow in the air but for the moment the temperatures are too warm for it to reach sea level. We're curving south-east on the great circle course for an imaginary mark of 57S 120W and going like a rocket.

Day 9: Saturday, January 2. Noon position 54.31S 149.31W
    Day's run 316 miles. Course 080 degrees.
    Wind W 20 knots. Barometer 984.

Snow showers during the night as we blasted to 316 miles noon to noon, equalling *Ceramco*'s best. It's now very cold and the spray hitting exposed parts of the body when on deck is quite painful. I got a shock when on the wheel early today, surfing down big seas. A whale surfaced 20 feet away on our starboard bow. Fortunately, he moved aside and we creamed past him.

Flyer has closed to within 20 miles of us. They must be driving their boat particularly hard and well because *Ceramco* isn't exactly hanging around. Conny sounds like he's perking up judging by our chats on the radio. I guess he's just been suffering the 'apres Auckland blues' along with the rest of us. We're still managing to hold off the doughty Dutchman, but I don't know for how much longer. *Euromarche* has dropped back to 90 miles astern.

Day 10: Sunday, January 3. Noon position 55.23S 142.33W
    Day's run (23 hours) 250 miles. Course 065 degrees.
    Wind SW 15 to 20 knots. Barometer 970.

The barometer dropped alarmingly down to 970, the lowest reading I've ever seen. The standard reading for this part of the world at this time of the year is between 985 and 990. We don't expect 1000, but at the same time 970 is a touch on the low side. If it keeps going down the way it has in the last 21 hours (985 to 970) it will go right off the bottom of the scale.

We gybed four times last night and our course is now taking us only slightly south-east and we level out after the plunge south. In one of the heavy snow showers during the night, the wind changed direction dramatically, from the north to the south-west, and increased in strength. The gusts lasted only seconds but we were caught out and broached, out of control.

Chappy's watch let the brace run but it jammed. *Ceramco* lay on her side, water up over the side decks. It was the middle of the night and snowing hard. After a minute that seemed like hours, Molly braved the icy seas and groped around to let the sheet run (the winch was under water). Chappy bore the boat away while we pulled the kite down, struggling with material that was covered in slushy ice and snow. That did it. We would have to devise a safer method of getting rid of the spinnaker in a hurry. The answer was so simple we kicked ourselves for not thinking of it during the last leg. The system involves clipping the windward (lazy) spinnaker sheet into the tripping mechanism of the brace clip in the pole end fitting. The sheet is then lead aft to the spare weather coffee grinder drum. If we're caught by a squall from now on, the helmsman can judge the situation and, if necessary, call for the lazy sheet to be ground in hard, tripping the brace and releasing the kite to flutter harmlessly behind the mainsail, ready to be dropped. The system prevents us gybing so we'll use it only with the heavier kites which, we've found, are just as easy to drop and then rehoist after a gybe in extreme conditions. This solution would have saved us a great deal of nervous energy on the Cape Town-Auckland leg and will be a boon from here on. We know we can push the boat harder, confident of getting rid of the kite in a hurry if we strike trouble.

The bad news today was that *Gauloises* has broken her mast (the seventh spar failure so far) and been forced to cut the rig adrift once it had gone into the sea. They have turned north and are heading for Tahiti, 2500 miles away, with only spinnaker poles to use for a jury rig. Tahiti is about the only place they can go for shelter and assistance because of the prevailing wind and weather in these parts. It reminds us of the need for caution. I know some of my crew think I'm too conservative at times, but broaching and careering around half out of control is not the way to sail a yacht in these waters and win. It involves a good deal of seamanship to ensure that gear breakages are kept to a minimum. Breakages mean down time and down time we can't afford.

Out of the blue last night we got a call from English yachtsman David Cowper, sailing solo, non-stop the wrong way around the world (east to west against the prevailing winds) in his 40ft sloop *Ocean Bound*. He's already been around solo the normal way (west to east) and this is his encore. The position he gave us puts him several hundred miles due north at 40 South. He'd taken 50 days to reach Cape Horn from England, 7 days to round the Horn and now 40 days to reach his present position. We hope to reach Cape Horn in 10 days. David is headed for Stewart Island, off the southern tip of New Zealand, and then on south off Tasmania to South Africa before the long haul back up the Atlantic to England. He sounded happy to have someone to talk to. On *Ceramco*, with 12 crew, we often feel cut off from the rest of the world. Doing it all alone must be a different experience again.

It must have been our night for callers. We heard also from another solo sailor going around the world non-stop, this time west to east, the same as ourselves. He

Chappy dressed for chill.

was a Dutchman on a yacht called *Ilsastroma*. We last talked to him soon after leaving Cape Town, and here we were overtaking him after a stop of nearly a month in Auckland. You have to admire the courage and determination of these single-handers. We wished them both 'bon voyage' as we carved on towards Cape Horn, 2440 miles away to the east, doing speeds of which the solo men can only dream.

Day 11: Monday, January 4. Noon position 55.47S 134.40W
Day's run 270 miles. Course 060 degrees.
Wind WSW 25 knots. Barometer 988.

'*Flyer* sighted approximately 3 or 4 miles on starboard bow.' The 0415 log entry said it all. Here we were, 10 days and 2380 miles after the start, half-way across the loneliest stretch of water in the world, and *Flyer* is almost within shouting distance. She'd caught up in the light and variable stuff two nights ago and we didn't like that. But it was still quite a thrill to sight her through the early morning murk, sleet and snow. We tried calling Conny on VHF Channel 16 but got no reply. It wasn't until 0730hrs that we raised some interest and Conny confirmed that he had us in view. It's quite remarkable that we have come together like this after such a distance. We've obviously been following almost identical courses since that original split off the east coast of New Zealand. Now, can we hang on to him or better still beat him to the Horn.

The boys are looking forward to seeing their first iceberg but I don't fancy their chances. We're keeping quite a bit further north than previous Whitbread race fleets and may not encounter any at all. We're now getting weather maps from Argentina as well as Canberra, and the low pressure systems are all going through at about 60S. We seem to be ideally placed, at around 55S, to take advantage of them.

Flyer's appearance has really gingered up my team. They've been full of mischief today, their normal selves for the first time since leaving Auckland. Chappy was tied up in a spinnaker bag in the cockpit and left to mumble and complain to himself for a couple of hours. The torches had been dubbed 'Molly's babies' since it's his job to look after them. His somewhat paternal attitude to the Evereadies was jolted last night when Newt ripped the head off one of them.

Staggy has been taking a lot of stick — mostly about the number of females he was seen to escort in Auckland. One of them, it transpired, was an Air New Zealand hostess and a friend of Peter Montgomery. So, through Peter, we arranged a radio sched with Air NZ flight TE 5, on its way from Honolulu to Auckland, for tonight. We talked to the Boeing 747 for 15 minutes and Staggy was permitted a quick chat with his lady friend. The crew was unable to pipe us through to the passenger sections because the transmission quality unfortunately wasn't good enough.

The radio has been a continual source of light relief on this leg. We've a twice-weekly schedule with Radio Wellington, plus our appointments with Alan Sefton and Peter Montgomery. Lately, after the evening fleet chat shows, we've been talking to Noel Lloyd in Whangarei, on the Northland coast of New Zealand. A lot of yachts away on their Christmas cruises have been listening in and we've been kept up with all the gossip.

Pippa told us tonight of *United Friendly* having to put back to Gisborne with a damaged mast track. They'd attempted a repair at sea but the electric drill and pop-rivet gun had been accidentally dropped over the side by the man who was sent aloft. We've lost our own share of gear the same way — including two spinnaker braces and a number of 'Molly's babies'.

The stainless steel vang, which holds the hydraulic boom vang to the mast, factured today. We've lashed the vang in place temporarily but will have to figure out a way to repair it properly as soon as the weather improves and there is less solid water and spray coming over the deck.

Starting to blast again.

Day 12: Tuesday, January 5. Noon position 55.44S 125.32W
       Day's run 306 miles. Course 055 degrees.
       Wind SW 25 to 30 knots. Barometer 992.

Flyer still in sight on the starboard bow. We called Conny at 0900 hours and told him: 'I can see you.' He was astounded and sent someone up top to check before conceding that we were right on his tail. *Flyer* had set a kite and sagged away to the south, while held up, reaching with genoa and staysail, after our brief encounter yesterday.

The *Flyer* crew reported they had seen icebergs. Newt reckoned he did too. He shouted excitedly that he spotted a berg, just visible on the horizon to port. Later he had to admit: 'It put a kite on and f....d off.' It had been *Flyer*.

We've had two close calls with whales, coming within 30 feet of the boat, on successive days. Let's hope they don't get any more inquisitive.

I can't help but admire the crew. Staggy and Chappy have been pushing their watches to the limit and getting total response — as the day's runs reflect. I spend most of my time on navigation, weather, radio and tactics although I make a point of putting in a reasonable amount of time on deck and spell either of the watch leaders if they want a break or are feeling below par.

Jaws is always doing something, on deck or down below, checking mast fittings, resplicing wire braces or making up new reefing lines. He's absolutely first rate with experience and maturity way beyond his years. Don has had his share of problems but always bounces back. Two mornings ago, the loo was blocked. A rubber stopper from the underside of the seat had dropped down the bowl and jammed the outlet valve. He had to dismantle the entire system to find out what was wrong, clear and reassemble it — not an enviable job in rough seas. The first time it was used, by OC, it blocked again. Don had to repeat the whole process, flashing OC a few dagger looks while he did so.

It was sleeting this afternoon, not very pleasant for the watch on deck. I'm now into two sleeping bags and wearing all my clothes to bed. That means two pairs of socks (from the New Zealand Wool Board), a full set of woollen longjohns on top of normal underwear, T-shirt, a one-piece Helly Hensen polar suit, a pair of heavy corduroy trousers and a thick polo neck woollen jumper.

We've got condensation for the first time on this leg but it shouldn't get much worse. We haven't looked like running the heaters at all.

The generator began to cough and spit this evening so Newt stripped all the fuel lines, cleaned them, then sealed all the connections with special Epiglass 'goo'. It ran as sweet as a nut after that. So it should. It's brand new, installed in Auckland after the agents declared the previous one to be 'worn out'. This after only 300 hours of running and absolutely faithful maintenance.

Day 13: Wednesday, January 6. Noon position 55.25S 116.53W
       Day's run (23 hours) 301 miles. Course 055 degrees.
       Wind SW 20 to 30 knots. Barometer 997.

The day was greeted by the log entry: 'Dawn coming again — nice girl.' The 0600 entry 'And he's still there' confirmed that *Flyer* was in view.

Our 24-hour run from 1900hrs on the 5th to 2000hrs on the 6th (the clocks were put forward an hour) of 322 miles was a record for *Ceramco*. Conny must be equally delighted with *Flyer*'s progress but I bet he's wondering how the hell he's going to get rid of us. In the last week we've both logged 2016 miles averaging 288 miles a day, or 12 knots. There's no sign of it slowing down either. The breeze tonight is 20 to 25 knots from the SW and *Ceramco* is boiling under full main and the full-size 2.2oz kite.

We have definitely proved on this leg that the way to do well is to go the right way — which puts me in the hot seat. If I don't pay enough attention to the weather and call the right shots, I negate all the good work the crew is doing on deck. Conscious of this, I'm already pouring over large and clear weather maps from Buenos Aires in the Argentine, trying to build up in my mind the general pattern of the weather in and around the Cape Horn area and on up the east coast of South America, past the Falkland Islands to Mar del Plata. We still have a long way to go before it becomes pertinent, but we'll be fully conversant with the situation when we get there. So far on this leg we've called all the right shots. The Maori taniwha, presented to us by the Carbine Club in Auckland and fixed to the bulkhead below, must be working. (Note: a taniwha is a legendary sea god.)

I spoke to Mark Williams (a syndicate owner in *Ceramco*) on his yacht *Trauma* last night. *Trauma* was anchored at Great Barrier Island and Mark went into great detail about the size and number of scallops they were eating. Made us quite envious. His son Erle, of course, is a watch captain on *Flyer* and must have been a major influence in *Flyer*'s recovery.

Some of my crew have been discussing what they will do when this race is over — which, after all that has happened in the last 12 months or so, isn't that far away. Most are setting their sights fairly low, I feel. I'm certainly not. Although the responsibility, for the yacht, the crew, the shareholders, the New Zealand public, bears quite heavily at times, and I find myself saying that this will be my last Whitbread, I wouldn't have it any other way and I'll probably be talking of a bigger and better yacht for 1985-86 by the time we reach Portsmouth.

The boys have been granted their wish. Late last night we spotted our first iceberg. It was a big one, but was about five miles away to starboard — too far to detour for a closer look. No doubt the ice watch will be taken a little more seriously from here on.

Day 14: Thursday January 7. Noon position 56.49S 108.39W
Day's run 287 miles. Course 075 degrees.
Wind WSW 10 to 15 knots. Barometer 989.

Flyer is not in sight — strange thing to report at this stage of a race, 1400 miles from Cape Horn. But this isn't exactly a normal situation. Conny has held up to the north while we've continued on a more southerly track. Who's right?

Vonny took the morning watch to spell Don today. Don had the day in his bunk except when he prepared the lunch. He didn't have to show his face on deck until after dinner at 2000hrs. Vonny enjoys his break from the galley on such occasions and the spelled crewman has a chance to catch up on much needed sleep. I spelled Chappy last night on the midnight to 0400 watch. This meant he had all night in his bunk. I'll be doing the same for Staggy in the near future. On these occasions it has proved best for the crew trying to get a good sleep to take a pill prescribed by the doctor. These help you to get a good 12-hour kip. I use sleeping pills only occasionally but sometimes they are necessary, especially when one is all tensed up. The watch leaders have first option on a spell, but the offer is not always accepted. Staggy and Chappy have to spend all of their watches on deck whereas the men on their teams are given time off below to read or sleep, as long as they remain fully kitted up and ready for action at short notice.

Day 15: Friday, January 8. Noon position 56.29S 103.02W
      Day's run (23 hours) 185 miles. Course 055 degrees.
      Wind SSW 25 knots. Barometer 980.

A poor run by current standards, and a worrying time. It was light and variable for most of last night and this morning. *Flyer* is still in VHF range but we haven't seen her for more than 36 hours.

We dropped the main twice today, to replace a broken batten and then to replace the headboard carriage which was jamming on the mast track. The 'spelling' continues, the log noting: 'Jaws in galley for lunch — should be interesting. Vonny on deck, IN No. 4 sail bag.' Newt reckoned he looked like a leprachaun with elephantitus.

These sessions on deck have been good for Vonny. He had become extra quiet and was spending most of his time just cooking and reading. He'd run out of cigarettes and the boys put his mood down to withdrawal symptoms — from tobacco and liquor. When Simon produced a carton of Gauloises, it was like a miracle cure. Vonny has become cheery and extrovert again. Simon has him rationed to four cigarettes a day and gives him extra 'good guy' smokes if he turns on a special meal or a favourite pudding.

Jaws worked wonders in the cooking department, producing a delicious apple and apricot crumble, covered in hot custard, milk or cream, after a tasty pumpkin, onion and tomato soup.

Day 16: Saturday, January 9. Noon position 56.12S 95.21W
      Day's run (23 hours) 259 miles. Course 985 degrees.
      Wind SSW 20 knots. Barometer 985.

The Jaws' crumble must have thrown Vonny into a turmoil. This morning he was found preparing breakfast at 0500hrs instead of his usual 0700hrs. He's done

The Stagg watch, all back in the 'Members' stand'.

144

Fast sailing and big mileages, with Flyer *in sight.*

us proud though, toasted cheese sandwiches. He's been jealously guarding an enormous amount of New Zealand Cheese Board supplies ever since we left Auckland. The crew reckon we've got a list to starboard because the cheese is all stacked up on that side of the boat, on top of the icebox. Newt might have broken through though. He warned Vonny that any cheese left over when we get to Mar del Plata will be personally jammed up a certain part of the cook's anatomy. Suddenly, we're having cheese with everything.

The breeze is up again and we're reeling off the miles. Still no sign of Conny, although we're letting him know we're close by with regular chats on the VHF.

Day 17: Sunday, January 10. Noon position 56.05S 87.43W
Day's run 254 miles. Course 055 degrees.
Wind WNW 15 to 20 knots. Barometer 985.

A day of snow showers and reasonable progress under full main, 1.5oz or 2.2oz spinnakers. Conny came on the radio at first light to report he'd sent a man up the mast to look out for us. We were six miles astern. *Flyer* must have dropped down from her course during the night. In my view their holding further north has cost them quite a lot.

Day 18: Monday, January 11. Noon position 56.12S 79.04W
Day's run 291 miles. Course 070 degrees.
Wind NW 30 knots. Barometer 990.

Down to No. 5 jib and three reefs in the main tonight with the wind gusting 40 knots. The weather maps, very clear from Buenos Aires, indicate we could have this breeze for a while. The British Antarctic survey ship *Bransfield* passed us the news that New Zealand had beaten China 2-1 to reach the World Cup finals. Good on the Adshead boys.

145

Day 19: Tuesday, January 12. Noon position 56.05S 71.15W
        Day's run 275 miles. Course 067 degrees.
        Wind W 15 knots. Barometer 988.

Good progress in view of the rugged conditions. It suddenly stopped raining this morning as the wind dropped, and the sky cleared as the breeze backed into the west. We were 200 miles from Cape Horn and heading towards the Hermit group of islands under the big kite and full main. It had been a lousy night on the weather rail, solid waves breaking over the watch crew who had to be there for trim reasons. Coming down they were cold and wet — with damp sleeping bags to look forward to. Ah, the joys of long distance ocean racing.

We've been buzzed by military aircraft from both Chile and Argentina during the day. They were most friendly on VHF radio, welcoming us to their part of the world.

At 1710 hours 'Land ho', the log recording 'sighted just forward of the port beam — the 600ft high Islas Ildefonso.' Then, at 2000hrs: 'Flyer again in view — two to three miles ahead of port beam.'

Here we are, approaching the fabled Cape Horn after more than 4500 miles of racing through the Southern Ocean, and the opposition is only a couple of miles ahead. Unbelievable. We'd seen Conny in mid-afternoon. He was running fairly square while we were reaching up.

We could already feel the big swells for which Drake's Passage is either famous or infamous. I don't know whether we are relieved or disappointed that we should be making this landfall in such relatively calm conditions.

Cabo de Hornos — the very name has struck fear into the hearts of mariners for centuries. I quickly dug out my copy of Robin Knox-Johnston's *Last but Not Least* (published by A.H. & A.W. Reed) — his account of the 1977-78 Whitbread race on *Condor of Bermuda* — to reread what I consider one of the best descriptions of the waters we are in and the reasons they are legend.

I quote: 'Through most of its passage around the world the Southern Ocean is unrestricted in breadth and depth, averaging between 12,000 and 15,000 miles in width and 2000 fathoms (two miles) deep. Abruptly, as this huge river of water approaches South America, it is faced with a gap of only 600 miles between Cape Horn at the southernmost tip of South America and the northern end of Graham Land, a peninsula protruding out from Antarctica. This gap is called Drake's Passage as Sir Francis Drake was the first man to sail through it during his circumnavigation in 1582-85. He chose this way to avoid the Spanish outposts in Magellan's Strait, the route used by Magellan, which lies among the islands north of Cape Horn. The southernmost land mass happens to coincide with the northernmost point of Antarctica, and in addition the water shallows to less than 100 fathoms at the same place. The water mass in the Southern Ocean suddenly finds that it has to squeeze through a gap one twentieth of its size, and so, of course, it accelerates. Whenever a wave from deep water runs into a shallower patch it becomes compressed and its crests move closer to each other with the result that the waves get steeper. This is exactly what happens at Cape Horn, and one could expect unpleasant seas in that area on these grounds alone. But the Horn lies at 56 degrees south, so that stronger winds up to storm or hurricane force can also prevail, and this makes matters even worse.

'The Horn has such a tradition in our maritime history because, until the opening of the Panama Canal in 1913, it provided the last route by which sailing ships could compete economically with steamers. A steamship's engines just could

146

not be governed sufficiently to cope with the change in loads caused by the propeller being in the water one minute and turning in air the next, as the ship pitched in rough seas. The result was that until 1913, a sailing ship could, by rounding the Horn, travel as quickly as a steamer between Australia and Europe or the east and west coasts of the United States. Nearly everyone who went to sea in ocean-going sailing ships up to the First World War could expect to round the Horn and some sailing ships were still doing it in the 1930s. Even though sailing ships would sail as soon as they were loaded, they would prefer to round the cape during the summer months from November to March, thus avoiding the appalling winter storms from April to October. Beating around the Horn from east to west against the prevailing winds in winter time was a hazardous venture, and in 1905, of some 130 vessels that sailed from Europe to the American west coast, only 52 reached their destination without any trouble. Four were definitely wrecked and a further 49 were still unaccounted for, four months after they should have arrived, although most of them struggled in eventually.

'The passage from west to east is easier as you are usually running before the winds. Even so, following seas can build up to extreme heights, and yachts have been rolled end over end by larger than normal waves. Of course, it can also, on rare occasions, be calm.'

Day 20: Wednesday, January 13. Noon position 55.00S 65.18W
Day's run 230 miles. Course 030 degrees.
Wind NNW 15 to 20 knots. Barometer 988.

We rounded Cape Horn at 0550hrs GMT — 0150hrs ship's time — 30 minutes or two to three miles astern of *Flyer*. Her masthead light was just visible ahead despite the heavy rain. The winds were light and the seas slight. We hadn't had a Satnav pix for several hours so I'd asked the helmsman to harden up a little. Suddenly the Horn itself loomed ahead of us, directly ahead of our bow and barely discernible as a dark, misty shape. We bore away quickly to skirt the off-lying rocks then harden up again. We were only two miles off as we passed the Cabos and carried on towards the east. The winds were NE, blowing cold off the snow-covered mountain ranges of Tierra del Fuego away to windward.

We stayed on port tack for a while longer then dived inshore on starboard. Conny, for some reason, kept heading east, probably anticipating an easterly wind shift. It didn't come. The breeze instead went NNW and we cracked sheets to head towards the Straits de le Maire, across the mouth of the Beagle Channel.

At 0600hrs, someone asked in the log: 'Where is *Flyer*?' The answer, at 0800hrs, was 'Behind us!' The wind shift had put us in the box seat. We were inshore and 10 miles to windward of the Dutchman. We took some pleasure from the fact that although Conny was first past the Horn, we were the first actually around it and heading up the coast on the eastern side.

There seemed to be a lot of interest in our situation. A Chilean naval vessel called us on VHF. It had a French film crew on board. They never got their pictures because we were sailing faster than their craft could motor and they never caught up. Next came an Argentinian destroyer, on station to welcome us into Argentine waters. Then an aircraft with a radio reporter on board. I had to do an interview which he translated into Spanish and put out live on Radio Rio Grande in the largest population centre of Tierra del Fuego.

I got through to Radio New Zealand through Wellington Radio and spoke live on Wayne Mowat's 'Tonight' show, describing the Horn, fast disappearing astern,

It's the same scene on Flyer.

and the islands and coasts of Tierra del Fuego to an estimated 1 million listeners. Quite a privilege and one which helped make this particular rounding (my second) one of the highlights of my sailing career.

We made short work of the 105 miles to the Straits de le Maire, the crew toiling like demons to consolidate what could be a vital break on *Flyer* just 1100 miles

Chappy searches for Cape Horn.

from the finish in Mar del Plata. The breeze was up and down, 10 knots one minute then 30 knots the next as savage squalls ripped down from the mountains off to port. We had strong tide under us and this helped speed us to the north-east. The sail changes — from heavy No. 1 genoa to No. 3 and then No. 4, reefs in, reefs out — came thick and fast. The overfalls were heavy off the Bay of Buen Suceso so we gave Cape San Diego, the most south-eastern tip of the South American mainland, a wide berth. Our large-scale charts of the area showed eight-knot currents as well as overfalls at this point. As we zipped through the Straits de le Maire, the Island de los Estados was very clear to starboard, its jagged peaks reaching heights of 2600ft. The last time I was through here, on *Condor* in the 1977-78 race, those peaks were covered in snow. This time there was little or none to be seen. Even the shores of Tierra del Fuego had appeared green and brown, with only the odd patch of white.

Tierra del Fuego — Land of Fire — looks, on the charts, to be the most fascinating part of this remote point of South America. Many of the thousands of islands and channels are still uncharted, but the others ring loudly with history — Peninsula Dumas, Peninsula Hardy, Canal Cockburn, Canal Beagle, etc.

After Cape San Diego, the next land we can expect to see will bear the high-rise buildings and casinos of Mar del Plata.

With all the tension and excitement, plus navigation and tactics, required for the Horn rounding I was suddenly very tired. I took one of the Doc's sleeping pills and climbed into my bunk. At 2000hrs, Staggy woke me to ask: 'Do you want the good news or the bad?' The bad was that *Flyer*, from about 10 miles off our stern quarter to leeward, was now on the horizon to windward. The good news was that we had a bad crack in the mast at deck level, but hadn't lost the rig.

We'd been becalmed under an ominous black cloud formation. *Flyer*, seeing our plight, had sailed around the calm patch and was now six miles in front and slightly to the west.

Jaws had discovered the mast crack. He'd dreamt that there was one while off watch this morning. The dream bothered him and he decided to check the spar. Nothing was immediately amiss, but when he looked under the deck collar, which stops water running down the mast and through its entry hole in the deck, he found a six-inch split right around the front of the extrusion.

Jaws and Don immediately tackled a temporary repair, taping and screwing heavy alloy plates across the crack, then rigging a wire checkstay from the main boom gooseneck to the forestay fitting on the bow, tightening it up with a rigging screw borrowed from an under-deck tiebar system.

The crack had probably been caused by all the heavy spinnaker reaching we'd done, with the heavy loads imposed by the thrust of the spinnaker pole pushing aft. The repair should get us to Mar del Plata alright. But I've radioed New Zealand to have heavy alloy sleeves flown to Mar del Plata to make the job more permanent.

The Doc observed that our Hobbit (Jaws) didn't look too happy under his mushroom (the mast). Simon retorted: 'Neither would you if your mushroom was falling over.' Vonny, sleeping in one of the settee berths tonight, with his head tucked well out of danger behind a bulkhead under the switchboard, still wasn't safe. Newt, thrown off balance when the boat lurched, put a foot right in our cook's face. Vonny let loose with a string of oaths. Newt simply looked at him and replied: 'Vonny, if you sleep on the M 1 (Britain's busiest stretch of motorway) you must expect to be run over by a truck.'

Day 21: Thursday, January 14. Noon position 52.44S 64.39W
    Day's run 139 miles. Course 360 degrees.
    Wind NNW 10 knots. Barometer 995.

The log read: 'Our bloody bogey ocean.' We were back in the Atlantic of course and had been becalmed for much of the night.

No sign of *Flyer* and Conny's not talking on the radio. We've worked out to the west of the rhumbline in an attempt to be first to a westerly change that is forecast. We feel *Flyer* will go straight up the rhumbline to Mar del Plata, or even slightly east towards the Falkland Islands. The last time they would have seen us, at dusk yesterday, we were to the south-east of them, heading north. As soon as it was dark, we extinguished all lights and put a ban on torches while we scurried away to the west. This race isn't lost, or won, yet.

With less than 1000 miles to run, the log noted: 'OC went up the mast to replace a broken batten. Looks normal swinging around up there as if he's collecting coconuts.'

Day 22: Friday, January 15. Noon position 50.22S 63.54W
Day's run 145 miles. Course 005 degrees.
Wind NE 10 to 15 knots. Barometer 995.

A day notable mostly for some of the better log entries of the leg. They started with: 'I get tired of zips. Every time I wake, a zip — sometimes two. To go on deck, two zips — sometimes three. To take a piss, a fight with zips. Why didn't I invent bloody zips.'

With trim extra important now that we were on the wind in light airs, the log declared, in bold print: 'There appear to be spare bunks to windward — space available.' Then an advert which read: 'Windward aft bunk. Nice length. Comfy lee cloth. No sick stains. Good view. Prime real estate, next to skipper. See PJB for rates.'

To finish up, the quote of the day from Newt: 'Molly can't cross his legs for nuts.'

Day 25: Monday, January 18. Noon position 39.47S 57.46W
Day's run 242 miles. Course 025 degrees.
Wind NNW 20 knots. Barometer 1020.

The last three days have been variable with the wind predominantly from the NE — right on the nose. Extremely slow progress after our dash across the Southern Ocean. We seem to be making a thing of slow finishes.

The noon runs for the 16th and 17th were 183 miles and 267 miles respectively. We were hoping that Conny might have dipped out somewhere. We've neither seen nor heard from *Flyer* since the night of January 20. But we have just learnt, from Mar del Plata, that Conny is 30 miles from the finish line. We've still got 70 to go — so he's grabbed a jump of 40 miles, and there's no time or distance left to do anything about it.

Day 26: Tuesday, January 19. In Mar del Plata.

Flyer got the gun at 2021.56hrs last night (local time). By then we'd been headed, the breeze swinging from the NNW to the NE and gusting 30 knots. We were down to the No. 6 jib and hitting hard in a terrible sea kicked up by strong wind against the northward-running Falklands Current. There were a few anxious checks on the mast but the repair was holding up.

It was a difficult finish to find. The line was between two moles at the harbour entrance and we had to do a U-turn to port, once we'd found the end of the main sea wall. To add to the difficulty, the navigation lights were damned difficult to see against the backdrop of the waterfront with all its hotels and restaurants. Also, the harbour wall had been raised (not shown in the latest Admiralty or Argentine charts) and several of the navigation beacons were now inside and below the top of the wall — out of sight from seawards. But finally we made it, ducking into the harbour entrance, beneath the huge statue of Christ, at 03.39hrs — 7hrs 17min 04sec behind *Flyer*. The wind change had cost us probably three hours, but we easily had our time on handicap.

Pippa had found herself a boat to meet us despite the hour. There was Seffo too, plus the Kiwis from *Flyer*'s crew — Erle Williams, Grant Dalton, John Vitali, Joe Allen, Warwick Buckley and George Hendy. What a race. We've been so engrossed in our own private match race with *Flyer*, we've paid little attention to the rest of the fleet. *Euromarche* should be third home then probably *Charles Heidsieck*.

Jaws trims and thinks of lunch.

AUCKLAND TO MAR DEL PLATA

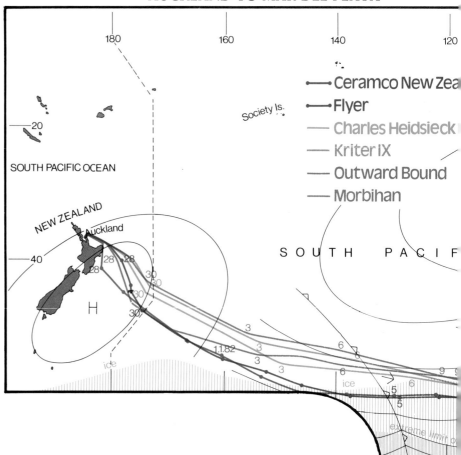

The final 1100 miles to Mar del Plata from Cape Horn, in mostly light headwinds, have cost us dearly. But we should have done enough to win the Roaring Forties Trophy which goes to the boat with the best corrected time from Cape Town to Mar del Plata, and that was one of our priority objectives when we originally sat down to commission a boat for this race — to be the fastest across the bottom of the world.

We'd covered 6000 miles from Auckland in 24 days 08 hours 39 minutes 24 seconds, averaging 10 knots. *Flyer*'s time was 24 days 01 hours 22 minutes 20 seconds. We'd had each other in sight for the best part of 10 days for 2500 miles. The match race of all time.

Molly dreams of the delights of Argentina.

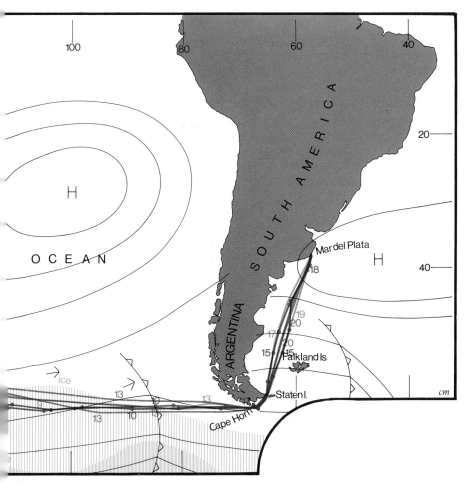

11. BABY BEEF AND BEAUTIFUL GIRLS

I must forth again tomorrow,
With the sunset I must be
Hull down on the trail of rapture
In the wonder of the sea.
— *Richard Hovey,* The Sea Gypsy

NO RECORD FOR *Flyer* this time. Mar del Plata was new ground for the race, the previous two Whitbreads having called at Rio de Janeiro, another 1000 miles to the north. But there was no doubting *Flyer* and *Ceramco* would have shattered the record had there been one. It had taken Eric Tabarly, in *Pen Duick VI* (racing this time as *Euromarche*), nearly 34 days for the Auckland-Rio leg in 1977-78, averaging 8.6 knots. We'd averaged 10 knots to Mar del Plata and, in effect, would have had 10 days up our sleeves had we been heading for Rio. We had reached Cape Horn three days ahead of *Pen Duick*'s time.

The wait for the handicap situation to clarify was just as tense as in Auckland. We'd beaten *Flyer* by 12 hours 10 minutes on corrected time, but we were unsure of how the rest of the fleet had been doing while we were struggling up the last 1100 miles from Cape Horn. We didn't have to wait long for the answers.

Euromarche was third to finish. We'd beaten her by 14 hours on corrected time. *Charles Heidsieck* was only 8 hours astern of *Euromarche* however and she pipped us by 4 hours 24 minutes.

The following morning a spinnaker was spotted off the coast making fast time towards the finish. It was a fractional rig — had to be *Challenger*. But, as the yacht got close enough to identify through binoculars, it proved to be Pierre Fehlmann's Farr design *Disque D'Or*. We owed him 83 hours. He crossed the line 57 hours after *Ceramco* and took over the handicap lead. If the 58ft *Disque D'Or* had made such good time, this leg would be a smallboat affair.

Sure enough, in the days that followed, the little ones had their day. Pierre paced the yacht club, inevitably with a clipboard under his arm, sweating on a leg win. It looked like he would do it as *Xargo III* and *Outward Bound*, the big threats, missed their deadlines. But in came the French 48-footer *Morbihan* to squeeze out *Disque D'Or* by 3 hours 50 minutes. *Xargo* was third, *Outward Bound* fourth, *Charles Heidsieck* fifth and *Ceramco* sixth.

We were thrilled for the *Outward Bound* crew even though they were disappointed at not winning the leg. Four days from the finish they were only 160 miles astern of *Xargo* and 100 miles ahead of *Morbihan*. In the following 24 hours, *Xargo* cleared out to a lead of 270 miles while *Morbihan* closed in to 30 miles astern. Digby had found his own private calm patch and there was nothing he could do. It had taken both *Outward Bound* and *Morbihan* between six and seven days to reach Mar del Plata from Cape Horn — the same time as it had taken *Flyer* and *Ceramco*. It was clear where the damage had been done.

Everyone's thoughts now turned to the final leg, 6149 miles back up the Atlantic to Portsmouth. The major honours were still delicately poised. The Auckland to Mar del Plata leg had been costly for *Kriter*. Andre Viant had suffered steering problems and *Kriter* had dropped off the pace. She was ninth on corrected time for the leg. Her overall lead of 7h 37m was gone and now she trailed *Charles Heidsieck* by 11 hours 21 minutes. *Flyer* was still third, having lost ground to *Charles Heidsieck* but closed in on *Kriter*.

The casualty list was still growing and now there were only 20 yachts, of the original 29, still in the race, even though some of the first leg drop-outs would rejoin us here. *Swedish Entry* and *Save Venice* had been left behind in Auckland — *Swedish Entry* with sponsor problems and *Save Venice* with serious hull damage. *Gauloises* had become the seventh dismasting of the race and had reached Tahiti, under jury rig, on January 27. *Licor 43*'s mast had gone again, breaking in four pieces when she was just 100 miles short of Cape Horn. The Spaniards organised a jury rig and made it to Mar del Plata on February 1. You had to hand it to them for determination. Then *Bubblegum*, the smallest boat in the race, struck trouble 180 miles from the Horn — a rudder bearing tearing away and ripping a hole in the hull. The rudder was abandoned and the crew plugged the hole with plaster of Paris bandages before using a spinnaker pole as a steering oar to get them to the safety at Punta Arenas in the Straits of Magellan.

The closest call was on *Rollygo*. Crewman Paolo Martinoni was whipped over the side by a flailing jib sheet when the boat was at 52 degrees south. It was pitch black in the middle of the night and blowing 30 knots. *Rollygo* was turned around on to a reciprocal course until Martinoni could be heard shouting for help. He was picked up at the third pass and none the worse for his unwelcome swim once he'd been stripped off and given a vigorous rub-down.

An 'all ships' alert went out for *European University Belgium* when she failed to

The Whitbread Invitation VII (from left). — Back row: Tony Fairchild (press officer), Geoffrey Boerne (Xargo III), Simon Gundry (Ceramco NZ), Yann Le Nabour (Euromarche), Ray Pogson (FCF Challenger, manager). Front row: OC Rutter (Ceramco NZ), Chappy Chapman (Ceramco NZ), Tony Taine (Outward Bound), Joe Allen (Flyer).

make radio contact for 11 days. Skipper Blondiau finally got through to his Belgian office to explain that the yacht had been knocked down and had rolled through 360 degrees. It had taken the crew a long time to sort things out and get the radio working again. *European University* finally made it to Mar del Plata on February 17, 35 days after *Flyer* and *Ceramco*.

For those of us already safe in port, Argentina was proving an interesting country to visit. Mar del Plata is the main seaside resort for the capital of Buenos Aires, some 450 miles away on the River Plate estuary. Inflation was rife and the local currency devalued so much that only the very wealthy could afford to holiday abroad. So Mar del Plata was jam-packed with wall-to-wall people, most of them devout sun worshippers.

The crew couldn't believe their good luck when, on the first morning in, they got their first sight of the astonishing array of beautiful females parading in and out of the Yacht Club Argentino's Playa Grande headquarters, all of them richly tanned and wearing slinky one-piece swimsuits straight from the fashion houses of Europe. Newt took one look and exclaimed, 'Miles and miles of vertical smiles'. But delight slowly turned to dismay for the hunters home from the sea when the ground rules become apparent. The girls were friendly and enjoyed the company of the race crews, but anything more involved was out of the question. In the six weeks we spent there, the boys reckoned they broke the world record for holding hands, but the 'scoresheet' remained clean. They had to take refuge in the extra-good steaks and highly palatable local wine that were to be enjoyed at very reasonable prices, thanks to the exchange rate for US dollars. The favourite eating house quickly became a restaurant close to the dock, called 'La Marca' where the specialty of the house was 'Baby Boeuf'. This was a steak which was anything but baby. It was big enough in fact to make even Jaws earn his keep.

The locals were helpful and friendly. This was the first time they'd hosted the race and they'd gone to a lot of trouble to cater for our needs. In some regards, they had no idea what our requirements would be, but anything that was needed was obtained — even if the delays were sometimes interminable.

The boats were moored in what in fact was an Argentine navy submarine base, with three of the navy's four subs in residence. There were strict rules to abide by and armed guards to enforce those rules. The high-profile display of sub-machine guns and sidearms was somewhat disturbing. Police and military personnel were everywhere.

Inevitably, there were a few incidents — particularly when the amount of noise you'd accept as normal in a New Zealand or English pub on a Saturday night

would bring in a riot squad. Venturing into the dock was a no-no, as Simon found out in a hurry. He borrowed the yacht club's runabout to take a group of children on a trip around the basin and was quickly warned back at gunpoint. The following night the guards, most of them young conscripts, thought they saw someone swimming in the water and making towards the submarines. They sent a few rounds into the water then did an armed check of the area where the boats were moored. The crews quickly got the message — no swimming allowed. Sometimes it was inevitable though, particularly as the likes of Newt, coming home from the beer tent, found it difficult to negotiate the climb down from the high dock wall to the bow of the boat below. He went in, fully clothed, three nights in a row before he discovered that the club ran a 24-hour shuttle service and it was much easier to climb aboard *Ceramco* from the club launch.

Eventually the days began to drag. The crews had done their tourist bit and seen all there was to see. They were also running short of money. Mar del Plata had three casinos, one of them reputed to be the biggest in the world. But they held little attraction. Simon provided some welcome distraction when he organised two teams from *Ceramco, Charles Heidsieck* and *Euromarche* to play in a rugby sevens tournament that was part of Mar del Plata's summer festival. *Daily Telegraph* journalist Tony Fairchild, in town to report the Whitbread race but a keen rugby man as well, wrote: 'How they managed to secure boots and shirts will remain a mystery. They looked more like a band of pirates than a rugby outfit and the fact that these multi-national teams both prefaced their games with the famous Maori haka doubled the interest in their performances. Sadly, the Whitbread second VII were beaten in their first match. But, then, they were composed of players who lacked the advantage of preparation aboard *Ceramco*. On the New Zealand yacht, while at sea, they played an imaginary game of rugby most evenings. They had to wait to be selected, then got kitted out and were psyched up before going out to play. After the demise of the 2nd VII, we didn't expect much of the first team. They couldn't really be expected to put up a good show against senior Argentine sides, one of which included three Pumas (Argentine rugby internationals). But they surprised everyone by reaching the semi-finals in which they went down by a narrow 6-4 margin. They missed a penalty attempt in the final minute and played for most of the second half with an injured player. Rear Admiral Charles Williams stumped up 500,000 pesos ($50) beer money and was as delighted with it all as were the players, but for different reasons. The Admiral appreciated how important the exercise had been as a way of building international friendship.'

Finally, it was time to go. Our mast had been repaired with the heavy cheeks flown in from Auckland and the boat stripped for anticipated light airs beating that lay ahead in the Doldrums. It was going to be quite a finish. *Charles Heidsieck* was in the box seat. She had to cross the Portsmouth finish line only 1 hour 54 minutes ahead of *Kriter* to clinch victory. *Flyer* had to make up 34 hours on handicap which meant she needed to finish 92 hours ahead of *Charles Heidsieck*. On the last leg, if conditions were right, she was capable of doing that.

Outward Bound, meanwhile, still had a good chance of making the top five and had her position as leading small yacht to maintain. *Ceramco* was out of this action. We were however the fastest yacht on corrected time across the Southern Oceans (from Cape Town to Mar del Plata) and had won the Roaring Forties Trophy. We had nothing to lose and would be going for broke on the final leg of the 27,000-mile journey.

AUCKLAND-MAR DEL PLATA

Elapsed Times

Boat	Hrs/Min/Sec
1. Flyer	577.22.20
2. Ceramco NZ	584.39.24
3. Euromarche	609.24.50
4. Charles Heidsieck	617.44.47
5. Disque D'Or	642.09.43
6. Kriter IX	649.24.42
7. FCF Challenger	652.37.03
8. Xargo III	662.48.52
9. United Friendly	667.45.51
10. Alaska Eagle	670.22.42
11. Outward Bound	694.51.35
12. Morbihan	697.56.02
13. Berge Viking	709.20.06
14. Rollygo	738.30.32
15. Skopbank of Finland	745.32.35
16. Traite de Rome	809.40.07
17. Croky	839.54.41
18. Ilgagomma	885.28.42
19. Walross	892.56.03
20. Licor 43	898.46.39
21. European University	1289.29.50

Corrected Times

Boat	Hrs/Min/Sec
1. Morbihan	527.56.17
2. Disque D'Or	531.46.46
3. Xargo III	538.17.31
4. Outward Bound	545.26.59
5. Charles Heidsieck	554.03.46
6. Ceramco NZ	558.27.35
7. Euromarche	568.33.46
8. Flyer	570.38.19
9. Kriter IX	573.04.55
10. Berge Viking	576.17.23
11. Skopbank of Finland	581.35.39
12. Alaska Eagle	583.53.02
13. Rollygo	586.15.05
14. Traite de Rome	615.11.22
15. Croky	641.33.28
16. FCF Challenger	652.37.03
17. United Friendly	655.10.59
18. Walross	709.45.43
19. Ilgagomma	736.04.06
20. Licor 43	818.47.46
21. European University	1090.29.27

Did Not Start: 33 Export, La Barca Laboratorio, Save Venice, Swedish Entry, Vivanapoli, Scandinavian.
Did Not Finish: Bubblegum, Gauloises 3.

Legs 1, 2 & 3 Elapsed Time

Boat	Hrs/Min/Sec
1. Flyer	2176.46.27
2. Charles Heidsieck	2333.08.02
3. Kriter IX	2386.45.49
4. Euromarche	2392.51.07
5. FCF Challenger	2407.41.10
6. Ceramco NZ	2452.58.43
7. Disque D'Or	2538.53.39
8. Alaska Eagle	2552.06.07
9. United Friendly	2606.35.12
10. Xargo III	2622.16.32
11. Berge Viking	2668.28.22
12. Outward Bound	2710.23.53
13. Morbihan	2782.11.17
14. Skopbank of Finland	2829.25.50
15. Rollygo	2849.20.09
16. Traite de Rome	2997.11.36
17. Croky	3044.49.20
18. Walross	3157.19.43
19. Ilgagomma	3213.32.11
20. Licor 43	3263.39.14

Legs 1, 2 & 3 Corrected Time

Boat	Hrs/Min/Sec
1. Charles Heidsieck	2120.25.21
2. Kriter IX	2131.48.43
3. Flyer	2154.17.00
4. Disque D'Or	2170.12.07
5. Xargo III	2203.05.14
6. Outward Bound	2211.20.56
7. Morbihan	2214.22.47
8. Berge Viking	2224.05.03
9. Euromarche	2252.49.50
10. Alaska Eagle	2262.34.21
11. Skopbank of Finland	2281.49.09
12. Rollygo	2340.46.32
13. Traite de Rome	2345.51.01
14. Ceramco NZ	2365.28.38
15. Croky	2382.17.43
16. FCF Challenger	2407.41.10
17. Walross	2543.03.41
18. United Friendly	2560.48.09
19. Ilgagomma	2714.29.14
20. Licor 43	2996.30.21

12. SUCCEED OR BUST

The Sun now rose upon the right,
Out of the Sea came he;
Still hid in mist; and on the left
Went down into the sea.
— Samuel Taylor Coleridge, The Rime of the Ancient Mariner

THE START TIME of 1500hrs allowed a lie-in before Pippa and I checked out of our small hotel and then a leisurely stroll down to the yacht club for an unhurried breakfast before reporting to the boat.

The morning was fine, but there were some dark and ominous clouds to the south-west that held the promise of a Pampero. I'd forgotten to buy two identical copies of *Time* magazine which I'd decided to use for a simple code system with Pippa for this last leg. The idea was for me to pick a line and quote a word. The number of that word in the line would represent a figure to Pippa at the other end of the radio-telephone link in England. In this way I could pass our accurate position without conveying it to the opposition. Tactics would be vital going back up the Atlantic and negotiating the Azores High. We didn't want Conny — or the Frenchmen on *Charles Heidsieck* and *Kriter* for that matter — to know what we were up to.

So my last hour on Argentine soil, for this visit anyway, was spent strolling back along the colourful Playa Grande beachfront, with its hut-like tents, clubhouses and sidewalk restaurants, to purchase the magazines and some ham rolls for lunch.

A tearful goodbye this time — thankfully the last of the race — before Pippa made her way to the pavilion from where she was to watch the start of the leg. The dockside was a seething mass of people as, at 1315hrs, we cut our mooring lines and reversed out into the basin. We'd been here nearly seven weeks and the lines, below the water, were a mass of weed and mud that we didn't want aboard at this late stage. As we backed away from the high, stone dockwall Chappy led the crew in a haka. The crowd loved it, started clapping halfway through and were still applauding as we motored away to the harbour entrance.

We'd had an over-long stay in Mar del Plata. The hospitality had been magnificent and the Yacht Club of Argentina people had really gone out of their way to cater for our needs — even down to installing a fibreglass swimming pool at dockside for us to wash sails in, the local fire brigade keeping the pool full — but we were still glad to be on our way. We're not tourists, the race is what this exercise is all about and we were itching to get on with it.

The Pampero didn't eventuate. Instead, the south-westerly did a 180-degree swing 20 minutes before the start to turn what had promised to be a kite run departure into a dead beat. The Cabo Corrientes waterfront was lined with tens of thousands of people, but I still managed to spot Pippa waving madly from the start pavilion, surrounded by the band.

The start itself was a shambles. The committee had laid the line incorrectly, almost up and down the course, and the seaward end was the only place to be. Consequently, everyone was there and there was a considerable amount of barging and banging and bad language as *Challenger* shouldered her way in at the outer buoy, *Berge Viking* clipped *Flyer*, and *Disque D'Or* did an emergency tack to avoid being cut in two by *Xargo*.

We kept our nose clean but were underpowered with the No. 4 genoa and one reef in the main. We changed to the No. 1 genoa and shook out the reef to get

'So, this is the way we'll go.'

moving and then as the breeze freshened, went back down through the wardrobe until we settled with the No. 4 and full main on port tack heading east.

Late this evening the only boats in sight are *Flyer* and *Challenger*, out on our port beam, and *United Friendly* below us, astern. The seas are a deep Atlantic blue as the coast behind us fades into the growing dusk.

Day 2: Sunday, February 28. Noon position 37.46S 54.16W
Day's run 158 miles. Course 090 degrees.
Wind NE 10 to 12 knots. Barometer 1023.

0700: '*Flyer* on port beam, *Challenger* on port quarter. Nobody else to be seen.' It had been a quiet night of first NNE winds, puffing occasionally to 25 knots, and then NE at 15 knots. We have continued all day on port tack hoping for an easterly change.

The quiet beginning is probably just as well as we've got some sickness on board. Staggy and the Doc have been vomiting after eating some cheese that disagreed with them and several others, including myself, are below par. In my case it's the remains of the flu, but we've all got some high living to recover from. Mar del Plata seemed to knock the crews around more than the other ports. Dysentry was fairly common and there were a few cases of 'social disease'. One of *United Friendly*'s crew broke an arm when he fell from a horse and a chap from *Ilgagomma* nearly drowned when, drunk, he fell into the dock on his way back to the boat. He was found floating face down and ended up in hospital for the night. Our mate Yvonne, from *Euromarche* has been flown back to France in a bad way. He was bitten by some insect while travelling near the Brazilian border and was subsequently very sick. His leg was still badly swollen when they put him on the plane.

Day 3: Monday, March 1. Noon position 35.51S 52.21W
Day's run 144 miles. Course 065 degrees.
Wind ESE 25 to 30 knots. Barometer 1024.

We've got the wind change we came looking for — it started to swing ENE early this morning and is now blowing 30 to 35 knots from the ESE. But we need everything we can get. The fleet chat show tonight revealed that we have stood too to the east and, for the moment, are down the pan. *Charles Heidsieck, Rollygo, Kriter* and *Disque D'Or* have gone up the shore at high speed on starboard in a completely different wind. They are now 60 miles ahead of us although a long way to leeward. This was a real kick in the bum for us, but now we're cracked off under the No. 5 jib and two reefs in the main, going like hell. Only time will tell whether we've been wrong. Everyone will have to make some easting at some stage or another and the weather charts indicate that we should continue to get better winds than the yachts further inshore. For the moment though we feel somewhat chastened.

Day 4: Tuesday, March 2. Noon position 33.25S 48.47W
Day's run 228 miles. Course 065 degrees.
Wind ESE 20 to 35 knots. Barometer 1024.

Rough and uncomfortable as we bang and crash our way northwards. Vonny's chicken casserole dinner stayed down last night — but only just, for some. The crew has been flat out with the endless stream of sail changes and reefs to counteract the frequent squalls going through. It has been a rapid transformation from the high life ashore to the reality of ocean racing. With the yacht on a permanent angle of 25 to 30 degrees, thrashing to windward in rugged seas, you tire quickly from the unending discomfort. The watch crews have taken to keeping sails on deck while so many changes are going on, the sails, in their bags, stowed on the weather deck. When the wind settles for any length of time, you can generally find two or three of the watch crew catching up with lost sleep. They are fully kitted in foul weather gear, hoods drawn closed, and they completely ignore the occasional heavy but warm spray as they slumber on.

We are recovering quickly and we feel we are in an excellent position tactically. The coast of Brazil, near Rio de Janeiro, is notorious for light winds, so the opposition inshore had better watch out.

A heavy rain shower this morning finally washed away the last of the Mar del Plata dust. The Pamperos raise enormous dust clouds on that part of the coast and the yacht was thick with it. The mast and fittings are now back to their normal colour though.

Day 7: Friday, March 5. Noon position 25.52S 39.05W
Day's run 236 miles. Course 065 degrees.
Wind ESE 25 to 35 knots. Barometer 1021.

The wind has remained in the ESE, with the occasional flick to the SE, for the last three days giving us runs of 250 miles, 204 miles and 236 miles. We've been laying course parallel to the Brazilian coast, making solid progress. At noon today we were only 1600 miles south of the equator, seven days' sailing at current speed.

We've been taking a lot of water down through the mast collar which, unfortunately, isn't a very good fit. The next fine day with no spray we will have to try and tape it up properly. On this angle of heel, the water doesn't reach the sump but ends up under the leeward bunks in the main saloon. Vonny has some sweet potatoes and cabbages stored there so they are a little damp right now. The rot is already setting into some of the food. The cabbages are starting to go bad and being soaked in sea water isn't going to improve their quality. We've had the floorboards up to pump the bilges dry, using a small, portable pump and sponges. A squirt of liquid detergent in the water that remained will keep things fresh down there until we repeat the process. This is going to be important as the temperatures rise in the tropics where conditions are ideal for all sorts of nasties which could mean stomach bug problems for the crew. Personal and boat hygiene must be kept at a high standard at all times.

I'm still sporting the cold I picked up two weeks ago in Mar del Plata so I'm not 100 per cent. Don has dysentry and vomiting, so is in his bunk. Lui has symptoms of the same complaints. On top of this, five or six of the boys are nursing colds. At least Vonny is bright and cheerful. I find it offensive that we should be sickly with shoreside ailments when we're out here in a clean, blue ocean which is covered with white horses, white trade wind clouds dashing across an inky blue sky above. *Ceramco* is leaping forward as though she fully appreciates the beauty of her environment and can sense that the finish of this race is beckoning.

The watches are the same as when we left Cape Town and Auckland. With Staggy are the Doc, OC, Jaws and Simon. Chappy has Newt, Molly, Lui and Don. They are working well to the same six-hour day and four-hour night watches we set out with. The humour is merciless. Simon has acquired the nickname Rope — for thick, hairy and twisted. The Doc's nickname is unprintable — a play on Dr Strangelove. Staggy's watch, dubbed the Staggettes on the last leg, are now the Faggettes (or Faggots).

163

Another dawn.

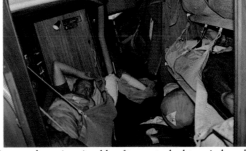
Vonny relaxes in a jumble of gear stacked to windward.

OC, Jaws, the Doc and Simon — still on starboard.

Pippa has arrived home in England after a good flight of only 16 hours. Modern air travel makes a mockery of distance. The same journey looks like it will take us more than a month.

Day 9: Sunday, March 7. Noon position 20.32S 35.19W
Day's run 159 miles. Course 360 degrees.
Wind light and variable. Barometer 1017.

We did 227 miles to noon yesterday but were down to 159 miles to noon today after a complete morning with the wind everywhere and heavy rain squalls.

The conditions have really tried the crew's patience and resilience. The log reads: 'Surely a record for amount of sail changes in two days — most of them unrecorded because we've been too bloody busy.'

The good news is that we are back in third place in the fleet. Only *Flyer* and *United Friendly* are ahead. Most of the other yachts are now stuck inshore with light headwinds and pushing the strong south-flowing Brazil current. *Flyer* has a lead of 160 miles. *United Friendly* is 80 miles ahead but is also 120 miles inshore from us. She could soon begin to slow down in fickle winds close to the South American coast. Maybe our initial tactics weren't so wrong after all.

Day 11: Tuesday, March 9. Noon position 13.52S 35.05W
Day's run 205 miles. Course 040 degrees.
Wind E 15 to 20 knots. Barometer 1017.

We have held on to *Flyer* in the last two days with runs of 194 miles and 205 miles, the wind filling in again from the ENE, going NE yesterday, and now east — most of the time blowing between 15 and 25 knots. The sail changes have continued unabated, slabs in and out of the main and switches up and down the headsail range from No. 1 to No. 3. *Charles Heidsieck* and *Kriter* are 50 and 60 miles astern. *United Friendly* is grinding to a halt in on the Brazilian shore. Since leaving Mar del Plata we have covered 2005 miles and have between 4000 and 4500 miles to go to Portsmouth.

At noon today we were 830 miles south of the point where we intend crossing the equator, working some 170 miles off the Brazilian coast on a course that will take us close to the Archipelago Fernando de Noronha. The routing charts show a marked decrease in calm and variable conditions on this track and hopefully we'll sneak through the Doldrums without too much bother. Our plan is to get north as quickly as possible on a course that will give us more reaching than those we expect most of the opposition will take. In the past, most yachts have kept well to the east when crossing the Doldrums, to be out to windward when approaching the Azores further up the North Atlantic. I prefer the possibility of getting a kite on and sailing fast. To be adopting tactics now for the Azores later on seems a pointless exercise. The North Atlantic weather maps, which we receive by Satnav from the UK, indicate a somewhat abnormal pattern. Usually there is a high pressure system, the Azores High, centred slightly to the south-east of the group.

Dr Agnew's 'Gunwhale Bum' clinic.

165

This pushes the low pressure systems up into the north. At the moment however the lows are crossing the Atlantic well below their normal route and if this pattern persists, life is going to be most interesting. My view is that the boats that get the equator crossing right and then past the Azores quickly, before the normal pattern re-establishes itself, will have the best chance of winning. With tactics becoming so crucial I quite expect most of the fleet to stop talking on the chat show, keeping their positions and circumstances a secret.

The fickle winds and heavy rain squalls the other day gave us the impression we were in the Doldrums already. But if we were, they were a long way south and have now retreated.

Day 13: Thursday, March 11. Noon position 07.12S 32.07W
Day's run 226 miles. Course 045 degrees.
Wind SE 20 knots. Barometer 1016.

Still on starboard tack but the wind is in the SE, freeing us enough to get the 1.5oz kite on at 1400hrs. We've been maintaining steady progress — 211 miles to noon yesterday and 226 miles to noon today. Now we should really start to smoke.

We really are thinking of applying to Guinness for the sail change record — but we can't remember the number we've done, there have been so many. We could have settled on one sail and accepted having to lug it through the squalls if it was too big, or losing speed in the lulls if it was too small. But we are racing to win, the crew is fit and keen and every second we gain now could be worth hours later on.

Staggy has very mild 'gunwhale bum' — spots on the behind caused by salty, sweaty clothes. They can be quite painful if not attended in the early stages. The Doc diagnosed 'creeping bum rot', a real shock to Staggy's vanity, and prescribed lying face down on the sails on the weather deck to expose bum to tropical sun. Staggy swallowed it hook, line and sinker, and did just that. Now he has trouble sitting down because of sunburn. The size and weight of Staggy's toiletry bag have always been the target for crew humour. In his present state, he must be getting quite worn out, the number of trips he makes to the loo to cream or powder his backside. Now the Doc, savouring every moment of this, has told Staggy he mustn't use the toilet below, but instead must strap himself to the pushpit to perform his daily functions. We all reckon Staggy wouldn't be worried in the least if he saw the state of Vonny's bum — even in normal condition.

Vonny has been wearing the same clothes since we left Mar del Plata 12 days ago. There has been mild concern about the grubby state of his T-shirt (Newt prefers the word 'filthy'.) Today the cook flicked a rotten tomato out through the main hatch, intending to dispatch the same to the ocean depths. Instead it splattered on both Newt and myself. We cornered him in the galley and, with a big, serrated diving knife, cut the offensive T-shirt from his back. He didn't move an inch during the operation, then carried on cooking in a replacement shirt which, although covered in dried paint, is at least clean.

The equator is less than 400 miles to the north and we are closing rapidly at 11 knots. It's a pleasant change from the Southern Ocean to have landmarks and targets. There was absolutely nothing for nearly 5000 miles between New Zealand and Cape Horn. Going up the Atlantic, we can pick our way past Rio, aim for Fernando de Noronha, cross the equator close to the islands of St Pedro and St Paulo, head for the Azores, and so on. It's only psychological, but it has a marked effect on crew morale when distances can be measured in, say, two Sydney-Hobarts or one Hobart-Auckland.

Day 15: Saturday, March 13. Noon position 00.27S 31.58W
    Day's run 180 miles. Course 015 degrees.
    Wind NE 15 to 20 knots. Barometer 1016.

The spinnaker lasted just 20 hours but helped us to a 227-mile run. By 1000hrs yesterday we were back to the big genoas as the wind went NE and blew only fitfully and the log recorded: 'Lightning to the NE! The ITCZ?'

It could be the Doldrums as we're still seeing plenty of high-energy electrical displays, the breeze hasn't known quite where to settle and our performance is down.

We had Rata Island, in the Fernando de Noronha archipelago, abeam at dawn yesterday but, through heavy rain, all we could see were the navigational beacons on the island's eastern shore.

The fact that we were headed by a cooler north-easterly was a good sign as it might mean we were through the Doldrums and out into the trades on the other side. If this was the case, we'd been either extremely clever in our approach or extremely lucky — or a combination of both.

The fleet was spread over an enormous distance. *Flyer* was 200 miles ahead but well to the east. Some of the tailenders were 1400 miles astern.

Today the signs continued to improve. The north-easterly piped up overnight to gust 30 knots with heavy rain, then the wind swung NNE and continued to blow hard. Tonight we're down to No. 3 with one reef in the main, convinced that we are through the dreaded ITCZ and making a decisive break on the boats astern.

The log notes: 'Simon going for the world non-stop sleeping record. Even 100mph flying fish hitting him in the dial can't deter his effort. Who said concrete is thick? Rope is thicker!' Then: 'Don E. filming while the Doc stars in and directs "Gunwhale Bum" — a new hit, horror movie featuring Chappy, Staggy, Molly and Jaws.' Staggy had been joined in the treatment room and Chappy is finding his affliction quite painful. The Doc is enjoying every minute of it, revelling in the power it gives him over his shipmates.

We crossed the line at 1600hrs this afternoon. The log reads: 'The equator passed under us yet again. Bump. Celebrated with raisin scones baked by the Doc.' Poor old Doc. It poured with tropical rain most of the afternoon and he decided to take a fresh water shower. He'd just finished covering himself in a beautiful lather of Badedas foam when the rain stopped completely. The only cure for that complaint was a salt water rinse-off.

The dry ice finally disappeared three days ago so we've run out of fresh meat now and have had to throw several packs of steaks over the side to stop them from jumping around inside the icebox. Eleven days of ice in tropical conditions was remarkable but from now on it's back to the tinned and freeze dried meats. Vonny has hidden away a few bottles of red plonk which he assures us is for marinating the dehydrated steaks, but the rest of us are sure most of it goes down his gullet.

Day 17: Monday, March 15. Noon position 06.16N 34.39W
    Day's run 232 miles. Course 360 degrees.
    Wind NE 20 to 25 knots. Barometer 1015.

'Sea conditions like Vonny's porridge — lumpy.' Nothing changes in that we are still heading north on starboard tack under No. 3 or No. 4 jibs with flattened main or one reef in. Yesterday's run was 204 miles, today's 232 miles. Our course sailed is close to optimum in that we are driving for speed with sheets started, to get away from this area as quickly as possible. There is no doubt now that we are through the Doldrums but we want to get well clear in case the ITCZ decides to chase us again.

'Forty winks before the mast,' by Don.

The Doldrums astern — we're out and clear.

We had the mainsail down today so that OC could replace the headboard slider tapes. The wires that Don had added previously were worn through as well. As soon as we rehoisted the sail the Nos 2 and 3 batten pockets blew off. Then, as *Ceramco* came off a particularly vicious sea with Simon hanging grimly to the windward wheel, the steering wires broke. On most yachts this would have been a major problem with considerable time lost, but with *Ceramco*'s twin wheels, independently rigged but also linked, it was just a nuisance. Simon switched to the still fully operational leeward wheel, Jaws replaced the broken wires with a new set, and we were back to normal without even slowing down. The twin wheel set-up paid for itself there and then.

Eleven flying fish came aboard during last night, improving the breakfast fare enormously. The standard menu had become muesli and 'frog in the hole' — the cook's specialty.

Because of the very long nights we have been running the generator for much longer periods than normal to keep up with the power consumption. Leaning over at a continual 25 to 35-degree angle for days on end on the starboard tack has caused problems with the cooling water intake for the BMW diesel that drives the big alternator. The only inlet we have is slightly to starboard of the centre line so Don has rigged up a connection down to leeward and the diesel now runs very satisfactorily.

Starboard tacks for three weeks can be boring.

A leak on the high pressure side of the desalinator pump that had been spraying water everywhere has been repaired by Don but to keep the intake to this pump always primed we have rigged up a temporary system. It entails a crew member using a small bilge pump to fill a 20-litre container in the main saloon with sea water. This is then drawn through the pump to produce fresh water.

Morale is high tonight. *Flyer* is only 60 miles to the north of us, although approximately 300 miles to the east. *Charles Heidsieck* is 200 miles to the south of *Ceramco* and 500 miles to the east. Time will tell which of us is right tactically. For me, it's northing that will count. Miles to the east, I hope, won't be much of an advantage.

The Plough is bright in the sky to the north-east of us and, for the first time, the Pole Star is clearly visible — one of the most useful navigational bodies in the heavens.

Day 19: Wednesday, March 17. Noon position 14.05N 35.54W
       Day's run 234 miles. Course 030 degrees.
       Wind ENE 25 knots. Barometer 1017.

Runs of 241 miles and 234 miles. The Azores are now only 1500 miles away. The Cape Verde islands, which we passed last September when heading south to Cape Town, are 600 miles to the east. Roughly 3000 miles to the finish — five Sydney-Hobarts.

Day 21: Friday, March 19. Noon position 21.42N 34.30W
       Day's run 232 miles. Course 035 degrees.
       Wind E 18 knots. Barometer 1021.

The sailing has been constantly fast in fresh winds and a moderately rough sea. We have put huge distances on most of our competitors. *Xargo* is 1000 miles astern, *Ilgagomma* 2000 miles back.

In the last two days (runs of 238 miles and 232 miles), we have been lifted and have curved east. *Flyer* has dropped down to the west. In the process, Conny has pulled ahead a little but we're still within 100 miles of him in terms of miles to run.

This afternoon produced a fright we could have done without. We were bouncing into uncomfortable head seas and hit one particularly hard. There was a double bang from the rigging and we turned to find that the wire runner backstay was starting to break. One third of the wire strands had already gone and the remainder could snap with the next big thump. The mast depends on these runners which take up much of the load on the centre of the spar and stop it pumping in a seaway. The helmsman quickly bore away across the seas while we winched the mainsheet in hard so that the sail accepted more of the load. We nursed the boat on the new heading until a spare runner backstay was rigged, then hardened up again to resume course. While changing the runner we had a near miss with a large, finned whale, clearing it by only a yard or so. Working on the theory that bad luck runs in threes, we sent Jaws aloft to check the rig — not everyone's cup of tea with *Ceramco* leaping around like a dinghy. To our relief, everything was okay. The two middle battens and batten pockets are still missing but we won't lower the mainsail to fix them until we strike more favourable conditions. The speed loss would be too great at this point in time. We're anticipating the wind will swing more south in the next day or so enabling us to get a kite on and make a high speed dash for the Azores.

Day 23: Sunday, March 21. Noon position 29.31N 31.23W
    Day's run 258 miles. Course 040 degrees.
    Wind SE 20 knots. Barometer 1024.

We got that south-easterly wind change at 0900hrs today, hoisted the 1.5oz kite and started to blast. The last two days have produced runs of 242 miles and 258 miles — good, but we want better. Portsmouth was 1850 miles away at noon today, the Azores 600 miles ahead.

The sloppy beam seas kicked up by the north-easterly, have been pushing *Ceramco's* stern around since we set the kite. The boat is now very light with food supplies well down, the diesel half gone and the water tanks kept at a moderate level.

The weather maps show a high pressure system at 28N 19W, drifting only slowly east. This is the Azores High — but further east than normal. An unseasonal low is coming in from the west at 28N. We're just beginning to feel the funnelling effects as the isobars squeeze up between the two systems.

We have been on starboard tack for 21 of the 22 days at sea since Mar del Plata — which must be another record for something (probably idiocy).

As the finish gets closer, the spirits are lifting. The end is in sight, not just of this leg, but of the whole race. The weather is what Newt would term 'chipper', so pre-dinner rum tots have become the fashion. Vonny seems to cook much better if he's given a large tumbler of rum before he's let loose in the galley.

The mainsail shape has been looking horrible, so today we dropped the sail for repairs. With the full crew on deck, the sail was lowered and spread over the central cockpit area. Lui and OC have already prepared new batten pockets with needle holes prepunched around the edges. With a team working on each pocket, the work was completed in short time. In one team, OC pushed the needle through from the top while Chappy, underneath, pulled it through with a pair of pliers. In the other, Lui did the pushing and Simon the pulling. The whole sail was checked over and the headboard slide webbings replaced before it was rehoisted as good as new. We're now ready for whatever the late winter winds of the North Atlantic have to offer.

Tonight we are running hard in a 25-knot SSE under the full-size 2.2oz kite with one reef in the main. We may soon have to go to a smaller spinnaker. *Ceramco* is averaging nearly 12 knots right on course, a bonus in an area where we could very well be becalmed.

Day 25: Tuesday, March 23. Noon position 38.12N 27.13W
    Day's run 284 miles. Course 045 degrees.
    Wind SE 20 to 25 knots. Barometer 1020.

The 284 miles was in 23 hours, following 280 miles to noon yesterday — the best sailing of the trip, but difficult at night. The heavy cloud cover has added to the darkness and the helmsmen have had their work cut out positioning the yacht for waves they frequently can't see. To help protect night vision in these circumstances, the shades are on all the hatches and ports and torch use has been cut to a minimum.

Yesterday morning produced one of the most magnificent sights of the race. We had several large finn whales chasing along behind us, criss-crossing *Ceramco's* wake only a couple of hundred yards back. The biggest mammals on earth, they were acting more like playful dolphins, catching up with us, blowing frequently as they surfed down the short, steep seas and clearly enjoying the chase. They kept it up for an hour before tiring of the game and heading off to the north while we charged on to the north-east, averaging 15 knots.

The wind increased to 40 knots last night and we were down to storm spinnaker and two reefs in the main, tight reaching. In these conditions we're using only the best heavy weather helmsmen and they've been working hard for every last ounce of speed, the crew trimming apace with them. The Doc noted in his log: 'What spectacular, crazy, race-winning sailing. Not much sleep for the off-watch crew, blasting under spinnaker, no moon, cloudy sky and black horizon. Big waves coming on deck as *Ceramco* screams along through the seas. Communications difficult because of the wind.'

The wild ride continued until 0900hrs today when the wind moderated and came abeam. We dropped the kite and reached on at 11 knots under the No. 2 genoa, heading for the centre of the Azores.

By 1500hrs, the northern Azores island of Terceira was faintly visible, 15 miles away to port. The houses and hotels flashed white against the grey-green high mountain backdrop. We hadn't seen the 7800ft-high peak of Pico even though we'd been quite close earlier in the day. Only the puffy white clouds hiding its summit gave its position away.

The 23rd is Conny's 56th birthday so on the fleet chat show we gathered around the radio and sang the traditional song. This was well received, as were the 12 bottles of Heidsieck champagne I was able to give him. Conny owed us three cases

Lui tends to the mainsail batten pockets.

of Heidsieck for our work in the Southern Ocean when his radio receiver was playing up and he had to rely on *Ceramco* for reports of the rest of the fleet. Now he only owes us two cases.

Flyer has pulled away to be 157 miles directly ahead of *Ceramco*. This means we lead them on handicap by only 15 seconds. It's going to be close. *Charles Heidsieck* is dropping back fast. Tonight she was 305 miles behind. *Challenger* is 260 miles astern and *Disque D'Or* reckons that she has done only 70 miles in the last 24 hours (while we were doing 284) and is becalmed.

Only 1200 miles to Portsmouth — two Sydney-Hobarts — and there are a few signs of channel fever showing on board.

Day 27: Thursday, March 25. Noon position 44.17N 19.58W
        Day's run 240 miles. Course 060 degrees.
        Wind SSE 10 to 15 knots. Barometer 1021.

The wind has been only moderate for the last two days, still from the SSE, but we've managed another 494 miles up the track. That puts us 800 miles from the finish and 650 miles from the English Channel. It looks like we'll strike light airs before too long, there's a massive high pressure system ahead, extending from Norway to Ireland. Weather information from here on is going to be ultra-critical and I've been trying to get as much uninterrupted sleep as possible in order to be fresh if conditions become trying.

We've cut *Flyer's* lead to 140 miles and now have *Charles Heidsieck* 500 miles astern. *Kriter,* it seems, is 400 miles behind her. Those two were favourites to wrap up the overall handicap prize with this leg — but our mate Conny just might be doing a number on them.

The log today read: 'Where are the log pens' followed by 'Chappy's gone to get them — with the pencils.' The amount of pencil and pens that have gone missing since Mar del Plata is astounding.

It has been quite strange sailing into a big ENE swell with the wind blowing along it from the south-east. The gusts on top of the seas lean *Ceramco* over until her leeward rail is awash. But, in the troughs, she's sometimes aback.

Lui spent all last night in his bunk, trying to get rid of a sinus problem. Newt also had a full night's sleep and then took over the galley while Vonny did his deck watch. Lui baked fresh scones for morning tea — making quite a sight standing over the stove in his brightly coloured Argentinian yak wool hat, red puffa jacket, red wet-weather trousers and white sea boots. This lot was topped off by a Sonny Walkman tape set.

Newt's lunch of dehydrated beef and beans went down well too — down into the ocean, much to Vonny's delight. The meat hadn't been soaked long enough and resembled thick cardboard in texture and taste.

Day 29: Saturday, March 27. Noon position 48.52N 12.18W
        Day's run 206 miles. Course 090 degrees.
        Wind ESE 15 to 20 knots. Barometer 1016.

Our speed has been dropping slowly but surely — 218 miles yesterday, 206 miles today. But we're still making good progress despite a few calm patches that we felt had come to stay. The weatherfax shows a high approaching from the west. We've got our fingers crossed that we get in before that one links with the big one to the east.

Two afternoons back, Staggy's watch sighted what at first appeared to be a submarine periscope. It turned out to be a large, red navigation buoy, labelled

'M', floating free. Luckily we saw it before nightfall as we had to alter course to port to miss it. Would have made quite a bang in the dark.

Since then we have passed two more large buoys — one yellow and the other a huge, black ship mooring job which just about constituted a danger to navigation.

We tacked on to port tonight, for the first time in 27 days, then we heard the news that *Challenger* had lost her mast. It had broken in four pieces in what Les Williams reported as only moderate conditions off the Azores. The rig had to be cut adrift to avoid the pieces punching a hole in the boat, and they are left with only spinnaker poles and main boom with which to sail the 1200 miles between them and the finish. We wish them well, because we know just how they must be feeling.

Less than 400 miles to go and we're now trying to get north as we close the Western Approaches. Northerlies are forecast, then in two days' time, north-westerly gales. We might just need a blast from that direction if we are to save our time on *Flyer* which has been wriggling away in this light stuff.

Day 30: Sunday, March 28. Noon position 49.14N 09.17W
 Day's run 123 miles. Course 120 degrees.
 Wind NE 5 to 15 knots. Barometer 1013.

Radio conversation between Conny and myself. Conny: '*Ceramco,* this is *Flyer.* Peter, if ever I do this race again I will do it differently.'

PJB: 'How, Conny?'

Conny: 'In a much bigger and faster yacht. I'm tired of looking over my shoulder to find you biting at my heels.'

We weren't exactly snapping though. The breeze waffled all through last night and we were reduced to one of the lowest runs of the trip. But, while we were oozing along quietly in smooth seas, somewhat frustrated with our lot, the yachts behind were having it rough, battling 50 to 60-knot headwinds and extremely boisterous seas. I think our pea soup fog is preferable.

The Doc had a chance to show his skill today, opening up an abscess behind Molly's right ear. The infection had not responded to a heavy course of antibiotics so the knife was necessary. Molly, swathed in bandages, is feeling much more comfortable and back to his normal self after a couple of uncharacteristic quiet days.

What next. Instead of navigation buoys, we've now seen two growth-encrusted sailboards. If we were cruising, *Ceramco's* deck would now be piled high with 'finds'.

Discussing *Challenger's* predicament, Newt recalled the day a New Zealand farmer Warwick Jones, from near Auckland, approached Les at Marsden Wharf to sign on for the rest of the trip. The conversation apparently went:

Farmer: 'Gooday mate, I'm Warwick.'

Skipper: 'Oh really, do we know one another?'

Farmer: 'Not yet mate, but I'm the farmer joker who's joining *Challenger* for the second half of the race. Here's me $7000.'

Skipper (suitably impressed): 'Of course, welcome aboard.'

Farmer: 'Just one thing mate — I've got a pet bull, had him for ages and wondered if I might bring him along.'

Skipper (suitably unimpressed): 'This is a racing yacht, not a cargo vessel.'

Farmer: 'Pity. I put a bullet through the old bastard last week and chopped him up for your freezer.'

This dead beating in thick fog is nerve wracking. Thank goodness for the Satnav and a good depth sounder as we're now approaching the continental shelf and over the Great Sole Bank, approaching the Scilly Isles. I've been working out the tides for the English Channel. They'll be spring, so I hope we strike them right (and *Flyer* gets them wrong). We're roughly 150 miles behind them, but they must be getting away in these conditions.

Day 31: Monday, March 29. Noon position 49.52N 04.31W
Day's run 184 miles. Course 075 degrees.
Wind NNW 20 to 25 knots. Barometer 1013.

The breeze finally filled in late last night to blow away the fog and speed us on our way into the English Channel. It was light from the NNE at first but soon after midnight started swinging through the north, increasing all the time.

By 0900, with the news that *Flyer* had crossed the finish line at 0747hrs GMT, we were 18 miles south of Lands End, blasting with the No. 4 genoa and one reef, in 40-knot NNW squalls. We had 190 miles to go, and a deadline of 0338hrs tomorrow morning to beat *Flyer* on handicap on this leg.

It was going to be close, but we should make it. The Solent tides would turn against us just after 0100hrs in the morning. We had to be there before then to make sure.

We hugged the English shore to dodge as much tide as possible going past Start Point at the western end of Lyme Bay but still struck steep wind-against-tide seas and our speed across the ground dropped. With 110 miles to go, we had to average 9 knots but we'd soon be getting a boost from the channel tides and, hopefully, shoot up the Solent on a spring flood.

We roared on past Portland Bill, then across Christchurch Bay and past Anvil Point to enter the Needles Channel at 10 minutes before midnight. Our luck was holding. We were going to do it. We'd been headed slowly as the wind back from NNW to NNE but the average never dropped below 9.5 knots.

It was bitterly cold but who gave a damn. The whole crew was on deck, working like they'd just started a harbour sprint. Off Cowes, we caught up with the *Solent Scene*, once again the Kiwi support vessel. The folks were all there — Pippa, Tom Clark, Peter Cornes, Alan Topham, Seffo, John and Judy Glanville, etc. They gave us a rousing welcome and we could hear the festivities above the noise *Ceramco* made as we hardened up under No. 4 jib and two reefs in the main to tack for the finish line off Southsea Castle.

Finally, at 0056hrs GMT on Tuesday, March 30, we dipped across the line. We'd beaten *Flyer* by 2 hours 41 minutes 43 seconds on handicap. She beat us home by 17 hours 9 minutes 8 seconds — the furthest we'd been behind since Cape Town. We'd covered the 6600 miles from Mar del Plata in 30 days 6 hours 56 minutes 55 seconds.

For Conny and his crew, admirable adversaries, the long wait had begun to see whether they would win the race on handicap as well as being first home in every leg.

For us, the great adventure, the great race was over. There was the sobering thought, as we dropped *Ceramco*'s sails for the last time — we'd almost certainly never race our trusty machine again. She had to be sold and the crew would go their separate ways.

But this was no time to be sober. Ashore waited Pippa and the back-up team, and one of the biggest champagne breakfasts Gosport would see.

Approaching the Azores — trimming for speed.

Horse Sand Fort in sight, Flyer *approaches the finish.*

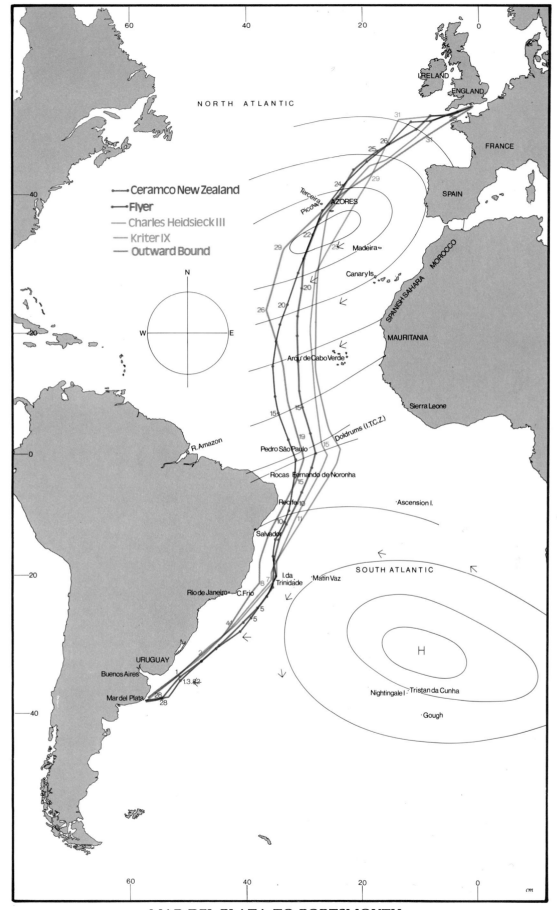

MAR DEL PLATA TO PORTSMOUTH

13. IN HINDSIGHT

*F*LYER ACHIEVED WHAT I always suspected Conny had at the back of his mind — the line and handicap double. *Charles Heidsieck* made the mistake of not paying enough attention to what *Flyer* was up to at the front of the fleet. They didn't cover the opposition, went too far to the east in anticipation of north-east trades, and missed the fresh reaching winds which *Flyer* and *Ceramco* picked up at the Azores. The difference was probably only 200 to 300 miles, but Gabbay lost as least that much to us by holding up to windward (to the east) while we were bolting north as fast as we could go.

When *Flyer* crossed the finish line, *Heidsieck* had 600 miles to go and had to average 7.6 knots to win. Under normal circumstances she would have romped home, but she struck strong headwinds and then light airs and missed her deadline by nearly 30 hours. To add insult to injury, *Kriter* beat *Heidsieck* into third place on handicap but not by enough to prevent Gabbay and his crew taking second for the race.

For us on *Ceramco*, although we won that final leg and so finished on a high note, it was very much a case of what might have been and if only.

We'd achieved much. In Auckland, we finished only 8 hours 23 minutes astern of *Flyer* and won the leg on handicap. In Mar del Plata, we were 7 hours 17 minutes astern of *Flyer* and finished sixth on handicap. In Portsmouth, we trailed *Flyer* by 17 hours 9 minutes and won on handicap.

Ceramco, designed to excel in the Southern Oceans, won the Roaring Forties Trophy for the best handicap performance from Cape Town to Auckland to Mar del Plata. Despite sailing 4000 miles under jury rig, we were third fastest yacht around the world, and broke *Great Britain II*'s record in the process (*GB II* went around in 134 days in the 1975-76 Financial Times Clipper Race and in 134 days 12 hours 22 minutes in the 1977-78 Whitbread. *Ceramco*'s time was 132 days 11 hours 55 minutes).

On corrected time for the three legs from Cape Town to Portsmouth, *Ceramco* beat *Flyer* by 29 hours 23 minutes 23 seconds (by 14 hours 31 minutes 30 seconds in Auckland, 12 hours 10 minutes 44 seconds in Mar del Plata and by 2 hours 41 minutes 43 seconds in Portsmouth).

When the mast went over the side we were pacing *Flyer* to Cape Town and, the way the results went, would surely have placed in the top three. But...

The mast came down — end of story. Conny won because his didn't, and because both *Flyer* and *Ceramco* were pushed to the limit in a manner none of us will ever forget. We set new standards for big ocean racers. The Whitbread race will be the better, and more exciting, for it.

Looking back, there are few things I would change in the situation that prevailed, least of all the crew.

The two watch leaders, Staggy and Chappy, went about their business in different ways — but achieved the same high results. Staggy changed a lot during the campaign, became more tolerant without compromising his own standards. I'm sure he's an even better yachtsman for the experience and much more accomplished at handling people. Chappy proved a natural leader and is a more rounded personality because of it. His greater appreciation of what was going on all around the boat was one of his main assets when, inevitably, he was compared with Staggy.

The Doc was precisely the mature influence I was looking for when I chose him and his refreshing enthusiasm never failed him.

Vonny produced some great meals in terrible conditions and some terrible meals in great conditions — I'm still not sure he didn't do a con job on us at the interview stage. His ability to be the butt of a lot of the cutting humour on board, and still hold his own in this department, made him worth his weight in gold.

Jaws was everything I knew he would be — always reliable, ever-ready to go up the mast no matter what the weather was doing, and liked by everyone. His maturity and competence were amazing in one so relatively young.

Don got quite stroppy at times when the tension of heavy air running and lack of sleep got to him. But his character always came through and his readiness to tackle anything at any time made him invaluable.

OC too could get stroppy. He's more highly strung than, say, Jaws. But he is an exceptional all-rounder with the nerve and stomach to tackle jobs which would make most people blanch.

Lui rubbed some people the wrong way ashore — probably because he drifted away to do his own thing, whatever that was. But on board he was first class and a tower of strength up on the bow. Few people knew that he is something of a dab hand at martial arts — but they do now. Nobody ever got the upper hand of him physically.

Molly is another all-rounder, happy to tackle anything — from going up the mast to diving under the boat to check the bottom. He also proved an excellent helmsman and an extremely good-natured companion. His dress habits left a bit to be desired at times however.

Simon had the last laugh on everyone who predicted he would foul up. He was totally dedicated and fully deserved his 'Personality of the Race' award. He worked hard on his image and came out right on top. Plus he was enormously strong and ever enthusiastic.

Newt — well he made the whole selection procedure worthwhile. He was the last one chosen and turned out one of the best. His humour was non-stop and this was important to morale. On top of that he was more than able around the boat and meticulous about everything he did.

It was significant that *Ceramco* and *Outward Bound* were the only two boats to do the race without a change of crew whatsoever. That says a lot for character and commitment.

Will we do it again? I can only speak for myself. On this, my third Whitbread, I frequently said it would be my last. I have to settle down sometime, particularly as Pippa and I want children. But there lingers this feeling of unfinished business. Most of my convictions about this race, manifested in *Ceramco* and her crew, were proved correct. I know what should be done to progress a step further again and so the temptation will be there.

Our race with *Flyer* will be a hard act to follow however, and I'm not sure that Conny will find the motivation to put another boat and campaign together. He will be pushing 61 years of age by the time the 1984-85 race comes around. But there is no fiercer competitor in deep-water ocean racing. This was emphasised when, after the race finished in Portsmouth, he finally revealed that he'd suffered a heart attack seven days out of Cape Town on the second leg. Aboard *Ceramco*, we had our suspicions that all was not well. He was so subdued on the radio. *Flyer*'s doctor, Julian Fuller treated his skipper and was concerned enough to suggest heading for Perth or Adelaide. Conny wouldn't hear of it. He was quoted as saying: 'If *Ceramco* had known about my health problem they might have pushed harder still, and how the hell would we have kept them down. We had to stay ahead and, so long as they didn't know anything, it was okay. If the worst had happened, and I had died at sea, then my crew would have put me over the side as is the tradition. Perhaps *Ceramco* would have seen me drifting by, but that would have been the only indication they would have had that all was not good with Conny.'

So, who knows. With that sort of determination, Conny could be back too for what would be the 1984-85 edition of the great race. If this proves to be the case there will again be no limit — on the adventure or the fun.

MAR DEL PLATA-PORTSMOUTH

Elapsed Times		Corrected Times	
Boat	Hrs/Min/Sec	Boat	Hrs/Min/Sec
1. Flyer	709.47.45	1. Ceramco NZ	700.14.05
2. Ceramco NZ	726.56.24	2. Flyer	702.55.48
3. Charles Heidsieck	832.26.24	3. Kriter IX	759.01.43
4. Kriter IX	836.31.48	4. Charles Heidsieck	767.30.08
5. Euromarche	838.37.33	5. Alaska Eagle	772.17.23
6. United Friendly	847.48.39	6. Rollygo	776.05.40
7. Alaska Eagle	860.50.45	7. Outward Bound	776.34.07
8. Disque D'Or	906.07.58	8. Xargo III	791.57.23
9. FCF Challenger	919.46.01	9. Berge Viking	792.49.14
10. Xargo III	920.53.45	10. Disque D'Or	793.33.10
11. Licor 43	927.19.48	11. Euromarche	794.47.50
12. Berge Viking	928.29.27	12. Traite de Rome	798.07.40
13. Outward Bound	928.55.37	13. Morbihan	801.01.58
14. Rollygo	931.21.25	14. Skopbank of Finland	805.17.38
15. Skopbank of Finland	972.28.42	15. Croky	833.17.00
16. Morbihan	974.23.00	16. United Friendly	833.18.46
17. Traite de Rome	997.28.33	17. Licor 43	845.46.14
18. Croky	1035.33.04	18. Bubblegum	895.56.42
19. Walross	1097.57.01	19. Walross	908.32.22
20. Bubblegum	1104.24.47	20. FCF Challenger	919.46.02
21. La Barca Laboratorio	1135.00.01	21. European University	942.41.52
22. European University	1144.36.34	22. La Barca Laboratorio	1058.13.23
23. Ilgagomma	1287.15.11	23. Ilgagomma	1134.53.41

FINAL DETAILS

Elapsed Times		Corrected Times	
Boat	Days/Hrs/Min/Sec	Boat	Days/Hrs/Min/Sec
1. Flyer	120.06.34.14	1. Flyer	119.01.12.48
2. Charles Heidsieck	131.21.34.35	2. Charles Heidsieck	120.07.55.29
3. Ceramco NZ	132.11.55.38	3. Kriter IX	120.10.50.26
4. Kriter IX	134.07.37.42	4. Disque D'Or	123.11.45.17
5. Euromarche	134.15.28.42	5. Outward Bound	124.11.55.03
6. FCF Challenger	138.15.27.12	6. Xargo III	124.19.02.37
7. Alaska Eagle	142.04.56.52	7. Morbihan	125.15.24.45
8. Disque D'Or	143.13.00.28	8. Berge Viking	125.16.54.17
9. United Friendly	143.22.23.50	9. Alaska Eagle	126.10.51.44
10. Xargo III	147.15.10.18	10. Euromarche	126.23.37.40
11. Berge Viking	149.20.57.51	11. Ceramco NZ	127.17.42.43
12. Outward Bound	151.15.19.30	12. Skopbank of Finland	128.15.06.47
13. Morbihan	156.12.34.17	13. Rollygo	129.20.52.12
14. Rollygo	157.12.41.33	14. Traite de Rome	130.23.58.41
15. Skopbank of Finland	158.09.54.32	15. Croky	133.23.34.43
16. Traite de Rome	166.10.40.09	16. FCF Challenger	138.15.27.12
17. Croky	170.00.22.24	17. United Friendly	141.10.06.55
18. Licor 43	174.14.59.02	18. Walross	143.19.36.03
19. Walross	177.07.16.44	19. Licor 43	160.02.16.35
20. Ilgagomma	187.12.47.22	20. Ilgagomma	160.09.22.55

TROPHY	AWARDED FOR	WINNER
Whitbread Trophy	First on Handicap	*Flyer*
R.N. Club & Royal Albert Yacht Club Trophy	Second on Handicap	*Charles Heidsieck*
Royal Thames Yacht Club Valsheda Trophy	Third on Handicap	*Kriter IX*
Whitbread Small Boat Trophy	Winner on Elapsed Time for the Small Boat Division	*Outward Bound*
Roaring Forties Trophy (Presented by the R.N.S.A.)	First on Handicap for Leg 2 and 3	*Ceramco New Zealand*
Portsmouth City Council Trophy	First on Elapsed Time	*Flyer*
Omino Di Ferro Trophy (Presented by Rollygo)	Best Yacht on Handicap - 3 good Legs to Count	*Ceramco New Zealand*
Race Committee Award	Best Personality of the Race	Simon Gundry
Charles Heidsieck Cup	Outstanding Seamanship	*Croky*
Dr Mogens Bugge Medical Challenge Cup	Most Courageous Act	Roberto Vianello
Kodak Award	Best Photograph of all Leg Winners	*Ceramco New Zealand*
Rank Trophy	Best Kept Log	*United Friendly*
Flyer Cup (Presented by C. van Rietschoten)	Yacht maintained in best condition throughout the race	*Disque D'Or*
Lady Mackworth Trophy	Yacht with best Handicap time whose Crew has included a Lady on each leg	*Xargo III*

The citations for the special awards read —

Outstanding seamanship: 'Although *Croky* was one of the smallest boats in the race, the skipper was always prepared for any eventuality and the yacht emerged from the race unscathed. For all four legs she arrived looking efficient and with everything functioning.'

Most courageous: 'For his outstanding courage and fortitude during the second leg. Despite severely frostbitten feet, Roberto Vianello resisted the temptation to put into port, carried on for another two weeks in considerable pain to complete the leg and then required hospital treatment on arrival in Auckland.'

Outstanding personality: 'For Simon Gundry's outstanding and enthusiastic contribution to international relations and to the general well being of the crews.'

APPENDICES

FIRST WHITBREAD ROUND THE WORLD RACE — 1973/74
Course: Portsmouth — Cape Town — Sydney — Rio de Janeiro — Portsmouth
AROUND THE WORLD RACE RESULTS —
Handicap Distance 27,120 Nautical Miles

	Rating	Elapsed Time Days/Hrs/Min/Sec	Corrected Time Days/Hrs/Min/Sec
1. *Sayula II*	42.4	152/09/11/08	133/12/32/43
2. *Adventure*	40.2	162/19/06/30	135/08/03/45
3. *Grand Louis*	43.4	162/01/19/41	138/14/52/06
4. *Kriter*	50.6	156/14/10/03	141/01/53/35
5. *Guia*	34.9	177/19/23/48	142/19/20/40
6. *Great Britain II*	69.02	144/10/43/44	144/10/43/44
7. *Second Life*	55.6	161/02/02/47	150/08/06/19
8. *CS & RB*	37.1	187/00/21/46	155/06/57/06
9. *British Soldier*	43.8	179/19/49/53	156/20/53/19
10. *Tauranga*	39.1	185/20/42/52	156/22/23/43
11. *Capernicus*	33.0	204/19/48/50	166/19/01/22
12. *33 Export*	44.2	197/10/02/24	174/22/28/22
13. *Otago*	41.7	203/21/31/14	178/08/49/10
14. *Peter Von Danzig*	42.1	204/15/30/55	179/14/50/40

SECOND WHITBREAD ROUND THE WORLD RACE — 1977/78
Course: Portsmouth — Cape Town — Auckland — Rio de Janeiro — Portsmouth
AROUND THE WORLD RACE RESULTS — 26,950 nautical miles

	Rating	Elapsed Time Days/Hrs/Min/Sec	Corrected Time Days/Hrs/Min/Sec
1. *Flyer*	48.4	136/05/28/47	119/01/00/00
2. *Kings Legend*	48.4	138/15/47/23	121/11/17/23
3. *Traite de Rome*	35.7	154/20/58/12	121/18/50/59
4. *Disque D'Or*	46.2	142/00/37/48	122/10/56/23
5. *ADC Accutrac*	46.9	145/15/28/11	126/20/18/36
6. *Gauloises II*	38.1	156/23/00/36	127/07/54/35
7. *Adventure*	37.5	158/14/12/35	128/02/54/28
8. *Neptune*	44.3	152/05/33/35	130/11/52/48
9. *B&B Italia*	41.5	157/05/34/48	132/02/22/47
10. *33 Export*	39.7	164/15/31/47	133/00/31/11
11. *Tielsa*	50.0	148/13/22/11	133/00/36/00
12. *Great Britain II*	68.4	134/12/22/47	134/10/43/11
13. *Debenhams*	41.3	161/05/05/23	135/19/49/48
14. *Japy Hermes*	45.1	164/01/29/23	143/06/00/00
15. *Heath's Condor*	68.8	143/01/41/59	144/00/09/35

DAMAGE TO YACHTS DURING WHITBREAD ROUND THE WORLD RACE 1981/82

		Leg
Rollygo	Rod lower shroud parted (Mast lost)	1
	Wire lower shroud parted	4
	Intermediate stainless steel pin sheered (12mm)	
Ceramco	Intermediate shroud parted (Mast lost)	1
New Zealand	Mast split at deck level	4
Charles Heidsieck	Forestay bottle screw parted	1
Kriter IX	3 runner mast fittings parted	1
	1 runner parted	4
	Both hull steering pulleys pulled away	3
FCF Challenger	Mast split at upper shroud connection	1
	Lower shroud parted (Mast lost)	4
	Boom broken	2
	Intermediate shroud parted	3
33 Export	Lower block backstay disintegrated (Mast lost)	2
Licor 43	Lower shroud parted (Mast lost)	2
European University		
Belgium	Cap shroud parted (Mast lost)	2
Gauloises 3	Shroud parted (Mast lost)	3
Disque D'Or 3	Mast cracked at deck level	2
	Boom broken	2
	Stanchions pulled out of deck	3
Outward Bound	Mast cracked at deck level	3
Bubblegum	Chain plate parted	1
	Deck moulding lifting	1
	Forestay parted	1
	Steering wheel spokes broken	2
	Rudder lower pintle bearing housing sheared	3
	Steering cables parted	1
Croky	Shrouds observed before parting	2
	Steering wheel broken	
Flyer	Boom broken	2
	2 winches disintegrated	2
Save Venice	Boom broken	2
	Keel loose	2
Skopbank of	Spinnaker pole broken	4
Finland	Boom broken	1
Scandinavian	Shroud problems (retired)	1
La Barco	3 keel bolts parted	4
Laboratorio	Cap shroud parted (Mast lost)	1
	1 keel bolt parted	4
	2 lower shrouds parted	
Swedish Entry	Forestay parted	1
	Forestay fitting broken	2
Ilgagomma	Forestay parted	4
	2 lower shroud fittings parted	4

This list is not comprehensive, as I observed far more damage than is reported, mainly to booms, blocks and winches.

MEDICAL REPORT

Long distance ocean racing is both physically and psychologically demanding. At times various members of the crew became quite irritable. Mood changes of this sort were most apparent during the two Southern Ocean sections of the race, when we experienced sustained hard running conditions in big seas. Although *Ceramco's* main cabin was well insulated, the noise, shuddering movement of the vessel and the occasional broach were all factors which made sleeping difficult. Insomnia therefore was the usual cause of irritability. A night off watch (the skipper standing in) and a short acting barbiturate sedative invariably resolved the problem.

The object at all times was to keep the yacht moving at peak performance. This priority remained uppermost in the minds of everyone throughout the entire 27,000-mile journey. Whilst on watch, if a crewman appeared particularly weary and a tack was taking longer than usual to complete, there was always someone alongside offering assistance. In view of this entirely selfless and supportive approach it was not surprising that, despite the absence of territorial privileges on board, a hot-bunking system and difficult living conditions, the situation remained harmonious during the 134 days at sea.

In preparing a medical list for a lengthy voyage on an ocean racing yacht, one is very much aware of the limited amount of space available for equipment and the problems created by excessive weight. It is also helpful if, when a medical problem is encountered, one can quickly find the appropriate supplies. For this reason I assembled my kit in watertight plastic containers. They were numbered and an index was stuck inside the medical locker door.

In our circumstances, accidental injury was much more likely to be a problem than disease states. The medical equipment was assembled with this in mind. The detailed inventory is listed. In the previous Whitbread race there were several severe injuries. A *33 Export* crewman severely fractured a thigh, a *Great Britain II* crewman was caught in the bight of a spinnaker brace and sustained a severe crush injury of the abdomen. We were fortunate that there were no such serious injuries on *Ceramco New Zealand.* In part I believe this was due to Peter Blake's insistence on crewmen wearing safety harnesses and clipping themselves on in heavy weather. One crew member required stitches for a lacerated eyebrow, but this injury was sustained in port at Mar del Plata. The occasional bruise and minor burn from the galley stove were hardly problems.

We had a number of crew suffer from gastro-enteritis during the first leg. This problem was traced to a contaminated filter in the fresh water supply line. Several crew developed influenza symptoms shortly after leaving Mar del Plata and in the final stages of the race Richard MacAlister developed an infected cyst behind the left ear which required surgical drainage and antibiotic treatment.

'Gunwhale Bum' is a well-known minor affliction of yachtsmen and is caused by buttock abrasions which become painful when wet with salt water. These commonly become infected, possibly as a result of scratching. We were fortunate in having a desalination plant and a plentiful supply of fresh water. Regular washing, the use of absorbment powder and cotton underwear minimised this tropical malady. However, few of our crew were troubled with it and one was able to recognise both the creeping and galloping form of the disease. Cure was usually effected by painting the area with alcohol and baring the buttocks to the sun.

In summary, only trivial problems were encountered and we could easily have managed without a medically qualified person. Apart from the fact that such a decision would have deprived me of an amazing and fulfilling experience, there is always uncertainty concerning the possibility of ill health and for this reason, and the skipper's peace of mind, I think, when possible, it is desirable to have a doctor as a crewman during an exercise of this nature.

Trevor Agnew

MEDICAL SUPPLIES

PACK 1:
Minor Trauma
Dressings
Sutures
Tinc. Iodophor
Local anaesthetic
Syringe
Scissors, dissecting forceps and
  needle holding forceps.

PACK 2:
Major Trauma
Oropharyngeal airway
I.V. giving sets x 2
Oropharyngeal suction & catheters
Butterfly needles x 2
Sphygmomanometer
Angiocaths x 2
1 Tourniquet
Syringes & needles x 4
Gloves x 2 pair
I.V. Ketamine. 2G.
Major Trauma Prep. pack
Xylocaine
E.Z. Surgical scrub

PACK 3:
Intravenous Solutions
Plasma Substitute (I.P.P.S.) x 2
Barts Solution. 2L.
Normal Saline. 2L.
I.V. Giving sets x 2

PACK 4:
Surgical Instruments (Major Trauma)
Spencer Wells forceps x 6
Rubber drains
Retractors x 2
Chest drain with flutter valve
Scalpels x 2
Non toothed & toothed dissecting
  forceps
Assorted ligatures & needle holding
  forceps
Scissors. 2 pair

PACK 5:
Intravenous & Oral Antibiotics
I.V. Flagyl
I.V. Ampicillin
I.M. Gentamycin amps.
I.M. Cephradine amps.
I.V. Cloxacillin
Amoxycillin Caps
Bactrim tabs
Ampicillin Caps
Flagyl Suppositories

PACK 6:
Skin
Vaseline
Lanoline
Tinea powder & cream
Johnsons prickly heat powder
Assorted sun protection creams

PACK 7:
Sea Sickness
Tabs marzine 50mg x 200
Tabs Stemetil 5mg x 50
Inj stemetil 12.5mg x 10
Suppo. stemetil 25mg x 10
Lytren powder. 6 packets

PACK 8:
Gut, Muscles & Joints
Salt tablets - dextrose covered CIBA
Multi vitamin & Vitamin C tablets
Tabs gastrobrom
Tabs Lomotil
Tabs Codeine phosphate
Tabs dulcolax
Caps indomethacin
Suppos. indomethacin
Finalgon cream

PACK 9:
Pain Relief & Sedatives
Tabs Sol Aspirin
Tabs Paracetamol
Tabs migril
Pethidine Tabs 100mg x 50
Omnopan Amps 20mg x 10
Pethideine amps 100mg x 10
Tabs soneryl 100mg x 100
Tabs Mogadon x 50
Tabs Valium 2mg x 50

PACK 10:
Ears, Nose & Eyes
Lacryl soln x 10
Cough Lozenges x 100
Nasal decongestants
Eye pads x 4
Local anaesthetic soln.
Bismuth gauze packing
Nasal Speculum & packing forceps

PACK 11:
Dental Pack
Model kryptex
Oil of cloves
Zinc oxide powder
Dental forceps
Ledermix paste
Dental probes & mirror

Assorted reamers
L. Anaesthetic & syringe & needles
Wire for banding teeth.
PACK 12:
Fracture Kit
Hare traction splint
Plasto material
Triangular bandages x 2
Finger splints
Cotton wool bandages

GENERAL RULES FOR THE SHIP

1. In port duty crew member to be responsible for keeping ship tidy, head cleaned and general security above and below decks.
2. No smoking below decks at any time.
3. Hospitable ship and almost anyone welcome aboard. Introduction of guests to the skipper is appreciated.
4. The cook may ration certain foods, beverages and other articles.
5. After using the stove, make certain the gas supply is turned off.
6. Power is scarce: always switch off lights after use.
7. Switch off tape recorder after use and replace tape in original box.
8. No personal gear to be left lying around the decks, cockpits or down below.
9. Watches run from 0-4, 4-8, 8-14, 14-20, 20-24hrs.
10. Night watches are called 20 minutes before the watch starts and crew members to be on deck 5 minutes before changeover.
11. Day watches are called 40 minutes before the watch starts and meals should be ready 30 minutes before watch starts.
12. Cleaning below decks is done by the 'off' watch.
13. Cleaning of dishes, etc. is done by a member of the 'off' watch.
14. The 'on' watch crew should always remember that the 'off' watch crew is trying to sleep.
15. Shirts to be worn when sitting down below.
16. All questions and requests for interviews from the press to be referred to the skipper.

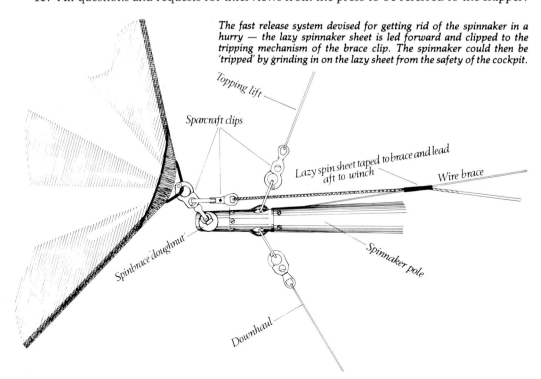

The fast release system devised for getting rid of the spinnaker in a hurry — the lazy spinnaker sheet is led forward and clipped to the tripping mechanism of the brace clip. The spinnaker could then be 'tripped' by grinding in on the lazy sheet from the safety of the cockpit.

Topping lift

Sparcraft clips

Lazy spin sheet taped to brace and lead aft to winch

Wire brace

Spinbrace doughnut

Spinnaker pole

Downhaul

GEAR
Spares carried on board

1 x main halyard: (wire and rope, already spliced), would double as main topping lift, genoa or spinnaker halyard or extra spinnaker brace.

1 x spinnaker/genoa halyard: (wire and rope, already spliced), would double as spinnaker brace, main halyard or runner backstay.

1 x outboard reefing line: (rope covered wire and rope), required only after breaking mast.

1 x spare steering wire set: (for first three legs), two spare sets carried on fourth leg and both used as replacements, changed at sea.

Running Gear

Genoa sheets: Two spares, total of four on board. These doubled as spinnaker pole preventers when heavy running.

Spinnaker braces: For 1st and 4th legs, 1 spare (total of three on board). For 2nd and 3rd legs, 2 and 3 spares (totals of 4 and 5 on board). These were slightly longer than necessary and, on the two Southern Ocean legs, all were reterminated and spliced at least once. On two separate occasions, without retaping, these lasted approximately three days before breaking while in use.

Spinnaker sheets: At least three spares carried each leg (total of five on board). An extra coil of braid, uncut but suitable for spinnaker sheets, was carried on legs 3 and 4.

Assorted ropes and lines: Two light spinnaker sheets for each leg plus reefing strops, handy billies, lashings and a roll of mousing material.

Halyards: All new in Portsmouth and Cape Town. In Auckland, the main halyard and two spinnaker halyards were replaced (new wire, old ropes respliced). In Mar del Plata, main halyard, two spinnaker and two genoa halyards replaced. On the 2nd and 3rd legs, both spinnaker halyards were reterminated at least once, if not twice, each per leg because of spragging through wear and chafe.

Tools and Equipment

Talurit handles with changeable heads to match rigging (6mm x 8mm).

Bolt cutter heads (to fit Talurit handles).

Wire cutters for rigging plus smaller set for taking snips at larger wire sizes.

Tap wrench (clutch type) with assorted taps and drills and mechanical fastenings.

Soft head hammer.

Makita cordless drill.

Impact driver.

Oil stone.

Siezing wire.

Portable vice.

Pop rivetter with interchangeable $\frac{3}{16}$in and $\frac{1}{4}$in heads.

Usual spanners, screwdrivers, hacksaws, pliers, vicegrips, files etc.

T-section alloy strips, pre-drilled, suitable for repairing boom and, if necessary, spinnaker poles. Spare sleeving for repairing spinnaker poles (never used).

12 x 8mm talurits were sufficient per leg, even when we broke the mast. We carried 8 x 6mm talurits per leg for the reefing lines.

FOOD LIST — LEG 1

U.H.T. (Longlife) Milk	112 pts	Mint sauce	2 bottles
U.H.T. (Longlife) Cream	10 x 7 ozs	Chutney/sweet pickle	6 jars
Dried Milk	4 x 3 lbs	Horseradish	2 jars
Flour	20 lbs	Soy sauce	2 bottles
Sugar	48 lbs	Tabasco	2 bottles
Rice	25 lbs	Chilli	2 bottles
Baking Powder	1 x 400g	Mustard	6 small jars
Salt	2 x 700g	Curry	5 tins
Pepper	4 x 50g	Parmesan Cheese	4 tubs
Coffee	6 x 1100g	Gelatine	1 pkt
Tea Bags	500	Suet	1 pkt
Milo	4 x 1100g	Vanilla essence	1 bottle
Cup of soups	126 boxes	Spaghetti	36 x 450g
Marmite	6	Macaroni	18 x 450g
Jam	8	Raisins	4 lbs
Peanut Butter	8	Dates	4 lbs
Honey	8	Dried apricots	4 lbs
Cooking Oil	1 gallon	Instant potato	10 pkts x 225gm
Vinegar	2 bottles	Dried peas	18 bags x 400gm
Cornflour	2 x 400g	Dried beans	18 bags x 400gm
Gravy mix	4 tins	Muesli	10
Custard Powder (instant)		Cornflakes	10
Herbs	various	Desiccated coconut	4 lbs
Spices	various	Boiled sweets	42 pkts
Tomato sauce	2 x 2 litres	Toffees	2 small sacks
Tomato paste	24 small tins	Chocolate	200 x 225g
Mayonnaise	2 large jars	Chewing gum	72 pkts
Treacle	2 tins	Fruit drink (powdered —	
Syrup	3 tins	orange flavour)	20 x 650g
Stock (instant)	6 tubs	Biscuits — sweet	42 pkts
Worcestershire sauce	4 bottles	savoury (ships biscuits)	4 large tins

TINNED

Sweetcorn kernels	15 x 450g	Apple & orange juice	4 cases
Sweetcorn creamed	15 x 450g	Corned beef	36 x 340g
Bean salad	14 x 310g	Canned stew (Butlands)	15 lge x 12 men
Baked beans	18 x 820g	Tinned butter	60 lbs
Tomatoes	18 x 790g	Tinned processed cheese	16½ lbs
Beetroot	12 x 820g	Tuna	42 x 185g
Carrots	6 x 450g	Sardines	36 x 100g
Peaches	8 x 820g	Eggs	42 doz.
Pears	8 x 820g	Bread — fresh	15 cut loaves
Pineapple	10 x 820g	Bread — longlife	50 cut loaves
Apricots	8 x 820g	Cheese (Mature cheddar)	30 lbs
Apple pie filling	10 x 567g	(Rich) fruit cakes	
Self saucing steamed		(Devonport Yacht Club)	17
pudding	36 x 380g		
Condensed milk	12 x 379g		
Reduced cream	12 x 200g		

MEAT

Corned silverside	9 lbs	Smoked ham	1
Pork chops	12 large	Salami	6 x 24"
Sirloin steaks	36 x 10 ozs	Bacon (rolled 1 piece)	20 lbs
Ham steaks	12 large	Sausages	168
Lamb chops	16	24 medium	
T-Bone steaks	days	12 x 12 ozs	
Stewing steak		32 lbs	
Minced steak		16 lbs	
Chickens		4 large	
Rolled roasts		2 x 8 lbs	

13 days Dehydrated/freeze dried meat, assorted packs for 12 men. i.e. Cubed steak, minced steak, sirloin steaks.

13 days Butland Tinned meat. Tins containing quantities for 12.

FRUIT & VEGETABLES

Potatoes	112 lbs (390)	Tomato	42 lbs (assorted grades of ripeness)
Onions	86 lbs (260)		
Cabbages	30		
Cauliflower	12	Peppers	20
Carrots	40 lbs	Celery	10 heads
Pumpkin	4 large	Spring onions	2 lbs
Courgettes	12 lbs	Oranges	1 case
Spinach	6 lbs	Grapefruit	1 case
Garlic	1/4 lb	Bananas	20 lbs
Parsley	1/2 lb	Apples	2 cases
Lettuce	16	Lemons	10
Cucumber	12		

GALLEY EQUIPMENT/DOMESTIC

Roasting trays	2	Jiffy	3
Saucepans	2	Windowlene	1
Skillets (teflon coated)	1	Teak wax	2 tins
Pressure cookers	2	Wash powder	4 large
Pie dishes	2	Dettol	6
Bread tins	2	Milton	1
Spud masher	1	Fly spray	1
Ladle	1	Scourers	4
Large spoons	3	Sponges	4 large
Knives	4	J-cloths	6 packets
Can opener	3	Dishwashers	2
Spud peelers	3	Scrub brushes	2
Cheese grater	1	Long handled broom	1
Egg whisk	1	Toilet brushes	2
Wooden spoons	2	Rubber gloves	1
Oven gloves	1	Clothes pegs	1 packet
Kitchen scissors	1	Matches	6 large packets
Sieve	1	Plastic bowls	1
Measuring Jug	1	Buckets	2
Rolling Pin	1	Dustpan	1
Mixing/salad bowls	3	Stiff brush	1
Garbage bags	50	Tea towels	12
Plastic/freezer bags	100	Vaseline	2
Clingfilm wrap	4	Oven cleaner	1
Aluminium foil	4	Air-fresh	1
Paper towels	42	Pepper grinder	1
Loo rolls	60	Insulated mugs	12
Water containers	2	Cutlery of each	12
Disinfectant	4	Crockery of each	12
Wash-up liquid	6 x 900ml	+ spare knives etc.	

LIST OF SYNDICATION OWNERSHIP

Share No. Name/s	Share No. Name/s
1 W.N. White	40 The Devonport Yacht Club Executive
2 J.M. Foster	Syndicate No. 2
3 P.J. Cornes	— B. Holmes
4 B. & J.H. Blake	— A. Kemp
5 Hood (NZ) Ltd	— G. Bendall
6 Hood (NZ) Ltd	— E. Kemp (Mrs)
7 D.K. Ross	— B. Westbrooke
8 H.K. Hattaway	41 G.W. Dunsford
9 D.H. Scott	42 Lake Taupo Yacht Club
10 R.B. Waddell (Mrs)	43 R.C. Murie
11 P.J. Blake	44 Royal New Zealand Yacht Squadron
12 P.J. Blake	45 Royal New Zealand Yacht Squadron
13 The Devonport Yacht Club Executive	46 H. & J. Towle
Syndicate No. 1	47 Sir William Stevenson K.B.E.
— B. Holmes	48 Ken D. Butland
— A. Kemp	49 D. Levene
— G. Bendall	50 Jordon Sandman Smythe & Co
— E. Kemp (Mrs)	51 D.I. Bigg-Wither, California, USA
— B. Westbrooke	52 Maxwell Industries Ltd
14 R. Von Kohorn	53 Sarah Easen & Russell Cochrane
15 R. Von Kohorn	54 NZ Express Transport Ltd
16 H.L. Julian	55 W.A. Laurie
17 M.H. Wiseman	56 William Ritchie
18 J.W. McKenzie	57 Weiti Boating Club
19 L.W. Tattersfield	58 Mr & Mrs C.R. Bidwill
20 Mr & Mrs D. McNeil	59 Mana Cruising Club
21 B. Farr	60 Kenneth Webley
22 Barker Textiles Ltd	61 Mark M. Williams
23 J. & M.B. Foster	62 N.W. Williams
24 A.A. Angell	63 Royal Port Nicholson Yacht Club
25 W.S. Wilson	64 D.J. Alison
26 J.A. Carmichael	65 A.J. Butcher
27 R.W. Scherer	66 Peter & Wendy Willcox
28 P.G. Neary	67 Sea Nymph Boats Ltd
29 E.S. Coutts	68 P.S. Bromily
30 P.G. Sheehan	69 Marlene Cresswell
31 D.P. Winstone	70 Brian Michael Horrocks
32 G.F. Gair	71 Randall B. Peat
33 P.J. Faire	72 R.H. Walker
34 N. & H. Foster, Guernsey	73 B.W. Ewing
35 C.R. Blair	74 John & Els Vandersyp
36 R.H. Duder	75 F.C. Lytollis
37 J. Gifford	76 L.V. & P.M. Berthelsen
38 L.H. Julian	77 Charles K.H. Webley
39 A.B. Griffin	78 J.H. Taylor & P.A. Rigg

79 L.V. & P.M. Berthelsen
80 Joanna Wooffindin
81 Hamilton Yacht Club
82 Alan T. Gibbs
83 Banks Peninsula Cruising Club Inc
84 Gisborne Yacht Club
85 Air Fresh International
86 Panmure Yacht & Boating Club
87 New Plymouth Yacht Club
88 Jack McIntyre
89 Warren Tuohey
90 Takapuna Boating Club
91 Wakefield Bros. (NZ) Ltd
92 Diana M. Walker
93 The First Dockyard Syndicate,
   Devonport
   — R. J. Graham
   — P. MacDonald
   — W. Fenton
   — G. Tattersall
   — S. Graham
94 Les & Graham Castles
95 Donald & Mary St Clair Brown
96 Auckland Multihull Sailing
   Association
97 John A. Neil
98 Glenda R. Neil
99 Bill Bean & John Field
100 The Devonport Yacht Club
101 The Royal NZ Navy Sailing Club
102 Ralph Roberts
103 Kath & Vaughan Chapman
104 John H. Dale
105 Premier Plastics Ltd
106 Tokoroa Yacht Club Inc.
107 Mr A.F. Hall
108 The Unclutchables, Warkworth
109 Canterbury Yachting Association
110 B. Rive
111 New Zealand Wines & Spirits Ltd
112 Auckland Motor Yacht Club
113 International Order of the Blue Gavel
114 Nelson Yacht Club 5 Syndicate
115 T. Maxwell de Denne
116 R.L., S.E. & G.R. Allport
117 Royal Akarana Yacht Club
118 M.G. Howard
119 Ajax GKN (Screw Division)
120 Variant Owners Association
121 Auckland Coin & Bullion Exchange
122 Tamaki Yacht Club Syndicate
123 Wanganui Sailing Club
124 R.W. Stanton
125 A.F. Laity
126 W.G. Beckett

127 John & Judy Glanville, Hampshire,
    UK
128 C.K. & P.P. Woodhead
129 Alexander, Bennett, Warnock &
    Mellsop
130 Alexander, Bennett, Warnock &
    Mellsop
131 Hutchison Hull & Co
132 C.L. Smith & K.M.P. Smith
133 Outboard Boating Club of Auckland
134 K. Butland
135 Thomas Edwin Clark
136 Thomas Edwin Clark
137 L.E.G. Richardson
138 Banks Peninsula Cruising Club
    Syndicate
139 James Hardie & Co. Pty Ltd
140 J.O., J.K., H.J.O. & H.A. Lusk
141 Flag Ship Committee Syndicate
142 John M.W. Archibald
143 Simon R. Archibald
144 G.T. Durrant
145 Kenneth Duthie Butland
146 An Auckland Plastics Syndicate
147 The Crew of *Ceramco New Zealand*
148 H.L. Homer
149 David Lee & Jim Wood
150 A.N. Harvey
151 Brendon A. Gilmore Ltd
152 Table I Syndicate (*Whispers II*)
153 Elysium & Unicorn Syndicate
154 Betelgeuse Muritai Syndication
155 Brookbanks Bros.
156 Napier Sailing Club
157 Peter Coote
158 The Chinaman Syndicate
159 Tauranga Yacht & Powerboat Club
    Syndicate
160 Citizens of Nelson
161 Metropolitan Life
162 Metropolitan Life
163 Paint Aids Ltd
164 Paul Jeremy Drake
165 Ralph Russell Newton
166 Michael Neville Drake
167 Kawerau Yacht Club Inc.
168 City of Napier
169 City of Napier
170 Robert John Cox &
    Terence Robert Coxon
171 Arthur O. Baldock
172 The Electric Construction Co. of New
    Zealand Ltd
173 Francis Henry Reynolds
174 W.M. Kember

175 Goodyear NZ Ltd
176 Robert Arthur Owens
177 Manukau Timber Co. Ltd
178 Craddock Fibreglass (1977) Ltd
179 New Zealand Optical Limited
180 Gary Forsyth & Capt. Warren Wood
181 Tim R. Nicholls
182 Nu-Look Windows E/C Ltd
183 Quality Bakers HB Ltd
184 Greg & Vilma Beacham
185 B.M. & N.R. Gabbot
186 T.E. & M.E. Andrews
187 Ron & Mona Willis
188 J.E. Langley & P.C. Feltham
189 K.J. & A.C. Laird
190 Pussers Ltd, British Virgin Islands,
    West Indies
191 Pussers Ltd, British Virgin Islands,
    West Indies
192 Chris James Hensley
193 Nirvana Syndicate
194 Beryl Barnard
195 Robert Gilbert Yellowlees
196 E.W. & G.V. Hargreaves
197 John Greville Holmes
198 E.A. Moody & P. Spackman
199 A. Peterson, J. Zidich, N. Page,
    T. Plummer, D. Blair
200 Wemyss & Associates
201 Doug McKee & Colin Geddes
202 H. Smith, P. Bennett & Others
203 Torrent Bay Syndicate
204 Tony Kirk
205 D.R. Winstanley
206 Lee Caldwell
207 Bill Gibbons
208 D.R. & B.J. Winstanley
209 Max Gregory
210 Peter Fish
211 John Miller Syndicate
212 Gus Blithe
213 Robertson Engineering Ltd
214 D.C. Dewhirst & D.C. Holdaway
215 Pat & Gavin Wright
216 Margaret & Wayne Lucas
217 Olive Field
218 Lester D. Higgins
219 R. Cameron & Co. Ltd
220 Doreen Ann Anderson
221 Derek Morrison
222 Duncan Bruce Kibblewhite
223 William Mark Thomas
224 Laddie & June White
225 Paul Trevethick
226 Norah Stagg & Richard Crawshaw

227 Gerhard Ammermann
228 Dominion Containers Ltd
229 L.R. Allen
230 Manawatu Standard Ltd
231 A.J. & S.C. Robb
232 Leonard James Priddle
233 Joyce Stella Dowsett
234 John & Catherine Edwards
235 Robertsons Ltd
236 E.T. Hornsby Earthmovers Ltd
237 McCulloch Menzies Wellington
    Moths Syndicate
238 Michael R. Evans
239 Barbara M. Nolan
240 Timothy Michael Herrick
241 Rheem NZ Ltd
242 Phase 2 Owners Syndicate
243 Cox & Dawes
244 8 O'Clock Newspaper
245 Broadbank Corporation
246 Richard Fitzgerald MacAlister
247 Mike & Pam Carter
248 Harry & Norah Foster, Guernsey
249 Peter John Fergusson Hardley
250 Chemical Resources Co. Ltd
251 A.F. Fish
252 Foveaux Crossing Syndicate
253 NZ Cement Holdings Ltd
254 Robert Fenwick
255 C.E. Fordham
256 Nylex Fletcher Ltd
257 Williams & Kettle Ltd
258 Smith & Smith Ltd
259 Z. Milich
260 Moyes & Groves Ltd
261 Faye Lorna Gillard
262 Lea & Wayne Gillard, Robyn &
    Haddie Kaire
263 Graham Canmore Inwood
264 Bowater Motors (1980) Ltd
265 David Kidd
    David Chartres
266 T.T. & J.A. Miano (N.Z.) Ltd
267 Mr & Mrs Les Hutchins
268 Graham Stimpson
269 A.J. & M.M. Sheard
270 Ken & Joy Lee
271 Quinten Simpson
272 UEB Industries
273 Timaru Yacht & Powerboat Club
    (Syndicate)
274 Airport Inn
275 R.J. Jones
276 N.Z. Insurance Co.
277 Heards Ltd

278 Heards Ltd
279 James Dick Ellis & Family
280 C.M. Aitkenhead & Sons Ltd
281 Endeavour Services Corporation Ltd
282 New Lynn R.S.A. Syndicate
 — B. McKinlay
 — F. Brown
 — F. Hitchcock
 — D. Calder
 — J. Hunt
283 Allan & Dianne Swan
284 The City of Wellington
285 New Lynn R.S.A. Syndicate
 — R. Kendall
 — J. Wynn
 — L. Kendall
 — K. Tebay
 — K. Reynolds
286 J.E. Timpson
287 Veronica Kalkman
288 Nathan Liquor Division
289 Nathan Liquor Division
290 M.C. Vautier
291 Mr & Mrs A.J. Wedd,
 Mr & Mrs L.S. Richmond
292 Frank Percival Wills
293 Mainzeal Corporation Ltd
294 Mainzeal Corporation Ltd
295 L.D. & M.M. Fenton
296 Zipper Clipper Syndicate
297 Auckland Co-op Taxi Society Ltd
298 Kenneth William Staton
299 Staff of Diversey Wallace Ltd
300 Desmond W. Hurley
301 John Graeme Sinclair Reid
302 Ross Roofing Ltd
303 The Waitemata Syndicate, Henderson
304 Sir Robertson Stewart CBE
305 Joy Butland
306 Mrs C.S. Frewen
307 P.M. Martin
308 South Auckland Caravan Centre
309 Robert E. Duhnke Jr., Seattle, USA
310 D.L. Hazard
311 Oregon Paint Co. Ltd
312 J.V. Riddell
313 H.T.W. Nolan
314 Olga Mary Faire & Peter Robert
 Moule
315 Waitaki NZ Refrigerating Ltd
316 J.B. Hay
317 C.K. & P.P. Woodhead
318 James Farquhar Cleland
319 Donald M. Calder
320 Adrienne Harding

321 Selwyn Buckingham
322 Gerald S. Hall
323 Charles & Jessie Tyndall, British
 Columbia, Canada
324 Robinson Toomey & Partners
325 Fruit Distributors Ltd
326 Kesteven Cother Saxton
327 Sheila Patricia Glendining
328 North Shore Outboard Boating Club
329 Timaru Yacht & Powerboat Club
 (Syndicate No. 2)
330 Carter Holt Holdings Ltd
331 Countrywide Building Society
332 Margaret R. Till
333 Haughton-McRae-McRae-Powell-
 Larsen
334 Colin Williams Reynolds
335 Porirua City Council
336 Majorie Irene Lilley
337 Amco Oil Syndicate
338 Read & Gibson Ltd
339 Team McMillan Ford
340 G.R. Cornes & E. Beckett
341 P.K. Rive, Comalco Extrusions Ltd
342 P.K. Rive, Comalco Extrusions Ltd
343 Thomson Hilton Leys
344 The Children of Goldfield Special
 School
345 South British Group of Companies
346 A. & J. Keyworth
347 R.G. Ellis
348 Noton (N.Z.) Ltd
349 T.R. Burton
350 Nona Ross
351 S.W.A.P.D. Syndicate
352 H.E. Buchanan
353 Frost & Manning
354 R.B. Pohe
355 Canterbury Frozen Meat Co. Ltd
356 C.J. Lovegrove
357 A.H. Irwin & M.J. Walsh
358 Durafort Investment Ltd
359 B.E. & O.C. Mackay
 R.H. Champion
360 J.R. Williams
361 Independent Newspapers Ltd
362 J.G. Lloyd, M.E. Buchanan, M.G.
 Barrott, W.A. Hayes, J.R. Bee
363 L.W. & M.L. Stevens, P. & I.R.
 Cowie, W. Chilton, R.C.G. Stewart,
 O.W. Potts & Sons
364 Trotter & Co. (Glenfield Intermediate
 School)
365 The Lotus 9.2 Association
366 Papatoetoe Rotary Club Members
 Syndicate

367 E.D.P. Division, Post Office,
Wellington
368 Hutt Club (Inc.)
369 Marsden Alexander Motors Ltd
370 Kapiti Boating Club No. 1 Syndicate
371 Les Evans
372 J. & G. McDougall
373 A.W. Rawnsley
374 Richard Jamieson
375 E.J. Linklater & 30 other Feilding
Rotarians
376 John Gault Syndicate
377 Colin & Isabel Leitch & Family
378 A.K.L.R.S.T.E., Air New Zealand
International Reservations Staff,
Auckland
379 William David Angwin
380 Kapiti Boating Club No. 2 Syndicate
381 John Charles Fair
382 Chris McMullen
283 Eric Wing
384 Jack Alexander McLeod Kean
385 William Lewis Murphy
386 Eileen Joan Greenhalg
387 Eileen Joan Greenhalg
388 H.J. Bull
389 Leonard & Dingley Ltd
390 Embecon Pty Ltd
391 South Pacific Credit Card Ltd
392 South Pacific Credit Card Ltd
393 Trev's Team Syndicate, C.I.R. Dept,
Greenlane Hospital, Auckland
394 Fisher & Paykel Social Club
395 North Shore Rugby Football Club
396 Peter Rimington Brown
397
to
402 Kohimarama Yacht Club
403 Buttle Wilson & Co.
404 Kohimarama Yacht Club
405 Charles Wiffen Ltd
406 Devonport Yacht Club
407 Kapiti Boating Club Inc. No. 3
Syndicate
408 Christopher Tait Horton
409 Pilkington Ceramco Syndicate
410 Frederick Clarence Lytollis
411 Ken & Joy Lee
412 Ken & Joy Lee
413 W.D. Lucas
414 Warren Blake
415 Benjamin David Robertson
416 Peter Shorter
417 Healing Industries Limited
418 Healing Industries Limited

COMPANY CONTRIBUTORS TO *CERAMCO NEW ZEALAND*

Adidas
Air Fresh International
Air New Zealand Ltd
Akarana Engineering Ltd
Alcan N.Z. Ltd
Alliance Freezing (Southland) Co.
Anchor Distributors Ltd.
Anodising Engineers Ltd
Apollo Press
Auckland Crane Company
Auckland Coin & Bullion Ltd
Auckland Harbour Board
Auckland Star
Aulsebrooks Ltd
Austral Abrasive Products Ltd
Australia & New Zealand Banking Group
Autocrat Sanyo N.Z. Ltd
B.J. Ball (NZ) Ltd
Bank of New Zealand
Beardsley Pearce Ltd
David Barker
Beechams (NZ) Ltd
Bing Harris Ltd
Len Birth Photography
Blue Boats
Boatcall
Boehringer Ingleheim Ltd
W.H. Bond & Company
R.L. Bowden & Company
Bowring Burgess Marsh McLennan
  Fenwick
David Brett Ltd
B.P. New Zealand Ltd
British Airways
Dennis Brown Motors
John Burns Ltd
Butland Industries
Ken Butland Ltd
John Edward Butler N.Z. Ltd
Cadbury Schweppes Hudson Ltd
Canterbury Apparel Ltd
Caravan & Leisure Land Ltd
Carter Holt Ltd
Caxton Printing Works
Cerebos Foods (NZ) Ltd
Chloride Batteries NZ Ltd
Citizen Watches Ltd
Clarke & Matheson Ltd
Colgate Palmolive Ltd
Collins Stationery
Columbus Maritime
Cooks Consolidated Services Ltd
Corbans Ltd

Cox and Dawes Ltd
Craven Engineering Ltd
James Crisp Ltd
Neil Cropper Ltd
Crown Lynn Potteries Ltd
Dale Freightways Ltd
Danforte Laboratories
Dean Graphics
Design Gallery
'Devco' Products Ltd
Devonport Yacht Club
Dominion Containers Ltd
Andrew Donovan Ltd
Dorlon Products Ltd
Douglas Pharmaceuticals Ltd
T.J. Edmonds Ltd
El Duane
Eta Foods Ltd
Eveready Batteries Ltd
Faberge
Feltex Cordage Ltd
Feltex Thermaform Ltd
Fibremakers Ltd
Fisher & Blundell Ltd
Foodtown
Forman Insulation Ltd
A. Foster & Company
Francis Publishing Ltd
Garman Holdings (Sax Altman)
Garnet Keene Ltd
Gisborne Harbour Board
Great Outdoors Company Ltd
W. Gregg & Co.
Hansells N.Z. Ltd
H.B. Confectionery
Healing Industries (Epiglass)
Heards Ltd
Heerdergen Foundry Ltd
Hodder & Stoughton
W.E. Holmes Ltd
Hutcheson Wilson & Co. Ltd
Industrial Chemicals
Johnson & Johnson Ltd
Klissers Farmhouse Bakeries Ltd
Kodak N.Z. Ltd
Lane Walker Rudkin Ltd
Leader Press Ltd
Leopard Breweries Ltd
Levi's
Lewmar Marine (UK)
Lidgard Rudling
Lion Breweries Ltd
Loadlift Equipment Ltd

Lockley Offset Printing Ltd
Lucas Industries Ltd
Lyttelton Harbour Board
Macbeth Manufacturing
Marine Power & Service
Marine Stainless Fittings Ltd
Mathias Meats N.Z. Ltd
Mauri D.Y.C. Foods
McFarlane Fisheries Ltd
McMillan Ford
Merrell Wm. S. Company
Mesco Gas Ltd
Metropolitan Life
Mill Valley
Millar Patersen & Co. Ltd
Moray Industries
Morris Black & Matheson Ltd
Napier Harbour Board
Nelson Harbour Board
Nestles N.Z. Ltd
Neville Newcomb Ltd
N.Z. Ambulance Officers Training School
N.Z. Apple & Pear Marketing Board
N.Z. Dairy Board
N.Z. Industrial Gases
New Zealand Rotary & Lions Clubs
N.Z. Tube Mills
N.Z. Wines & Spirits
N.Z. Wool Board
New Zealand Yacht & Sporting Clubs
N.Z. Yachting Magazine
North Shore Times Advertiser
Oasis Industries
Ocean Pacific Ltd
Don Osborne & Associates
Charles Palmer & Co. LTd
Panmure Businessmen's Assoc.
Penguin Books Ltd
Pussers Ltd (British Virgin Islands)
Quality Packers Ltd
Quickstik Limited
Radio New Zealand Ltd
Reckitt & Coleman Ltd

F. Renshaw Ltd
Richardson-Merrell
Riddell Marine Components
B. Rive
Roche Products N.Z. Ltd
Rotary Yachting Fellowship
Rothmans N.Z. Ltd
Royal N.Z. Naval Sailing Club
Royal New Zealand Yacht Squadron
Rutherford & Williams (NZ) Ltd
Sanford Ltd
Sanitarium Health Food Company
Sea Bee Air
G.D. Searle (NZ) Ltd
Seaspray Magazine
Sebaggo Incorp. U.S.A.
S.G.S. N.Z. Ltd
Shore Sails
Smith Biolab Ltd
Smith & Nephew (NZ) Ltd
South East Asian Advertising
Southern Communications
N.W. Stevens Ltd
Superior Distributing Co. (USA)
Television New Zealand
Teltherm Industries
'The Shirt Club'
3-M
Timaru Milling Company
W.F. Tucker Ltd
Union Carbide NZ Pty Ltd
Union Shipping Group
Waitaki NZ Refrigerating
James Walker Ltd
Warwick R. Walker Associates
Warner - Lambert NZ Ltd
Brian Weaver Ltd
Weldwell NZ Ltd
Wellington Harbour Board
Whangarei Harbour Board
Williams & Cranwell Ltd
Wrightson Wines & Spirits

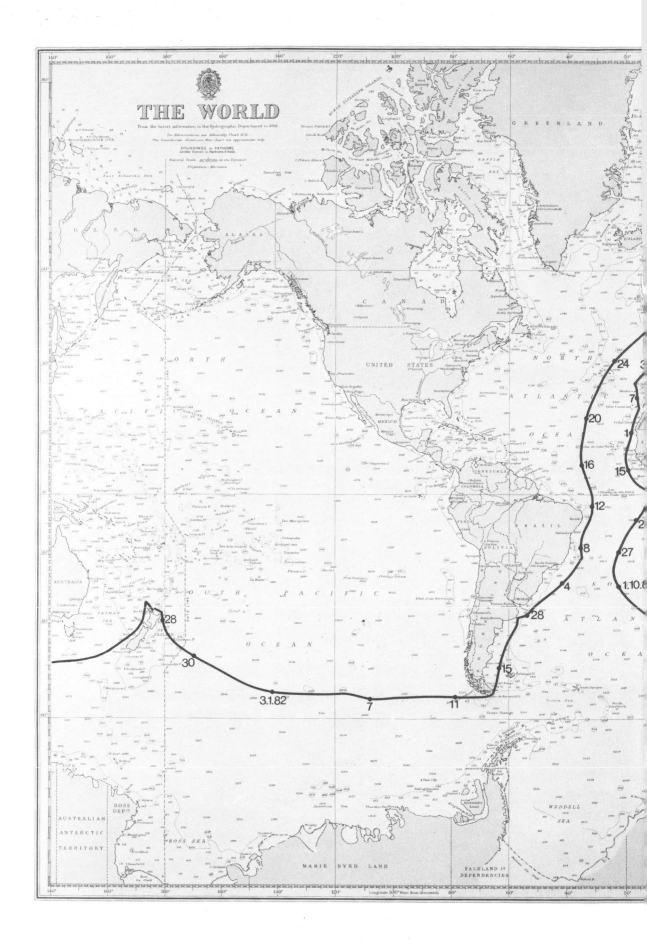